ON QUEER STREET

By the same author

HUGH DAVID

On Queer Street

A Social History of British Homosexuality
1895–1995

HarperCollins*Publishers*

HarperCollins*Publishers*
77–85 Fulham Palace Road
Hammersmith, London w6 8jb

Published by HarperCollins*Publishers* 1997
1   3   5   7   9   8   6   4   2

Copyright © Hugh David 1997

The Author asserts the moral right to
be identified as the author of this work.

A catalogue record for this book
is available from the British Library

ISBN 0 00 255595 6

Set in Monotype Bembo by
Rowland Phototypesetting Limited
Bury St Edmunds, Suffolk

Printed and bound in Great Britain by
Caledonian International Book Manufacturing Ltd, Glasgow

for

ADAM JOHNSON

and Pip Bryce, Alex Mahoney,
Felix Rice and
Joselio Gomes da Silva

Tod und Verklärung

Contents

Introduction

I once kissed a man who'd once been kissed by Lord Alfred Douglas.

That a man now in his mid-forties is thus only two pecks away from Oscar Wilde in a fantastically apostate succession is interesting principally for the light it throws on the size of what is now commonly referred to as 'the gay community'. For although week after week the number of venues – bars, clubs, restaurants, discos, shops, gymnasia and saunas – taking advertisements in the columns of *Time Out*, the *Pink Paper* and half a dozen other magazines which cover the London gay scene gets larger and larger, the core market which they purport to serve actually gets smaller with the publication of every new piece of 'sexology'.

Born in the mid-1950s, I was brought up with the idea that Kinsey had *proved* that around one in ten men was homosexual; that gayness was, indeed, no more freakish – and statistically no more abnormal – than left-handedness. In this I was one of the lucky ones: enlightened doctors decided that my own south-paw leanings needed no correction, while the social and political climate of the 1960s, 1970s and early 1980s saw to it that – whatever empirical trialling at school and university told me – tendentious ideas that one in ten men was (or had once been) gay were never put to the test.

Now we know better. The most recent British figures (Penguin/ Blackwell Scientific Publications, 1994) suggest that, for all his super-American thoroughness, Kinsey got it badly wrong and, alas, homosexuals make up no more than 4 per cent of the adult male population of Britain. They thus number hardly more than one million, the equivalent of the inhabitants of a small provincial city. Contrary to popular opinion, they have roots in every social class; but, like Jews and Afro-Caribbeans, through a mixture of aspiration and expectation, they have gravitated towards the 'safety' of certain professions and positions in society.

That, despite being castigated as 'shirt-lifters', 'brown-noses', 'Quentins', 'gay boys', 'poofters' or just plain 'queers' and hampered by any number of now-unimaginable legal and social obstacles, so many attained social prominence was one of the reasons for my writing this book. That in total those men – the Cowards and Beatons and Ortons of public record – numbered no more than a few score and that, by implication, there were hundreds of thousands who couldn't or wouldn't achieve this and whose names didn't appear in either the social columns or the county court records, rapidly supplanted it.

Despite the success in the 1930s and 1940s of the Mass Observation project, it is only in the past few decades that the study of 'oral history', and specifically the collection of the reminiscences of ordinary people, has gained legitimacy. It has been outstandingly successful in reclaiming the quotidian reality in particular of working-class lives, the texture of everyday existence. While some attempt has previously been made to preserve the unique experience of homosexual men (notably by Kevin Porter and Jeffrey Weeks, to whose book *Between the Acts* I am particularly indebted), this has tended to concentrate on the atypical posturings of that social and literary *beau monde* and the sordid tales of 'cottaging' and acts of gross indecency which year after year titillate and appal the occupants of the press boxes in police and magistrates' courts. Even today, on the ever-expanding gay scene, there is a growing realization that such snapshots falsify the wider picture and, indeed, that some of the more *outré* manifestations of the scene itself might actually demean the undoubted but more mundane achievements of 'gay liberation':

> There is danger lurking in the way we are represented in the media. In a misguided attempt to illustrate gay diversity, we highlight tiny minorities which obscure ordinary gay life.
>
> Drag kings, SM dykes and technobabes only widen the gap between heterosexuals and ourselves. Their images give the impression of freakish behaviour, at odds with the representation of competent gay people in respected professions.[1]

It is these 'competent gay people' and the surprising continuity of the lives they have led behind that metonymical 'freakish behaviour' with which this book is primarily concerned – that and the impact which, marginalized, persecuted and belittled, they have nevertheless had upon the whole of society.

I have not attempted to twist history in accordance with the wishes of those who would complicate a sexual orientation with radical dialectic, or to over-simplify it into a cautionary tale of rise and hubristic fall. AIDS and, as we must for the foreseeable future accept, the enduring presence of HIV have fundamentally changed both public and private conceptions of homosexuality; but the over-tidy, journalistic notion of the twentieth-century homosexual's giddy, switch-back metamorphosis from derided Queer into barely tolerated Homosexual, politically correct Gay Man and finally stigmatized AIDS 'victim' is both superficial and downright wrong.

This book is neither a political history of gay liberation nor an attempt to set any social or cultural agenda: writers such as Antony Grey and Alan Sinfield are better qualified to attempt such things than I. I make no apology for not mentioning every action group, every nuance of thought, every signal event which has caused ripples in the gay community since the beginning of the century. Nor have I seen any need to accede to the demands of the radical Left and refer to the subjects of this book as 'queers'. A militant rejection of the words 'homosexual' and even 'gay' smacks more of dogma than utility, and in what follows I have chosen to refer to 'homosexuals', using the term as neutrally as possible, except in later chapters where 'gays' seemed more appropriate. For rather different reasons, I have also consciously ignored the lesbian history of the period, except where it coincidentally overlaps with my own material. Until very recently it was a completely different story; no less worthwhile, no less worthy of telling – but not perhaps by a male author.

In much the same way as I did in a previous book on London bohemianism, I have tried in this book to describe what life was like, how it felt to be a member of a discrete sub-group within society, and to do so by allowing men who were actually a part of things to tell their own stories.

Most of these were given to me in one-to-one situations by individuals who volunteered their services; the majority of the interviews were tape-recorded. I encouraged the interviewees to be as frank as possible and to consider the emotional and domestic as well as the sexual side of their lives. Many – senior Establishment figures, actors, ex-prisoners, teachers, rent-boys – responded with astonishing candour, and early on I decided that, in those extracts from their reminiscences which were to appear in this book, I would make no cuts on the grounds of the language they used or the sexual explicitness of their material.

Many of the men were speaking of their homosexuality for the first time and from positions in which their frank revelations could be extremely compromising. Because of this, all their names have been changed: pseudonyms are indicated in the text by their inclusion within inverted commas ('John'). Occasionally, too, partners' names and specific locations in the stories have been altered or omitted at the speaker's request. In one or two cases I have also agreed to complete anonymity.

I am grateful to all these men – quite as much to those who merely pointed me in the right direction and whose memories are the 'voices off' in the drama which follows, as to those from whose experiences I have directly quoted.

This book is dedicated to the memory of five men, all of whom died from AIDS-related conditions during the period of its creation. Each was, to a greater or lesser extent, a friend of mine; none, at the time of his death, had reached the age which I am now.

If the memory of their lives and manner of their deaths were the initial inspiration for the book, the generosity of many other people helped it on its way. I am particularly indebted to Dudley Cave, Hugo Greenhalgh, Antony Grey, Simon Ingram, Francis King, the Lesbian and Gay Switchboard, Jim Lovendoski, Michael Mara, Will Parry, Mike Port, Richard Pyatt, Mike Sansom, Peter Sowerbutts, Peter Tatchell, David Tolliss, David and Rosy Walker, Richard Wellings-Thomas, Adam Wilkinson, and Christopher Whelan and the staff at Body Positive, London.

Not for the first time, Edmund Hall proved an invaluable friend. He willingly shared ideas and contacts during much of the time I was researching this book – even though he was fully occupied with the writing of his own parallel study, *We Can't Even March Straight* (Chatto & Windus, 1995).

As always, my agent Bill Hamilton brokered an amicable deal, introducing me to Michael Fishwick, Sophie Nelson, Rebecca Lloyd and a demanding but enthusiastic team at HarperCollins. All have kept faith with me, a troublesome computer and a text which was initially envisaged as a 'quickie' to mark the 100th anniversary of the imprisonment of Oscar Wilde, but rapidly grew into something bigger.

Martyn Ives and Testimony Films generously made over research material to me. David Prosser and All Out Productions gave me more help than I could reasonably have expected; Central Television and Channel Four Television also acted as selfless go-betweens. As ever, the staff of the London Library was efficient, informative and indulgent.

Hugh David
London, November 1996

PART ONE

Heroes and Villains

1 ~

'For the Public Benefit'

THE DEFENDANT AWAITING SENTENCE in the dock of the Central Criminal Court at the Old Bailey in London was a forty-year-old Irishman.

Four years previously a friend described him as rich, tall and handsome. Only four months previously the description remained substantially true. If anything, he was 'bolder, stronger, bigger'.[1] He was at the very pinnacle of his profession and, ostensibly at least, a pillar of late Victorian society. He was a married man living in considerable style with his wife and two young sons in an expensive four-storey house in Tite Street, Chelsea. He seemed to define and personify the spirit of *fin de siècle* London. He was invited to dine at high tables; and dined, indeed, at the very highest. He was lionized in the press and mobbed in the streets.

Now, though, on the morning of Saturday 25 May 1895, all that had gone. Although he towered above the barristers and clerks who filled the well of the court – he stood a full six feet three inches in height and was, according to George Bernard Shaw, 'a giant in the pathological sense' – Oscar Fingal O'Flahertie Wills Wilde cut a sad and rather pathetic figure. A certain puffiness masked the good looks; his once-immaculate hair was dishevelled. The dinner invitations no longer arrived; the mob had turned nasty and even started to spit; bankruptcy proceedings were about to begin. With bewildering rapidity, over the course of just six weeks he had been stripped of everything.

~

It all went back to a day in February 1895 when a card, addressed to Wilde and describing him as 'posing as a Somdomite [*sic*]' (or possibly as 'ponce and Somdomite' – the handwriting was difficult to read[2]), had been left at his London club. At that time, a century ago, no other accusation – of, say, excessive drinking, gambling, lying, or marital infidelity – carried such a weight of obloquy as that of sodomy. Sodomy; brought up on the Bible, that was what they called it. That or pederasty (*paederasty*, as the classically educated preferred); they seemed to see no difference. Men such as Wilde were 'inverts' or 'perverts'; once again, no one was too concerned with the difference.

The card had been lying around at the Albemarle Club for ten days before Wilde received it. Stung, he brought charges for criminal libel against the man who had left it – the Marquess of Queensberry, the father of his young companion Lord Alfred Douglas, familiarly known as 'Bosie'. Queensberry in turn entered, as he had to, a Plea of Justification, saying that the card had been left openly at the club – and thereby legally 'published' – since he knew that Wilde had 'corrupted and debauched the morals' of a number of young men. Wilde

> was a man of letters and a dramatist of prominence and notoriety and a person who exercised considerable influence over young men [and had committed] sodomitical practices for a long time with impunity and without detection wherefore it was *for the public benefit and interest* that the matter contained in the said alleged libel should be published and that the true character and habits of the said Oscar Fingal O'Flahertie Wills Wilde should be known [in order] that the said Oscar Fingal O'Flahertie Wills Wilde might be prevented from further committing such offences . . .[3]

The case opened on 3 April and, on that day at least, things had gone well – or tolerably well – for Wilde. A letter he had written to a male friend ('You are the divine thing I want') was read aloud in court. 'Is that an ordinary letter?' asked Queensberry's counsel. 'Everything I write is extraordinary. I do not pose as being ordinary, great heavens!' Wilde replied. That evening he told friends: 'The working class is with me – to a boy!'

The next day, however, the persiflage became more laboured when the man endeavouring to establish that he was not a 'somdomite' was questioned about his relationships with a succession of those boys:

Were these young men all about twenty? – Yes; twenty or twenty-two. I like the society of young men.

What was their occupation? – I do not know if these particular young men had occupations.

Have you given money to them? – Yes. I think to all five – money or presents.

Did they give you anything? – Me? Me? No!

Among these five did Taylor introduce you to Charles Parker? – Yes.

Did you become friendly with him? – Yes, he was one with whom I became friendly.

Did you know that Parker was a gentleman's servant out of employment? – No.

But if he were, you would still have become friendly with him? – Yes. I would become friendly with any human being I liked.

How old was he? – Really, I do not keep a census.[4]

Already, the game was up, and everyone but he seemed to know it. Names were being mentioned. There was every possibility that the defence would put faces to anything up to ten of them – ten were certainly identified in Queensberry's Plea of Justification – given further provocation. But it was not until the following afternoon that Wilde conceded and the case was withdrawn. He was not in court to hear the judge rule that 'it was true in substance and in fact that the prosecutor had "posed" as a sodomite'.[5]

～～

It could be argued that what has come to be known as the First Trial of Oscar Wilde, those three days in April 1895 which so captivated London society – they thronged the public galleries of the Old Bailey – changed the lives of British homosexuals more profoundly than anything else in the next three quarters of a century. They were certainly taunted with cries of 'Oscar, Oscar!' right up until the beginning of the First World War.[6]

Every generation needs its own heroes, and for three or four generations of gay men Wilde seemed to more than fit the bill.[7] Indeed, until the emergence or 'outing' in the last twenty-five years of a more divergent range of role models – W. H. Auden, Alan Turing, Guy

Burgess, Rock Hudson, Sir Ian McKellen, Chris Smith, MP, the black footballer Justin Fashanu – he was about all there was. While serving an eighteen-month prison sentence in the mid-1950s after what became known as 'the Montagu case', the homosexual writer and journalist Peter Wildeblood found that his fellow-inmates still automatically bracketed him with Wilde.[8] Wilde's campness ('To write, I must have yellow satin'), the brittle archness of *The Importance of Being Earnest* and the lush prose of *The Picture of Dorian Gray* played no small part in defining the dialect of the tribe: 'All women become like their mothers. That is their tragedy. No man does. That's his.'[9] By contrast, the selfishness and spite apparent in *De Profundis* have been overlooked. The prose sings, but the sentiments expressed are less than noble: 'The very bread and water of prison fare you have by your conduct changed. You have rendered the one bitter and the other brackish to me. The sorrow you should have shared you have doubled, the pain you should have sought to lighten you have quickened to anguish.'

Wilde's decision to sue for libel was another example of this less celebrated side of his character. It was both wilful and suicidal, a pettishly arrogant act seemingly born out of a mistaken belief that (as Queensberry had suggested) he really did enjoy some 'impunity'; that his public position somehow put him above the law. Friends such as Frank Harris (and even the artist Henri Toulouse-Lautrec, who happened to be in London at the time) had early on tried to disabuse him of this and urged him to drop the case against Queensberry. On holiday in January 1895, Wilde had run into André Gide in Algiers. The French writer went even further than Harris and suggested that Wilde remain abroad, beyond the jurisdiction of English law:

He spoke about returning to London; the Marquess of Q[ueensberry] was libelling him, demanding he go back, accusing him of fleeing.

'But if you do go back, what will happen?' I asked him. 'Do you know what you are risking?'

'It's better never to know that . . . My friends are quite extraordinary. They advise prudence. Prudence! But I can't have any of that. That would be going backwards . . . I must go on as far as possible . . . until I can't go any farther . . . until something happens . . . something else.'[10]

Wilde left for London the following day and, even after he was made aware of the contents of Queensberry's Plea, with its compromising list of names and dates and places, he insisted on ploughing on with the case. Egged on by, and perhaps blinded by, his infatuation with the handsome but immature Bosie, he seems to have refused to consider the wider implications of this course of action. For if he lost, Queensberry's allegation that he was 'posing as a somdomite' would be substantiated. Furthermore, the evidence adduced could well suggest that he was more than merely 'posing' and prompt a far more serious criminal prosecution.

In the event, that was, of course, exactly what happened.

As we have seen, Wilde was not in court on the final day of the trial. He was, however, well aware of what was going on – and, more importantly, of what was expected of him.

There is no way of proving it, but it seems likely that Wilde would have known of the death of Peter Ilyich Tchaikovsky in St Petersburg a mere eighteen months previously. In circumstances extraordinarily close to Wilde's own – the composer was at the height of his fame but an unhappily married homosexual threatened with exposure – in October 1893, just eight days after the first performance of his sixth symphony (the 'Pathétique'), he had committed suicide, in all probability by consciously drinking cholera-infected water.

'The past is another country', L. P. Hartley was to write. 'They do things differently there.' They did; in Britain in 1893, 1895 or, for that matter, virtually any year up to and including 1967 (when male homosexual acts were legalized) suicide was a rare and desperate escape route for the cornered 'sodomite'. A different code obtained: on the morning of 5 April 1895, the day on which Wilde withdrew his case against Queensberry, his wife Constance told a friend, 'I hope Oscar is going away abroad.'

This was not a quaint, romantic notion. Imbued with a sense of Victorian propriety, Constance knew that this was the Decent Thing for her husband to do. Only a few years previously the solicitor representing a titled man involved in a homosexual scandal with which Wilde was certainly familiar (but completely unconnected) had noted, 'I am informed on what I believe to be the most reliable authority that it is the intention of the police to apply for a warrant for his arrest *unless he resigns his appointments and goes away*'.[11]

Now Wilde's lawyers, too, were extolling this course of action, volunteering to filibuster on his behalf in court – even to the extent of letting the young men give evidence – to allow him time to catch a train to Dover and then the ferry to Calais. Frank Harris advised, 'They're going to bring up a string of witnesses that will put art and literature out of the question. Throw up the case and go abroad and, as an ace of trumps, take your wife with you!' Remarkably, even Queensberry had contacted Wilde to say, 'I will not prevent your flight' (although he had gone on to add, 'but if you take my son with you, I will shoot you like a dog').[12]

France – Paris, Calais, Dieppe, Deauville and other convenient Normandy ports, as well as Rouen and Monaco – had long been a second home to those British homosexuals affluent enough to escape there when things got uncomfortable at home. Wilde, who spoke very tolerable French, had been a frequent visitor ever since he first set foot in Paris (chaperoning, or chaperoned by, his mother) as a nineteen-year-old in 1874. In 1883 he had even contemplated settling permanently in the French capital, but his money ran out and after only four months he returned to London.

Now, with a warrant already issued for his arrest, it was everywhere expected that he would cross the Channel again and, in effect, do that decent thing. At this stage no one, not even Queensberry, wanted to punish him further – and still less to make a martyr out of him. At the end of the trial the judge wrote a note to Queensberry's counsel, the formidable Edward (later Sir Edward) Carson, congratulating him on the fact that his 'searching crossXam' had rendered it unnecessary for 'the rest of the filth' – by which he meant the inevitably graphic testimony of the boys – to be made public.[13] (Some years earlier, writing in connection with a similar case, the Attorney General of the day had noted that 'it is greatly to the credit of the reporters of the Press that they almost invariably refrain from reporting [cases of this description]'.)[14]

On an official level at least, it seems clear that the whole matter of *Reg.* v. *Queensberry*, as the libel case was officially listed, was something of an embarrassment; a necessary but unfortunate occurrence, some-thing to be swept as far – and as quickly – under the carpet as was possible. Even the police were more than usually compliant in the eventual and inevitable execution of the warrant for Wilde's arrest. Although they knew very well where he was, several hours elapsed before any action was taken.

Wilde, however, was playing a different game. 'I'll stay, I'll stay,' he repeatedly told those friends who remained loyal. 'One can't keep on going abroad, unless one is a missionary, or what comes to the same thing, a commercial traveller.' He should have been in court that day: instead he enjoyed a leisurely lunch and then, in the late afternoon, adjourned to the Cadogan Hotel. His friends were still urging him to go; a sympathetic journalist had already alerted him to the fact that the warrant had been issued . . . but in the end he did nothing. John Betjeman sums up the ensuing events accurately enough:

> He sipped at a weak hock and selzer
>   As he gazed at the London skies
> Through the Nottingham lace of the curtains
>   O was it his bees-winged eyes? [. . .]
>
> A thump, and a murmur of voices –
>   ('Oh why must they make such a din?')
> As the door of the bedroom swung open
>   And TWO PLAIN CLOTHED *POLICEMEN* came in:
>
> 'Mr Woilde, we 'ave come for tew take you
>   Where felons and criminals dwell:
> We must ask yew tew leave with us quoietly
>   For this *is* the Cadogan Hotel.'
>
> He rose, and he put down *The Yellow Book.*
>   He staggered, and – terrible-eyed,
> He brushed past the palms of the staircase
>   And was helped to a hansom outside.[15]

And that was what happened. (Betjeman was materially wrong only in his reference to the *Yellow Book.* Wilde was not reading the latest issue of the journal of high Aestheticism which had brought Aubrey Beardsley to prominence, but a copy of Pierre Louÿs's novel *Aphrodite,* which happened to have a yellow dust-jacket. Ironically, he never had

any direct contact with the magazine.)[16] Wilde was arrested, taken to
Bow Street police station, charged and then remanded in custody to
Holloway Prison.

'Society put up with a great deal that was illegal, and sometimes
did so knowingly,' wrote Richard Ellmann in his definitive life of
Wilde. But, he went on, 'countenancing illegality did not amount to
sanctioning it [. . .] and the atmosphere could change at any time.'[17]
It could. It did. It changed for Wilde at ten past six on the evening
of Friday 5 April 1895 when the two plain-clothed policemen were
shown into his room at the Cadogan Hotel.

It changed for many other people too. Along with the sexually tor-
mented homosexual poet Algernon Charles Swinburne and the artists
James McNeill Whistler and Aubrey Beardsley, Wilde had personified
the Aesthetic movement, a band of poets, would-be poets, artists and
socialites who had added significantly to the gaiety of the nation since
the late 1870s. There *was* an Aesthetic philosophy – it had its origins
in the precious atmosphere of Oxford University in the early 1870s,
in Immanuel Kant's notion of the essential disinterestedness of Art,
and in the later writings of Théophile Gautier and Walter Pater[18] –
but, in the popular mind at least, this was soon replaced by far cruder
slogans. The Aesthetes stood for 'Art for Art's sake', lilies and green
carnations, blue-and-white china and the concept of 'the house beautiful'. Out on the street, in London and in Oxford, they were immediately recognizable by their long hair and their affected, adjective-rich
vocabulary: '*blessed!*', they'd say; '*divine!*'; 'a *total* marvel!'; 'how *consummate!*'; 'what a *precious!*' . . .

Precious it all was; but, at the start, Aestheticism and self-proclaiming
Aesthetes such as Wilde were fondly indulged. In *Punch* magazine, at
the time a journal of real influence, a series of cartoons by the writer
(*Trilby*) and artist George du Maurier was benignly satirizing their
self-absorption as early as 1879. The following year the caption to a
cartoon entitled 'Nincompoopiana' had a society hostess, Mrs Cimabue
Brown, pointing out to a friend the Aesthetic painter Maudle: 'the
great Painter, you know. He had just painted Me as "Héloïse", and
my husband as "Abélard". *Is* not he *Divine?*'[19] In other texts, too,
'Aesthetes' were appearing, some with names such as Drawit Milde,

the Wilde Man of Borneo, Ossian Wildenesse and Oscuro Wildegoose which left no doubt as to their original inspiration.

It was all great sport. And soon leading members of the Aesthetes – and Wilde in particular – were also being good-naturedly lampooned in a series of popular but now forgotten West End hits. Wilde alone was the basis for the eponymous hero of a play tellingly entitled *The Charlatan* and for Herbert Beerbohm Tree's creation of the character Scott Ramsey in the comedy *Where's the Cat?* and the foolish Lambert Streyke in a long-running farce called *The Colonel* – ironically, this last work was written by F. C. (Sir Francis) Burnand, then also editor of *Punch*.

Wilde reached his Aesthetic apogee, however, when W. S. Gilbert and Arthur Sullivan abandoned what was planned to be a satire on the Tractarian movement in the Church of England and turned their attention instead to his 'greenery-yallery, Grosvenor Gallery' world of asphodels and *divine* blue-and-white china. With the principal subject of the satire occupying a prominent seat in the stalls, their operetta *Patience* opened at the Opéra Comique in London on 23 April 1881. No one was in any real doubt that one of its principal characters, the 'fleshly poet' Reginald Bunthorne, *was* Wilde. He certainly had by far the best patter-song:

> Though the Philistines may jostle, you will rank as an apostle in
>   the aesthetic band,
> If you walk down Piccadilly with a poppy or a lily in your
>   mediaeval hand,
>   And everyone will say,
>   As you walk your flowery way,
> 'If he's content with a vegetable love which would certainly not
>   suit me,
> Why what a most particularly pure young man this pure young
>   man must be!'[20]

Now, like *Where's the Cat?*, also largely forgotten, in the early 1880s *Patience* was hugely successful. There were eight encores on the first night; the original production ran for 578 performances, making it one of the most profitable of all the G&S Savoy operas. Wilde basked in the vicarious publicity it gave him and, kitted out in a new 'Aesthetic lecturing costume', embarked on an American lecture tour on the strength of it. But in truth *Patience* marked the beginning of – or, more exactly, the beginning of the beginning of – the end. The seeds of doubt are already there in Gilbert's libretto. Colonel Calverley and the Duke of Dunstable make an obvious point when Bunthorne first appears, followed by a 'Chorus of Rapturous Maidens':

DUKE: But who is the gentleman with the long hair?
COL: I don't know.
DUKE: He seems popular!
COL: He *does* seem popular![21]

But only minutes later Bunthorne himself is musing – '*aside, slyly*', according to the original stage directions – that he must seem 'Like a literary man/ Who despises female clay'.

Swept along by Sullivan's vivacious score and the high-spirited nonsense of the plot, the audience at the Opéra Comique may be forgiven for not rising to this level of textual exegesis. Even before *Patience* opened, however, readers of *Punch* were being offered a more disquieting view of Aestheticism – and of Wilde in particular. Du Maurier's cartoons had become increasingly savage; for all that he was an artist, physically Maudle had evolved into an unmistakable caricature of the playwright. As early as February 1881 du Maurier had him lounging slug-like next to the elegant, Pre-Raphaelite Mrs Cimabue Brown as he discoursed on 'The Choice of a Profession'. Hindsight only adds to the breathtaking audacity of the caption:

MAUDLE: How *consummately* lovely your Son is, Mrs Brown!
MRS BROWN (*A Philistine from the country*): What? He's a *nice, manly* Boy, if you mean *that*, Mr Maudle. He has just left School, you know, and wishes to be an Artist.
MAUDLE: *Why* should he be an Artist?
MRS BROWN: Well, he must be *something*!
MAUDLE: Why should he *Be* anything? Why not let him remain for ever content to *Exist Beautifully*!
(*Mrs Brown determines that at all events her Son shall not study Art under Maudle.*)[22]

Fully ten years before his arrest, then, Wilde was already the embodiment of the 'pansy'; the limp, lisping Aesthetic dandy. Everything he did, every word he wrote or uttered, was calculated to maintain this position. Life and art were melded in a thoroughly modern presentation of 'image', nowhere more so than in the 'House Beautiful' he created in Tite Street, Chelsea, as a calculated shock to High Victorian sensibilities (and a private snub to Whistler who had had the presumption to design a similarly exotic 'Peacock Room' as early as 1877).

There were no doors to any of the rooms at Tite Street, only tapestry curtains; and, in (literally) stark contrast to the more orthodox fashion for flock-and-mahogany, in the ground-floor dining room both the walls and all the specially made 'Grecian style' furniture were painted an unrelenting gloss white. The original 1884 architect's specifications were rediscovered in 1951 and throw an oblique but valuable light on Wilde at this time:

> *Library*. The walls to the height of 5′ 6″ to be painted in distemper dark blue. The upper part of the walls, cornice and ceiling to be pale gold colour. The woodwork throughout to be golden brown (russet).
> *2nd floor Bedroom front*. Pink walls, woodwork, ceiling; & 2 feet of top of walls under cornice apple green.
> *Drawing-room front*. Woodwork ivory white. Walls distempered flesh pink from skirting to cornice. The cornice to be gilded dull flat lemon colour gold and also the ceiling margin to Japanese leather, which latter will be provided by Mr Wilde.[23]

Even as the real-life equivalent of Lady Windermere's Parker or Algernon Moncrieff's Lane was showing visitors into his pink-and-gold drawing room (Lady Windermere, sir, the Duchess of Berwick, Lady Agatha Carlisle, Lady Plydale, Lady Stutfield . . .), Wilde had reached an uneasy apogee. Publicly, he was fêted as the man of mode, the man about town, the successful writer, the poet and the playwright. His dazzling fecundity at this period made sure of that: his *Poems* had been published in 1881, *The Happy Prince and Other Tales* in 1888; *The Picture of Dorian Gray* appeared in 1891, followed in quick succession by *Lady Windermere's Fan* (1892), *A Woman of No Importance*, *Salomé* (both produced in 1893), *An Ideal Husband* and *The Importance of Being Earnest* (1895). Privately, however, resentment at the style as much as the scale of Wilde's success was already festering. Not all the visitors to Tite Street left convinced of the beauty of the ménage. One noted that everything was 'bizarre and vulgar, even vaguely sinful'.

〜

All this bile came flooding to the surface as soon as Queensberry lanced the boil. Frank Harris later recalled that Wilde's arrest 'was the signal for an orgy of Philistine rancour such as even London had never known before. The Puritan middle class, which had always regarded Wilde with dislike as an artist and an intellectual scoffer, a mere parasite of the aristocracy, now gave free scope to their disgust and contempt, and everyone tried to outdo his neighbour in expressions of loathing'.[24] W. B. Yeats agreed. 'The rage against Wilde', he told H. Montgomery Hyde, 'was also complicated by the Britisher's jealousy of art and the artist, which is generally dormant but is called into activity when the artist has got outside his field into publicity of an undesirable kind.'[25]

And it wasn't just Puritan, middle-class 'Britishers'. Wilde's fame was such that details of Queensberry's accusations were well-known and widely reported throughout Europe. In March 1894, before the libel case even came to court, the playwright and Bosie were refused admission to a hotel in Monaco. Back in London, erstwhile colleagues and collaborators were also rushing to distance themselves from Wilde. John Lane, his publisher, abruptly removed all mention of his books from the firm's catalogue. Convinced that Wilde had been reading the *Yellow Book*, also coincidentally published by Lane, an angry crowd demonstrated outside its office. Windows were broken. 'It killed the *Yellow Book*,' Lane later recalled, adding wryly, 'and it nearly killed me.'

The hitherto successful run of *An Ideal Husband* at the Haymarket Theatre was terminated on the day after its author's arrest. (One disaffected member of its cast, the actor-playwright Charles Brookfield, had even supplied Queensberry's lawyers with material damaging to Wilde.) Performances of *The Importance of Being Earnest* at the St James's Theatre – which had opened to great acclaim on 14 February, a celebrity first night audience having braved one of the worst storms of the decade to be there – continued ... but with Wilde's name obliterated from all the playbills and posters outside the theatre.

Among the Establishment, Wilde's arrest raised equally uncomfortable questions. Five years previously, in the autumn of 1889, it had been heavily involved in another case whose social and political implications, were, if anything, even more convoluted.

Police investigations had led to suspicions that a house near Tottenham Court Road in the West End of London was being run as a male brothel. 'Observation has been kept on the house – 19 Cleveland Street', it was stated in the original report, 'and a number of men of superior bearing and apparently of good position have been seen to call there accompanied by boys in some instances, and on two occasions by a soldier . . .'[26] Among the 'men of superior bearing' were 'the heir to a duke and the younger son of a duke'. There was also the suggestion that Prince Albert Victor, familiarly known as Prince Eddie, the elder son of the then Prince of Wales, grandson of Queen Victoria and heir-presumptive to the throne, had been among the callers.

Most of the resulting 'trial' was conducted in private – in a blizzard of private letters and any number of off-the-record conversations which involved the Prime Minister, Lord Salisbury, the Director of Public Prosecutions and the Attorney General. There was nothing of substance which directly linked the Prince – 'PAV', as he was referred to for reasons of security – and the royal family to the case; but no one knew quite what to do with that 'heir to a duke' – actually Henry Fitzroy, the Earl of Euston – and, more particularly, that 'younger son of a duke'.

Lord Arthur Somerset was thirty-seven, a major in the Royal Horse Guards, the superintendent of the Prince of Wales's stables and a younger son of the eighth Duke of Beaufort. Now, in unprecedentedly graphic detail, the sworn statements of a number of 'boys' (most of them teenaged Post Office workers) were implicating him in what became known as 'the Cleveland Street scandal'. 'We got into the bed quite naked. He told me to suck him. I did so. He then had a go between my legs and that was all. He gave me half a sovereign,' said one. 'On one occasion at least I put my person into his hinderparts. I could not get it in, though I tried and emitted,' another recalled . . .[27]

A consensus obtained, however. Every bit as well as the legal authorities, Somerset knew the form: he resigned his commission in the army, relinquished his appointment in the Prince of Wales's household and slipped away to France – where he was to remain, at Hyères on the Riviera, until his death in 1926. It was what was expected of him, and a convenient and leisurely piece of face-saving for all concerned.

Somerset's resignation from the army was gazetted at the beginning of November 1889; a warrant for his arrest was not issued until 12 November: meanwhile he had left England as early as 18 October.

Quite simply, Somerset had gone, had been allowed to go, even *been urged to go*, because it would have been utterly unthinkable for the 'younger son of a duke' and, quite possibly, the elder son of the Prince of Wales to have been seen to be involved in a legal case turning upon evidence describing how 'boys' put their 'persons' into older men's hinderparts. Ranks had closed, and in Westminster and St James's, for a short time at least, it seemed that a scandal had been averted. Shortly after Somerset's flight Sir Dighton Probyn, comptroller to the Prince of Wales's household, made confidential contact with Lord Salisbury: 'I write now to ask you, to implore of you, if it can be managed to have the prosecution stopped. It can do no good to prosecute him. He has gone and will never show his face in England again. He *dare* never come back to this country.'[28] The Director of Public Prosecutions, Sir Augustus Stephenson, took a similarly pragmatic view. 'It is quite possible (in my judgement it is probable) that he will not return,' he noted. 'It may be the best thing that could happen.'[29]

Even in 1889, however, it was impossible to stop the 'truth' leaking out. Stories that a member of the royal family and other titled men were involved in the 'abominable' goings-on at Cleveland Street were soon swirling around London. The sometimes unreliable *Pall Mall Gazette* was the first to give them credence – and the first to pose unpalatable questions.

> The question which Sir Augustus Stephenson will have to answer is whether the two noble lords and other notable persons in society who were accused by the witnesses of having been the principals in the crime [. . .] are to be allowed to escape scot free [it thundered]. The wretched agents are run in and sent to penal servitude; the lords and gentlemen who employ them swagger at large and are even welcomed as valuable allies of the Administration of the day.[30]

Their patience finally exhausted, then, it was both Disraeli's 'upper ten thousand' and a baying mob of not-so-fortunates who, for their own reasons, arraigned Wilde and filled the public galleries to see the spectacle of 'their man' in the dock at the Old Bailey a mere eight weeks later. The trial began on 26 April, when Wilde and Alfred Taylor, the manager of what amounted to a male brothel and a man whose name had figured briefly in the previous libel proceedings, were formally charged with having committed acts proscribed under section 11 of the Criminal Law Amendment Act of 1885.

In view of its later significance and the part it was to play in the lives of homosexual men for another three-quarters of a century, it is perhaps appropriate here briefly to consider the Criminal Law Amendment Act and its notorious section 11, soon dubbed (by a lawyer) the 'Blackmailer's Charter'.

The Act had begun as a non-controversial House of Commons bill designed to raise the age of female consent (from thirteen) and curb the 'white slave trade' in girls sent against their will to work in foreign brothels. Indeed, it was formally entitled 'An Act to make further provision for the Protection of Women, the suppression of brothels and other purposes'. It was only when, after an unopposed second reading, Henry Labouchère, a wealthy radical MP and newspaper editor, proposed a last-minute amendment to insert a new clause headed 'Outrages on public decency' that the Bill attracted any real parliamentary attention.

For centuries acts of sodomy (or buggery, the English lawyers' preferred term) had been illegal. Buggery had been a capital office under English law from 1533 until 1861, when the maximum penalty was reduced to life imprisonment. In practice, however, cases had normally only been brought when 'public decency' was outraged. Labouchère's carefully (or carelessly) worded amendment sought to change all that and criminalize *all* aspects of homosexual behaviour. It was a catch-all measure. Specifics and such legal niceties as 'buggery' had no part in it. Instead, the amendment suggested vaguely that any man committing – and anyone helping him to commit – 'any act of gross indecency', whether in public or in private, should be liable to up to one year's imprisonment.

The amendment was debated on the floor of the House of Commons late on the night of 6 August 1885 and approved with only minor changes – one being a government amendment increasing the maximum punishment from one year's imprisonment to two. Thus it was that the 'Labouchère Amendment', the 'Blackmailer's Charter', came on to the statute book when the Criminal Law Amendment Act formally became law on 1 January 1886. For the record, section 11 read as follows: 'Any male person who, in public or in private, commits, or is a party to the commission of, or procures, or attempts to procure the commission by any male person of, any act of gross indecency shall be guilty of misdemeanour, and being convicted shall be liable at the discretion of the Court to be imprisoned for any term not exceeding two years, with or without hard labour.'[31]

Those sixty-eight words were the cross on which Wilde was to be nailed. He and Taylor were originally indicted on no less than twenty-five counts. The wording of those had been bad enough:

The Jurors for our Lady the Queen upon their oath present that –

1. *First Count*
OSCAR FINGAL O'FLAHERTIE WILLS WILDE on the fourteenth day of March in the year of our Lord one thousand eight hundred and ninety-three at the Parish of Saint John the Baptist Savoy in the County of London and within the jurisdiction of the said Court being a male person unlawfully did commit acts of gross indecency with another male person to wit one Charles Parker against the form of the statute in such case made and provided and against the peace of our said Lady the Queen her crown and dignity.

On and on they went, count after count, the dry legal language making even starker the nature of the charges:

that ALFRED TAYLOR on the said fourteenth day of March in the year of our Lord one thousand eight hundred and ninety-three at the Parish of Saint John the Baptist Savoy in the County of London and within the jurisdiction of the said Court unlawfully did procure the commission by the said Oscar Fingal O'Flahertie Wills Wilde being a male person of acts of gross indecency with another person the said Charles Parker [Count 2] . . . with another person the said Alfred Wood [Count 14] . . . that the said Oscar Fingal O'Flahertie Wills Wilde [. . .] did commit acts of gross indecency with another male person to the jurors aforesaid unknown [Count 18; Count 19] . . . with another male person to wit one Edward Shelley [Count 25].

In a transcript of the trial and subsequent re-trial[32] the indictment itself runs to more than eight pages. What followed, even in abbreviated form, fills another 146, a minute-by-minute account of six days which were to alter irrevocably the way in which English men and women saw the world.

The trial itself ('the Second Trial of Oscar Wilde') was an unsatisfactory affair. Sensational stories were aired but, after listening to tales the substance of which few of the members of the all-male jury can even have imagined, when it retired it was unable to reach any unanimous verdict. After four and a half hours of deliberation the foreman had to inform the judge: 'My lord, I fear there is no chance of agreement.'

Exasperated, the judge had no option but to order a re-trial. It was as a result of this ('the Third Trial of Oscar Wilde') that the playwright found himself standing in the dock of the Old Bailey on the afternoon of Saturday 25 May 1895. For the previous five days a new jury had listened to what was essentially the same evidence that their predecessors had heard. This time round, however, everything was more focused; and there were two crucial differences to the manner in which things were handled. The original twenty-five counts were reduced to a more manageable fourteen – and Taylor and Wilde were tried separately.

Despite the fact that Wilde's name appeared first on the indictment; despite an intervention from his counsel, Sir Edward Clarke, that a detailed examination of the malfeasances of Taylor would prejudice the jury against his more illustrious client, the new judge, Mr Justice Wills, decided to hear first the case against Taylor. According to the official transcript of the trial, Wilde was meanwhile 'taken below to the cells'.

To those in the court, he was gone but hardly forgotten. Before he had been on his feet for two minutes, Sir Frank Lockwood, the Solicitor-General, had drawn him back into the centre of the action in the prosecution's opening speech to the jury:

> . . . the first case with which I shall deal is that Taylor attempted to procure the commission of certain acts by Mr Oscar Wilde with a young man named Charles Parker. *I insist that no false delicacy will be allowed to prevent the whole of the details of what actually took place from being laid before you, gentlemen. It is your right to know what did take place, and nothing ought to be left to you to guess.*[33]

Although neither the original trial nor this re-trial was ever anything other than fairly conducted, the unofficial rules of engagement were quite different from those which had obtained during the earlier libel proceedings. No one now was holding back on the 'filth' and the evidence presented against Taylor served as little more than an hors d'oeuvre to the revelations which would be served up against Wilde.

Charles Parker was coaxed into telling the court how Taylor had introduced him, then aged eighteen, and his brother William to Wilde at a restaurant ('I think it was the Solferino') in March 1893. The four men then had dinner, for which Wilde paid, and fell into conversation. 'And then?' he was asked.

> Subsequently, [Parker replied] Wilde said to me, 'This is the boy for me! Will you go to the Savoy Hotel with me?' I consented, and Wilde drove me in a cab to the hotel. Only he and I went, leaving my brother and Taylor behind. At the Savoy we went first to Wilde's sitting room on the second floor.
>
> More drink was offered you there? – Yes, we had liqueurs. Wilde then asked me to go into his bedroom with him.
>
> Let us know what occurred there? – He committed the act of sodomy on me.
>
> With your consent? – (Witness did not reply.)
>
> Did Wilde give you any money on that occasion? – Before I left Wilde gave me £2, telling me to call at the Savoy Hotel in a week.[34]

Moments later, Parker recalled how, on another occasion, he and Taylor 'slept together in the same bed. Taylor called me "Darling" and referred to me as his "little wife". When I left he paid me some money; he said I should never want for cash and that he would introduce me to men prepared to pay for that kind of thing.'[35] He was only the first of a chain of prosecution witnesses. Among many others, the landlady of the house in which Taylor lodged until August 1893 described how no women seemed to visit him. There were only

> men, young men from sixteen to thirty. I have seen Alfred Wood there. He once stayed for three weeks. Others were Sidney Mavor,

Charles Mason, and Ernest Macklin. Mavor and Mason stayed there for nights with Taylor. There were frequent tea parties.

Who came to them, men or women? – Oh, always gentlemen. Taylor used to address his visitors by their Christian names – 'Charlie, dear', and 'Dear boy'.[36]

This was evidence against Taylor – but it still amounted to a pre-trial by implication of Wilde. Extraordinarily, the landlady was allowed to add, directly after the last answer quoted above, a further innuendo-laden sentence: 'I have heard Taylor talking to someone he called "Oscar", but I have never seen Mr Wilde there.'

On the second day of the re-trial, Tuesday 21 May, Taylor gave evidence in his own defence. A one-time pupil at Marlborough College, any of the public-school sangfroid he might once have possessed withered before the Solicitor-General's cross-examination. Pressed to say 'how many different men have shared your bedroom' – and name them – he mentioned six, five of whom were already familiar to the court. Sir Frank Lockwood did not press for details of the sixth ('I will spare your mother that') and concentrated instead on the details of Taylor's singular lifestyle:

Do you remember going through a form of marriage with Mason? – No, never.

Did you not tell Parker that you had? – Nothing of the kind.

No burlesque ceremony? – No, nothing.

Did you not place a wedding ring on his finger and go to bed with him that night as though he were your lawful wife? – It is all false. I deny it all.

Did you ever sleep with Mason? – I think I did the first night. Afterwards he had a separate bed.

Were you on terms of affection with him? – I don't understand your question. If you mean did I commit acts of indecency, I did not. I did not use that term.[37]

Wilde himself did not appear in court again until the following day, Wednesday 22 May, when the case against Taylor had been concluded. (Taylor was found guilty on two of the six counts with which he was finally charged. Sentencing was, however, postponed until the case against Wilde had been heard.)

Right from the start Wilde was on a hiding to nothing. The jury
– and a far wider public outside the court – had heard the details of
Taylor's behaviour, to which his had so effectively been yoked; now
his own 'Aestheticism' was to be weighed against the sterile strictures
of the Criminal Law Amendment Act. Charles Parker and other boys
paraded through the witness box, telling their stories of assignations
at the Savoy Hotel and elsewhere. Dense legal argument resulted in
one of the eight indictments specifically naming Wilde being dropped.
Two days passed. It was not until Friday 24 May that Wilde began
giving evidence on his own behalf. There was laughter in the public
galleries at some of his responses, but he hardly helped his counsel's
case when exposed to the witheringly accurate questioning of the
Solicitor-General:

Do you remember giving Mavor a cigarette case? – Yes. It cost
£4.

Did you give one to Charles Parker also? – Yes, but I am afraid
it cost only £1.

Silver? – Well, yes. I have a great fancy for giving cigarette cases.

To young men? – Yes.

How many have you given? – I might have given seven or eight
in 1892 and 1893[38] [. . .]

Did you know at the time that the Parkers were a valet and a
groom respectively? – No, and had I known it I should not have
cared.

You have no sense of social differences? – No.

You preferred Charles? – I make no preferences.

You like bright boys? – I like bright boys. Charles Parker was
bright. I liked him[39] [. . .]

How much money have you given Charles Parker in cash? –
Four or five pounds.

Why? – Oh, I give young men money with pleasure.[40]

In quite literally playing to the gallery like this, Wilde badly mis-
judged the mood of both the court and the public outside. In the
closing hours of the trial the judge, Mr Justice Wills, felt bound to
remark that 'To have to try a case of this kind, to keep the scales
even, and do one's duty is hard enough; but to be pestered with the
applause or expressions of feeling of senseless people who have no

business to be here at all except for the gratification of morbid curiosity, is too much.'

There was a certain inevitability about things, then, on that Saturday evening, 25 May 1895, as Wilde and Taylor stood in the dock for sentencing. The jury had been out for a little under three hours, but returned shortly before six o'clock with their verdict that Wilde too was guilty – on six of the seven counts on which he had finally been charged.

Mr Justice Wills made no secret of his feelings. Before they retired he had commiserated with the jury over 'the horrible nature of the charges' they had heard. Passing sentence, he was equally unequivocal:

That you, Taylor, kept a kind of male brothel it is impossible to doubt. And that you, Wilde, have been the centre of a circle of extensive corruption of the most hideous kind among young men, it is equally impossible to doubt.

I shall, under the circumstances, be expected to pass the severest sentence that the law allows. In my judgement it is totally inadequate for such a case as this. The sentence of the Court is that each of you be imprisoned and kept to hard labour for two years.[41]

Taylor need no longer detain us. Oscar Fingal O'Flahertie Wills Wilde, however, casts a long shadow.

Some kill their love when they are young,
And some when they are old;
Some strangle with the hands of Lust,
Some with the hands of Gold . . .

A sentimental notion of abstract love is at the heart of 'The Ballad of Reading Gaol', Wilde's meditation on the execution of 'C. T. W., Sometime Trooper of the Royal Horse Guard'. But if that could reach out and embrace strangers, the etiolated, reflexive passion which fires De Profundis is the author's alone. 'In prison and in chains', Wilde seeks to blame Bosie, and through him the world at large, for everything that has happened to him. The original manuscript (not published in its entirety until 1949) is cast in the form of a letter. Running to some eighty pages, it begins:

Epistola: In Carcere et Vinculis

H. M. PRISON,
READING.

DEAR BOSIE, – After long and fruitless waiting I have determined to write to you myself, as much for your sake as mine, as I would not like to think that I have passed through two long years of imprisonment without ever having received a single line from you, or any news or message even, except such as gave me pain.

Our ill-fated and most lamentable friendship has ended in ruin and public infamy for me, yet the memory of our ancient affection is often with me, and the thought that loathing, bitterness and contempt should forever take the place in my heart once held by love is very sad to me . . .

Loathing, bitterness and contempt *had* built up in Wilde's heart, however; a blind bewilderment too. He could not comprehend how and why everything had changed so fundamentally. Nor could he appreciate anything other than the personal implications of his imprisonment. Others could. Before the jury retired in the third trial Mr Justice Wills had told them: 'Whatever your verdict may be, gentlemen, it cannot leave things precisely as they were before this trial.'

Nor did it. Nor could it; guilty or innocent, the mere presence of Wilde in the dock changed the whole public perception of the homosexual. The level of resentment which had built up against him and the whole Aesthetic movement was reflected in the tenor of the press comment in the immediate aftermath of the trial. While *Reynolds's News* could not bring itself 'to gloat over the ruin of the unhappy man', virtually every other paper could, and saw wider implications in his personal tragedy. The *St James's Gazette* welcomed what it called 'a dash of wholesome bigotry'. 'Open the windows! Let in the fresh air,' cried the *Daily Telegraph*. But it was the *News of the World* which really got to the heart of the matter when it told its readers on 26 May 1895: 'The aesthetic cult, in the nasty form, is over.'

Over a period of a very few weeks, the substance which underlay all the smirks and innuendo-laden stories of Maudle and the other Aesthetes, real and fictional, had been made public. A bare eight years previously, in 1887, Wilde had been offered, and had accepted, the editorship of the *Lady's World: A Magazine of Fashion and Society* (commendably, one of his first actions had been to change the magazine's title to *Woman's World*) and the world at large had applauded what was seen as a shrewd career move. There were no knowing looks or contemptuous titters because there was then no automatic connection between Aesthetic effeminacy, 'artists', W. S. Gilbert's 'pure young men', 'vegetable love' and the dimly discerned, scarcely imaginable physical realities of buggery, sodomy or 'gross indecency'. Right up until his arrest Wilde was, quite literally, committing a crime which dared not speak its name. When the London *Evening Standard* reported the Queensberry libel case it spoke only of a card describing 'Oscar Wilde posing as —'. As Alan Sinfield has demonstrated,[42] Wilde himself quickly became the crime. In E. M. Forster's novel *Maurice* (written in 1914, but not published until 1971) the eponymous hero can do no better (or worse) than call himself 'an unspeakable of the Oscar Wilde sort'.

A prurient interest *was* taken at the Old Bailey in the stories of soiled sheets at the Savoy Hotel ('I found it necessary to call the attention of the housekeeper to the condition of Mr Wilde's bed. The sheets were stained in a peculiar way') and other dubious matters during Wilde's various trials. But chiefly because no one had heard such stories before. All along, the 'loathsome' nature of the defendants' behaviour was presented as a shocking, unexpected obverse to their outwardly 'sophisticated' yet materially conservative lifestyle. Memories of the Cleveland Street scandal still lingered; but it was Wilde's presence in the dock which tore away the last vestiges of the innocence of Gilbert and Sullivan's 'pure young men'.

During the earlier part of the trial Taylor's sometime landlady described in her evidence how his rooms 'were furnished sumptuously'; how he 'used to burn scent in them'; and how, because the curtains were never opened, the rooms were always 'lighted by different coloured lamps and candles'. Taylor's night shirt, she recalled, was fastened by a gold brooch pin. She had also, she mentioned, seen 'a woman's wig and shoes and stockings'. Naturally, much was made of this when Taylor himself gave evidence:

But there were articles of women's dress in your rooms? – No, there was a fancy dress for a female, an Eastern costume.
Was it made for a woman? – I think so.

Perhaps you wore it? – I put it on once by way of a lark.

On no other occasion? – I wore it too at fancy dress balls, at the carnivals at Olympia, at Covent Garden and at Queen's Gate Hall.

I suggest that you often dressed as a woman? – No.

You wore, and caused Mason afterwards to wear, lace drawers, a woman's garment, with the dress? – Hardly that. I wore knicker-bockers and stockings under a long open cloak which was fastened at the waist.

And a woman's wig, which afterwards did for Mason? – No, the wig was made for me. I was going to a ball as Dick Whittington.

Woman's stockings? – Yes.[43]

The Savoy Hotel, Covent Garden . . . stained sheets, permanently closed curtains, women's stockings . . . even in his summing-up, Mr Justice Wills effectively yoked together these potent images of an unhealthy coupling of the *beau monde* and the *demi-monde*:

The sums too which appeared on the [Savoy Hotel] bill are high for such a supper. I know nothing about the Savoy, but I must say that in my view 'Chicken and salad for two, 16 shillings', is very high. I am afraid I shall never have supper there myself.

I must state here that I wish that medical evidence had been called. It is a loathsome subject, but I make a point of never shrinking from details that are absolutely necessary. The medical evidence would have thrown light on what has been alluded to as marks of grease or vaseline smears. Then, with reference to the condition of the bed, there was the diarrhoea line of defence . . .[44]

The implications were inevitable. Far from being the innocent exemplars of 'purity', the Aesthetes had abruptly become 'buggers', 'inverts', 'perverts' or 'sodomites' – the neologistic term 'homosexual' was never used – whose newly revealed behaviour was 'abominable' and 'loathsome'.

'We know of no spectacle so ridiculous as the British public in one of its periodic fits of morality,' wrote Lord Macaulay. But that was in his three-volume collection of *Essays* which had first appeared in 1843. Half a century on, this latest fit of morality threatened to expose Wilde's circle to far more than mere ridicule. (That, they could take; the more conscientiously 'aesthetic' Aesthetes had been putting up with it for years in the streets of Oxford, the columns of *Punch* and the dining rooms of London.) Nor was it just Wilde's circle: his conviction opened up the very real possibility of a wide-ranging purge of homosexual men.

Not entirely surprisingly, a genteel sort of panic ensued. Hesketh Pearson has memorably described a 'holiday rush' of men who abruptly decided to take vacations of indeterminate length in all the familiar French resorts. Even before the opening of Wilde's final trial, a friend had written to the writer Edmund Gosse pointing out that, on one night, 600 men had boarded Dover–Calais ferries – ten times the usual number.[45] Dozens of Wilde's friends 'fell away', Richard Ellmann records.[46] Robbie Ross went to the Terminus Hotel in Calais, and then travelled on to Rouen. Lord Ronald Gower and more than one of the witnesses from the second trial also decided that they would be better off abroad.

For all his assertions that he would stay, whatever the consequences, Wilde too, when eventually he was released from custody in Reading Gaol on 19 May 1897, had little option but to leave the country. He died in Paris less than three years later, on 30 November 1900.

By then he was almost forgotten, and in Britain his *fin de siècle* Aestheticism and *Patience*'s 'greenery-yallery, Grosvenor Gallery' world were, quite literally, things of the past. A homosexual sub-culture remained, of course; but it was hugger-mugger, secretive and diffuse. Unmarried vicars and bachelor uncles were granted the token immunity they had always enjoyed: they were just 'so' or 'musical' or 'that way'. But the truth was out, and others were not so lucky. Erstwhile 'pure young men' were now 'bum-boys' and 'shirt-lifters', only interested in 'a bit of brown'. Wilde cast a long shadow.

2 ✒

'You and I are Outlaws'

THE LEAD ARTICLE in a small, ultra-conservative subscription magazine called the *Imperialist* which flourished during the Great War was
always the editor's hectoring 'As I See It' piece. In the issue of
26 January 1918 this was entitled 'The First 47,000', and its suggestion
of widespread moral and sexual deviance among the most eminent in
society would have astonished – or, more likely, frankly bemused –
the average man in the street, should he have chanced to read it:

> There exists in the *Cabinet noire* of a certain German prince [the article
> insisted] a book compiled by the Secret Service from the reports of
> German agents who have infested this country for the past twenty
> years. More than a thousand pages are filled with the names [. . .]
> of forty-seven thousand English men and women. The names of
> Privy Councillors, youths of the chorus, wives of Cabinet Ministers,
> dancing girls, even Cabinet Ministers themselves, while diplo-
> mats, poets, bankers, editors, newspaper proprietors and members
> of His Majesty's household follow each other with no order of
> precedence.[1]

Quite what prompted Noël Pemberton-Billing, the somewhat eccen-
tric Independent MP and founder-editor of the *Imperialist*, to write
this remains unclear – the very existence of what became known as
the 'Black Book' has never been proved. Published at a time when
Britain (and its Empire) was still at war with Germany, the piece may
well have been intended as no more than an exercise in jingoistic
propagandizing; the *Imperialist* was far from alone in highlighting
examples of the alleged beastliness of 'the Hun' at this time. The
article's fulminatory tone, however, at once indignant and ungram-

matical, suggests that Pemberton-Billing was pursuing a separate, private agenda. Eighteen months previously he had announced that his magazine would 'not only criticise but attack, without fear or favour, all those men and measures which make for the perpetuation of our past political follies'.[2]

With 'The First 47,000' he came as close as he dared to identifying not only 'those men' but also the underlying cause of 'our past political follies'. Sexual irregularity, he told his readers, was the prime qualification for inclusion in the 'Black Book'. Thus it is no surprise that he implicitly yoked together privy councillors and the rather contemptuously labelled 'youths of the chorus' (and paralleled this zeugma with the even more picturesque coupling of the 'wives of Cabinet Ministers' and 'dancing girls'). Nor is it insignificant that he chose to include 'poets' among those he seems to have been both damning and defending.

Three quarters of a century on, the thrust of his article seems alarmist and vaguely absurd. Stripped of its tub-thumping, however, it is vividly illustrative of the mood of the period. Pemberton-Billing was writing at a time when sex and all matters sexual were for the first time being seriously discussed. Quite independently, the medical and psychological theorizing which implicitly underpins our 'modern' thinking about everything from pregnancy to homosexuality and a tentative experimentation into the feasibility of relationships a world away from the received (but largely illusory) picture of the cosiness of nineteenth-century family life were subverting pink imperial certainties long before trouble in the Balkans more fundamentally clouded the horizons of those on whose Empire the sun never set.

Sigmund Freud had published *Die Traumdeutung* (*The Interpretation of Dreams*), arguing that dreams are little more than manifestations of sexual desire, in 1900. *The Psychopathology of Everyday Life* followed in 1904; *Three Essays on the Theory of Sexuality* in 1905. Marie Stopes's pioneering advocacy of contraception and the idea of family planning began in 1916 with the publication of her book *Married Love*. More insidiously, little more than ten years later Marguerite Radclyffe-Hall's novel *Adam's Breed* won the Femina Vie Heureuse prize; her better-known story, *The Well of Loneliness*, first appeared in 1928.

The intellectual climate was changing with bewildering rapidity. On 1 October 1913 Harold Nicolson, then an Oxford-educated British diplomat, was able to enter into what we would now call an open marriage with Vita Sackville-West. Even before it was celebrated he had described the arrangement as 'our amazing marriage', implicitly acknowledging that before the wedding he and Vita had mutually agreed on a relationship in which both would be free to pursue extra-marital affairs with members of their own sex. Honesty and openness were the only bench-marks (honesty and openness on such a scale that when their son Nigel Nicolson's book *Portrait of a Marriage* was published in 1973 a review was entitled 'Portrait of a *What?*'). The nature of Vita's enduring relationship with Virginia Woolf is well documented; not unnaturally perhaps, accounts of the intimacy and extent of Nicolson's more temporary homosexual dalliances are some-what more circumspect. A letter he wrote to Vita as early as 1919, describing the beginning of a liaison with the couturier Edward Moly-neux, graphically illustrates both the strength and the pussy-footing necessary for the maintenance of such a marriage. Writing from the offices of the British Delegation in Paris, Nicolson confided:

> I have got such a funny new friend – a dressmaker, with a large shop in the in the Rue Royale, a charming flat at the Rond Point (where I spent the *whole* of Saturday night – sleeping on the balcony) and about 10 mannequins of surpassing beauty. I am lunching at the shop today. My dressmaker is only 27 – and it is rather sporting to launch out into so elaborate an adventure at that age. Mar would like my new friend, I think – very attractive. Such a nice flat too. I think I shall stay there when and if I come back and not go to the Majestic. There is a spare room and I would pay for my board.[3]

In the aftermath of the Wilde trials – and it was a long aftermath; shockwaves continued to reverberate until well after the outbreak of the Great War – men like Harold Nicolson remained the exceptions rather than the rule. Freud and Freudian theory had yet to be adduced as contributory or mitigating factors in the increasing number of cases of 'immorality' and 'gross indecency' brought before the courts. Rather, just as they had in Wilde's day, money and social status cocooned the likes of Harold Nicolson. Meanwhile, more ordinary homosexual men were singled out and pilloried – and any boys displaying signs which could be interpreted as warnings of an incipient effeminacy were firmly directed towards the Victorian 'straight and narrow'.

The writer Beverley Nichols recalled how in around 1914 (when he would have been in his mid-teens) he was discovered by his father reading a copy of *The Picture of Dorian Gray*. 'You *pretty* little bastard! You *pretty* little boy!' his father shouted at him. 'Oscar Wilde! To think that my son . . .' And then he spat on the book and ripped it apart with his teeth. Nichols protested – disingenuously by all the evidence, since the book was a gift from an older, overtly homosexual friend – that he knew nothing about Wilde. The next day his father enlightened him. 'That is what the man did,' he said, handing his son a sheet of paper on which was written: 'ILLUM CRIMEN HORRIBILE QUOD NON NOMINANDUM EST'. Nichols *fils*, who went on to read Latin at Oxford, construed this as meaning, 'The horrible crime which is not to be named'.[4]

John Betjeman, too, experienced the measure of this anti-Wildean backlash and recalled how 'Oscar' had emerged as a new bogey-man-coming-to-get-you, the ultimate sanction for anxious upper middle-class parents, within a very few years of his death in 1900. A late but transparently autobiographical poem, 'Narcissus', explores Betjeman's mother's fears about her pre-teenaged son's (seemingly innocent) friendship with a similarly young boy named Bobby. Even before the Great War, some things were 'unwholesome':

> . . . when we just did nothing we were good
> But when we touched each other we were bad.

But it was not just that:

> And then she said I was her precious child,
> And once there was a man called Oscar Wilde.[5]

In an interview with his biographer Bevis Hillier (recorded in 1976) Betjeman elaborated on the extent to which what we would now call this homophobic prejudice clouded his childhood and schooldays:

When I was at Marlborough I discovered that Oscar Wilde was someone one ought not to mention; so naturally he had great attraction for me [. . .] Then I discovered that Lord Alfred Douglas was actually still alive. So I wrote to him from Marlborough.

[His replies] arrived from Belgium about once a week while I was on holiday in Cornwall.

[My father] said: 'You've been having letters from Lord Alfred

Douglas.' I couldn't deny it. 'Do you know what that man is?' I said: 'No.' 'He's a bugger. Do you know what buggers are? Buggers are two men who work themselves up into such a state of mutual admiration that one puts his piss-pipe up the other one's arse. What do you think of that?' And of course I felt absolutely sick, and shattered.[6]

The reactions of Nichols *père* and Betjeman *père* were not uncommon. Around the turn of the century homosexuals of all ages and classes felt cowed and helpless. Their proclivities now increasingly discussed in the new era of openness, they were still vicariously stigmatized by the obloquy which had been heaped on Wilde, while their public – and even private – behaviour remained circumscribed by the strictures of the Criminal Law Amendment Act. As, indeed, it was intended to be, now that the genie was out of the bottle: twenty-three men convicted of 'unnatural crime' were punished with fifteen strokes of the birch each in the twelve months between 1 November 1911 and 31 October 1912.

Not surprisingly, all this served irrevocably to change the nature of what, then as now, it is convenient but misleadingly simplistic to call the homosexual 'community'. Undoubtedly, among some of its 'members' it bolstered a new strength and defiance. But those brave Edwardians and Georgians who felt (in another wildly anachronistic phrase) 'glad to be gay' shared the same feeling of anomy which was to cloud the lives of a vastly greater number of homosexual men for the next two generations. The distinguished journalist and foreign correspondent Michael Davidson was one such. Born in 1897, he had recognized from an early age that his inclinations were predominantly pederastic, but his characterization of his own teenage feelings of isolation are wholly typical:

It was astraddle my 18th birthday that my first 'adult' sexual encounters occurred: that I discovered that grown-ups could behave just as I felt like behaving. I knew by now exactly what I wanted; and though the young men I lived among, in spite of their endless talk about women, now and then paired off in bed for bodily larks, I knew that this was mainly a boyish hangover and quite different from my own yearning. And *I still vaguely believed that I and Oscar Wilde – and, I suppose, that unlucky man at the Southampton swimming pool — were the only people since the age of Alkibiades to be* born *with this yearning.* Now I learned from experience that there must be quite a lot of men, and even women, who wanted boys . . .'[7]

This essential sense of *differentness* colours both the homosexual writing of the time and the more casual recollections of other men who, like Davidson, knew 'the scene'. It is immediately apparent in a clutch of *Last Poems* by A. E. Housman. It pervades the whole of *Maurice*, the posthumously published novel which E. M. Forster wrote, seemingly as an act of self-assertion, in 1913–14. It lingers, too, behind the cast of outsider figures, spies and strangers ('Look, stranger . . .') which populates the early work of such homosexual writers as W. H. Auden and Christopher Isherwood who were born in the twentieth century and did not come to prominence until the early 1930s.

Published in 1922, Housman's *Last Poems* were prefaced by a note from the author which concluded with the sentence: 'About a quarter of this matter belongs to the April of the present year, but most of it to dates between 1895 and 1910.' This is in itself of more than biblio-graphical significance: times — and Housman himself — had changed. By 1922 the man whom Max Beerbohm had memorably described as looking like an absconding cashier had largely tamed and subjugated the strangely asexual, almost Hellenic passion which had fired so much of his earlier work. The *Last Poems* show little of the wistful, if com-plaisant, innocence that had been largely responsible for the immense popularity of his first volume, *A Shropshire Lad*. George Orwell was later to recall that, as a teenager, he knew all of its sixty-three poems by heart. Tellingly, W. H. Auden explained why: better than any other English poet, in *A Shropshire Lad* Housman had expressed the true sensibility of the male adolescent.

The poems were certainly written from the heart. Housman had had his own lad, a man called Moses Jackson, a friend from university days with whom he had what has been called a 'passionate attachment'. But in 1887 Jackson had broken off the relationship, emigrated to America and — possibly even more galling for Housman — married.

'Think no more, lad; laugh, be jolly', *A Shropshire Lad* exhorted — although hindsight had already overlaid the phrase with a certain hollow irony. One of the later poems in that collection included the lines:

I too would be where I am not.
I too survey that endless line
Of men whose thoughts are not as mine.[8]

Another began:

When I came last to Ludlow
    Amidst the moonlight pale,
Two friends kept step beside me,
    Two honest lads and hale.

Now Dick lies long in the churchyard,
    And Ned lies long in jail[9]

In the *Last Poems* this tone was intensified to one in which private melancholy was transfigured by anger. The collection revealed with remarkable honesty how wretched the world still seemed to a cultured homosexual man more than a quarter of a century after Wilde's imprisonment.

It is even more remarkable since, at the time of its first publication, Housman, born in 1859, was in his early sixties and, outwardly at least, the fastidiously correct professor of Latin at Cambridge University. *Last Poems* bears an urgent, italicized epigraph beginning

We'll to the woods no more,
The laurels are all cut,
The bowers are bare of bay
    That once the Muses wore,

but one of the later poems, composed in around 1900, cuts through the bucolic, (pre-)Georgian lexis and seems to speak from the heart:

The laws of God, the laws of man,
He may keep that will and can;
Not I: let God and man decree
Laws for themselves and not for me;
And if my ways are not as theirs
Let them mind their own affairs.
Their deeds I judge and much condemn,
Yet when did I make laws for them?
Please yourselves, say I, and they
Need only look the other way.

But no, they will not; they must still
Wrest their neighbour to their will,
And make me dance as they desire
With jail and gallows and hell-fire.
And how am I to face the odds
Of man's bedevilment and God's?
I, a stranger and afraid
In a world I never made.
They will be master, right or wrong;
Though both are foolish, both are strong.
And since, my soul, we cannot fly
To Saturn nor to Mercury,
Keep we must, if keep we can,
These foreign laws of God and man.[10]

In choosing to write, albeit privately, a novel with an explicitly homo-sexual theme at this time, then, E. M. Forster was venturing into a no man's land. Not for nothing was *Maurice* wistfully dedicated to 'a Happier Year'. Hedged around no less than Housman by the admit-tedly caricatured prospect of 'jail and gallows and hell-fire', and by the all-too-potent spectre of 'law' and 'the laws' (the words appear five times in Housman's poem), Forster nevertheless decided to make the best of things. He explained in 1960 that 'a happy ending was imperative. I shouldn't have bothered to write [the novel] otherwise. I was determined that in fiction anyway two men should fall in love and remain in it for the ever and ever that fiction allows.'[11]

That last sentence is important. It exactly encapsulates the sentiments of the post-Wildean homosexual. (Forster, born in 1879, was sixteen at the time of the Wilde trials; thirty-four and, like his protagonist, still closely tied to his mother when he began work on *Maurice*.) There are two implicit *idées*: that 'two men should fall in love and remain in it'; and that – at least until the turn of that 'Happier Year' – such a situation could obtain only 'for the ever and ever that fiction allows'. The tone is simultaneously optimistic and despairing.

So, too, is the novel's. A brave, if slight, work ('publishable – but worth it?' Forster noted, having re-read and slightly re-written it in 1960), its heart is very clearly on its sleeve. Although it has far more in common with such of Forster's earlier novels as *The Longest Journey* (1907) and *A Room with a View* (1908) than with his later and more densely symbolic *A Passage to India* (1924), it is also incomparably more open and honest than any homo-erotic or homosexually inclined novel actually published at this period. Even *The Loom of Youth* (1917), Alec Waugh's then notorious story involving a public school 'pash', is fey in comparison.

In a fractured narrative (four parts; forty-six short chapters, some of which run for little more than half a page) *Maurice* tells the story of the eponymous Maurice Hall's progress through public school and Cambridge to superficial commercial eminence in London and ulti-mate sexual fulfilment. Even before he was out of his teens, Forster tells us, Maurice had recognized his own sexuality and realized that he was trapped and floundering in a threateningly alien world. While still at school he had 'longed for smut, but heard little and contributed less, and his chief indecencies were solitary [. . .] he desisted from these after the novelty was over, finding that they brought him more fatigue than pleasure'.[12] Masturbation, the silent serial-adoration of fellow-pupils and the development of strategies for self-protection came to dominate his waking life. But nothing is wholly satisfactory. He is in 'the Valley of the Shadow of Life', and remains in it 'longer than most boys' . . . until he goes up to Cambridge, indeed; until he encounters a fellow-student, the upper-class Clive Durham, in the Dean's translation class. Then, suddenly, everything seems to fall into place:

> Mr Cornwallis observed in a flat toneless voice: 'Omit: a reference to the unspeakable vice of the Greeks.' Durham observed afterwards that he ought to lose his fellowship for such hypocrisy.
>
> Maurice laughed.
>
> 'I regard it as a point of pure scholarship. The Greeks, or most of them, were that way inclined, and to omit it is to omit the mainstay of Athenian society.'
>
> 'Is that so?'
>
> 'You've read the *Symposium*?'
>
> Maurice had not, and did not add that he had explored Martial.
>
> 'It's all there – not meat for babes, of course, but you ought to read it. Read it this vac.'[13]

Inevitably, 'a breath of liberty' having fired Maurice's passion, the two embark on an affair – but one chastely constrained by the *Symposium* and its platonic protocols: 'They walked arm in arm or arm around shoulder now. When they sat it was nearly always in the same position – Maurice in a chair, and Durham at his feet, leaning against him. In the world of their friends this attracted no notice. Maurice would stroke Durham's hair.'[14]

It is not altogether surprising that the young men's sedate behaviour 'attracted no notice' – nor that the reader is actively encouraged to believe that Maurice rather wishes that it would. ' "You and I are outlaws," ' he tells Durham, optimistically, on one occasion. ' "All this" – he pointed to the middle-class comfort of the room – "would be taken from us if people knew." '[15] This is the theme which Forster wishes to explore. Explicitly, in *Maurice* he pits sedate, acceptable, socratic, hair-stroking notions of homosexuality against a much more carnal reality in exactly the same way as D. H. Lawrence was to test the ideal of Love on the annealing-stone of sex in *Lady Chatterley's Lover* (1928). It was only because Constance Chatterley was such a 'good fuck' that her husband's gamekeeper, Mellors, stayed with her (and vice versa). More decorously than Lawrence, Forster pursues this reality in *Maurice*. (Tellingly, the word 'fuck' occurs only once in the novel – but that is once more than in the whole of the *oeuvre* which was published in his lifetime.)

Maurice Hall wants that same good fuck, and it quickly becomes apparent that he is not going to get it from Clive. Down from Cambridge, pursuing independent careers in the City and at the Bar respectively, the men rapidly fall into a convenient but asexual and frustratingly suburban respectability:

Maurice's habits became regular. He ate a large breakfast and caught the 8.36 to town. In the train he read the *Daily Telegraph*. He worked until 1.00, lunched lightly, and worked again through the afternoon. Returning home, he had some exercise and a large dinner, and in the evening he read the evening paper, or laid down the law, or played billiards or bridge.

But every Wednesday he slept at Clive's little flat in town. Weekends were also inviolable. They said at home 'You must never interfere with Maurice's Wednesdays or with his weekends. He would be most annoyed.'[16]

Outwardly, the two live 'like other men' and have 'as much happiness as men under [their] star can expect': 'What a solid young citizen [Maurice] looked – quiet, honourable, prosperous without vulgarity. On such does England rely,' Forster comments. But there, along with his later depiction of Maurice and Clive's pat, conventional version of bachelor 'perfection', he is at his most scornfully ironic. His portrait of their relationship is only too redolent of the crusty, pipes-slippers-housekeeper-and-no-questions relationships enjoyed by Sherlock Holmes and Dr Watson in Arthur Conan Doyle's stories and Henry Higgins and Colonel Pickering in George Bernard Shaw's *Pygmalion* (1912). It is all a sham, Forster is saying; and in the final chapters of the novel he wastes no time in shattering it with a powerful plea for honesty, openness and sexual liberation.

Maurice, the 'Outlaw', rebels against all that an increasingly strait-laced, puritanical Clive stands for. In particular he comes to hate his former friend's dishonesty and self-deception – the way in which he denies his own 'criminal morbidity'; his insistence that 'the sole excuse for any relationship between men is that it remain purely platonic'; his schoolmasterly, Arnoldian notions of 'the ideal man – chaste with asceticism'. Forster colludes in all this by consigning Clive to a living hell ('He has annoyed me,' he notes). He marries him off to a girl called Anne and into a domesticity that is 'temperate and graceful'. Once again, the irony is heavy and deliberate. The novel gives ghastly glimpses of a marriage in which, unlike manly Cambridge 'sets' – or even Bloomsbury drawing rooms – 'much could never be mentioned. [Clive] never saw [Anne] naked, nor she him. They ignored the reproductive and the digestive functions.'

<hr>

There were, of course, forces far stronger than the mere dictates of the plot and an author's need for a 'happy ending' behind all this. Out of sheer personal pain and longing, in Maurice Hall the reserved and reticent Forster created almost the exact antithesis of himself. Maurice was 'someone handsome, healthy, bodily attractive, mentally torpid, not a bad business man and rather a snob'.[17] He was Forster's paradigm of the 'ideal' homosexual (though far, as we shall see, from his own concept of the ideal man). Retrospectively, we can also see him as the first convincingly *real* homosexual hero of twentieth-century fiction.

He is as fully rounded as *A Passage to India*'s Dr Aziz – and, crucially, he goes through the same dark nights of fear and self-loathing as comparable real-life figures of his age and class. He sees doctors, hoping for a 'cure' that will make him just as 'normal' as Clive. 'Might it not be better to alter [my] temperament and toe the line?' he asks himself, adding that he has 'only to keep away from boys and young men'.

But he cannot and, increasingly lonely and solipsistic once he has accepted that Clive is no longer interested in him, he decisively throws off the subfusc in a desperate search for the 'perfection' which only one of those 'beloved' boys or young men can bring. In a manner in which his creator could not, this 'unspeakable of the Oscar Wilde sort' takes his life (or certainly his liberty) in his hands and sets out to crash through the barriers of class and convention into elemental territory where, he is sure, happiness and fulfilment are to be found. 'Perhaps', he tells himself, 'among those who took to the greenwood in old time there had been two men like himself – two. At times he entertained the dream. Two men can defy the world.'[18]

It is at this point that Forster knowingly takes *Maurice*, too, into the realm of dreams (or at least of the unpublishable) and the book becomes a personal manifesto. Its final chapters tell how, during a family week-end, the newly emboldened Maurice only narrowly succeeds in sub-duing sudden, fiercely sexual longings for a teenaged fellow-guest. It is a close call, and one that finally confronts Maurice (and the reader) with an unsettlingly graphic view of the chasm which separates roman-tic notions of 'outlaws' and 'the beloved' from what we would soon learn to call the 'Freudian' urges of 'the wildwood'. 'Was it', Maurice worries, appalled at this indication of the real nature of his proclivities, 'conceivable that on Sunday last he had nearly assaulted a boy?'

Well, yes. Bravely and uniquely, in the few pages he devotes to this episode Forster was addressing one – possibly the greatest – of the homophobic prejudices which had been given new currency by the arrest and conviction of Oscar Wilde less than twenty years previously. The notion that there was an essentially paedophiliac side to homo-sexual behaviour had been one of the canards which lay behind many of the public reports of the Wilde trials. 'Were these young men all about twenty?' the forty-year-old Wilde had been asked. 'Yes; twenty or twenty-two. I like the society of young men,' he had guilelessly replied. That brought it into the public consciousness, but it had never been far from the homosexual sensibility. (The cant word 'chicken', generally applied to a child of either gender for at least two centuries, became an enduring part of homosexual argot as a specific description of an under-age catamite at around this time.)

Images of a Ganymede – we might almost say a Bosie – a beautiful, compliant, cup-bearer to an older, more powerful man, run through literature from classical times to the present. As recently as 1980 Anthony Burgess began his novel *Earthly Powers* with the breathtakingly audacious sentence: 'It was the afternoon of my eighty-first birthday, and I was in bed with my catamite when Ali announced that the archbishop had come to see me.' A generation earlier, in his autobiography *The World, the Flesh and Myself*, Michael Davidson had gone, if anything, even farther in a frank defence of his own proclivities. Somewhat unconvincingly, he put it all down to

> an inveterate 'motherliness', the broody fussiness with which I've coddled all my boys – plaguing them about warm underclothes or changing their wet socks, and trying to 'feed them up' after they were already full [. . .] I know that in all my relationships, other than the most casual, I've been driven just as much by a passionate protectiveness as by sexual interest – the second, for all I know, may be an extension of the first, as a mother gets sensual pleasure out of suckling. And even during actual bodily play, *my* pleasure – beyond the mental joy of seeing and touching, which is intense – comes from a consummate privity to *his* pleasure; if that's absent, the whole process seems absurd and pointless.[19]

In the years immediately following the Wilde trials the publication of material such as this would have been unthinkable. Wilde's courtroom one-liners were in themselves raw reminders of the recently discovered 'loathsome' side of homosexuality: somewhat surprisingly, A. E. Housman's rather disingenuous references to 'lovely lads' in *A Shropshire Lad* seemingly went unremarked when the collection was first published in 1896.

Forster cannot quite bring himself to deny the *potential* of the Zeus-Ganymede model as the basis of a homosexual relationship in *Maurice*. Indeed, brief as it is, his account of his hero's momentary temptation by the ambivalently drawn and seemingly complaisant 'schoolboy' Dickie Barry is the most explicitly 'erotic' passage in the book. It describes how, one Sunday morning, Maurice was sent up to the youngster's bedroom to rouse him for breakfast. He went upstairs 'with the tread of an older man' and opened the door:

> The boy, who had been to a dance the night before, remained asleep. He lay with his limbs uncovered. He lay unashamed, embraced and penetrated by the sun. The lips were parted, the down on the upper was touched with gold, the hair broken into countless glories, the body was a delicate amber. To anyone he would have seemed beautiful, and to Maurice who reached him by two paths he became the World's desire.[20]

'Uncovered', 'unashamed', 'embraced', 'penetrated', 'glories', 'beautiful', 'desire' . . . the sheer lushness of the vocabulary conveys the power – and importance – of what Forster is trying to say. Maurice is attracted to the boy, and for the whole of that Sunday it seems likely that he will yield to temptation. In the afternoon he 'got arm in arm with [Dickie], and extracted a promise for tea. It was kept.' There was one further tryst, too:

> They met once more – at midnight. [. . .]
> The variety of developments are endless, and it so happened that [Dickie] understood the situation perfectly. If Hall insisted, he would not kick up a row, but he had rather not: he felt like that about it.
> 'I'm above,' panted Maurice, not daring. 'In the attic over this – if you want anything – all night alone. I always am.'
> Dickie's impulse was to bolt the door after him, but he dismissed it as unsoldierly, and awoke to the ringing of the breakfast bell, with the sun on his face and his mind washed clean.[21]

'It so happened . . .': there is a curious, fairy-tale patness about the way in which Forster saves Maurice from himself. It *was* a close call; and by the following Friday Maurice is profoundly grateful for Dickie's bluff decency – and agonizing over the reasons which lay behind what had so nearly happened:

> His feeling for Dickie required a very primitive name. He would have sentimentalized once and called it adoration, but the habit of honesty had grown strong. What a stoat he had been! Poor little Dickie! He saw the boy leaping from his embrace, to smash through

the window and break his limbs, or yelling like a maniac until help came. He saw the police –

'Lust'. He said the word out loud.[22]

꧁꧂

Within little more than three pages Forster thus both discusses and dismisses the idea of boy-love: had his words appeared in print more immediately, they might even have gone some way towards disentangling the frequently malicious yoking of pederasty and homosexuality which was an enduring feature of newspaper reports of homosexual cases in the post-Wilde era. It is frankly and almost matter-of-factly done – not least because the subject was of little interest to him. It is clear from P. N. Furbank's *E. M. Forster* and other biographical material both modern and contemporary that the likes of Dickie Barry held little appeal for Forster himself. Nor, as *Maurice* makes clear, did 'lovely lads' even have much of a place in his dream world where 'two men should fall in love for the ever and ever'. Ironically, the differentiation between homosexuality and pederasty which a Victorian or Edwardian would have made is easier to appreciate now than it would have been a generation or more ago. In the wake of the decriminalization of homosexuality in 1967, the emergence of AIDS and the even more recent public concern at the possible extent of child sex abuse, both subjects have received considerable media attention, with the result that the ignorant or sometimes wilful confusion of the two is markedly less widespread than it used to be. Here and in the following pages it is important to maintain this distinction. Whatever else they were, and in common with the other men featured in this book, Wilde and Lord Arthur Somerset were not pederasts. Bosie, Charles Parker and the wretched procession of Post Office 'boys' and valets with whom their names were linked were in their late teens or older (Bosie was twenty-one, for instance, and Parker eighteen) when they first became involved with them. Similarly, the majority of A. E. Housman's 'lovely lads' were serving soldiers, while even their Sicilian contemporaries, the Taormina 'peasant-boys' whom Baron von Gloeden (1856–1931) photographed in 'Socratic' poses, were very plainly post-pubertal.

Far more central to the idea of the 'lovely lad' and the whole notion of 'man love' then, as now, was the lower-class origin of the 'loved

one'. Indeed, the appeal of 'a bit of rough' or 'rough trade' in general
– and the risks of a physical relationship with a sexually pliable
working-class young man which transcends but simultaneously
reinforces class boundaries – has always been central to the homosexual
experience. Wilde, again, enjoyed 'feasting with panthers' – *'Did you
know that Parker was a gentleman's servant out of employment?'* – and he
was neither the first nor, despite everything, the last. Closer to our
own times, J. R. Ackerley, Tom Driberg, W. H. Auden, Christopher
Isherwood, Beverley Nichols, Denton Welch and many others found
consolation, if not real love, down in 'the wildwood'. Indeed, the
walk-on role of the frequently anonymous 'little lad', the 'golden boy',
the 'baby-boy' or the ubiquitous 'secretary' is one of the century's most
enduring. Financially vulnerable, frequently unemployed, these inamor-
ati were 'available', 'to be had' ('TBH' in the parlance of the day) and,
though often fundamentally heterosexual, willingly complaisant.

There were, famously, guardsmen to be had in London; but there
were also tram-drivers, lift-boys, waiters, barmen, sailors and (in
Forster's case) policemen. Uniforms conferred special status – as John
Gambril Nicholson's poem 'Your City Cousin' (included in a 1911
collection called *A Garland of Ladslove*) had made very clear:

> Smart looking lads are in my line;
> The lad that gives my shoes a shine,
> The lad that works the lift below,
> That lad that's lettered GPO.

Out of town, the rough, manly tweeds and corduroys of agricultural
workers (far more numerous before the Second World War than they
are today) also had their appeal. With all the leaden sentimentality of
Gambril Nicholson, in 1866 an anonymous country squire had written:

> Among the yeomen's sons on my estate
> A gentle boy would at my mansion wait:
> And now that time has almost blanched my hair,
> And with the past the present I compare;
> Full well I know, though decency forbade
> The same caresses to the rustic lad,
> Love, love it was that made my eyes delight
> To have this person ever in my sight.

More than half a century later, the writer Denton Welch recalled how, as an eighteen-year-old in the summer of 1933, he had gone alone on a walking tour of the West Country. A sixteen-year-old farmer's boy had rebuffed his advances, but then a young farmer riding 'a huge horse' stopped him. Wouldn't he like to jump up and have a ride? Welch did, and found himself settled in front of the saddle, between the farmer's legs: 'I could smell his clothes – the mingled tobacco, beer, horse and sweat that clung to them; and I could tell how hot he was, for I was pressed hard against him as he reached round for the reins. I could even feel his heart beating into my back [. . .] I felt the hard press of his thighs and legs along my own.'[23]

❦

'Funking of intimacy', Forster noted in 1951 when he read an unpublished version of Welch's journals which included that passage. And with some justification: a third of a century (and two world wars) previously, he had easily bettered what he called Welch's tone of 'sham-innocence and cock-teasiness'.[24] The final chapters of *Maurice* had explored the true nature of what was, and had never been other than, a class-based, essentially predatory form of proprietorialism. They had described the reality which lay behind Welch's evocation of that working-class, *Cold Comfort Farm*-ish scent of tobacco, beer, horse and sweat and his suggestive mention of the 'hard press of his thighs'.

On the surface this seems perverse. *Maurice* was, after all, written a year or more before Welch was so much as born. But it is a mistake to assume that 'gay liberation' advanced on a smooth, accelerating curve which brought it from the nadir of the 1890s to the relative tolerance and commercial success it came to enjoy in the 1970s and early 1980s, before the identification in Britain of the human immuno-deficiency virus (HIV) and the first reports of deaths related to Acquired Immunodeficiency Syndrome (AIDS) both shattered confidence and bolstered popular prejudice. And, as we have already seen, it is an even bigger mistake to see homosexual men as having ever been a cohesive group within society. This is the error Noël Pemberton Billing made in lumping together his privy councillors and 'youths of the chorus' among 'The First 47,000'. Even among the outlaws there was always squabbling in the camp. If the Forster of 1951 now sounds avuncularly *knowing*, even condescending, in his reaction to what Welch had written (and Welch had died in 1948), it is important to note that, irrespective of the age difference between them, the two men sprang from markedly different traditions. To Forster, Welch must have seemed maladroit, an ingrate, a cock-teaser for whom thighs were only thighs and sex was only sex.

As *Maurice* makes clear, more than a decade before Welch was even approaching adolescence a wholly different homosexuality had emerged; one which, although it embraced the ideal of the 'golden boy', even in the early years of this century stood out in stark contrast to the effete effusions of Aestheticism. The novel concludes with a hymn to the very 'intimacy' in which Welch's *faux-naïf* innocence plays no part. It is an ecomium to corduroys, to the rough and to the same wildwood which D. H. Lawrence would unwittingly echo a decade later in *Lady Chatterley's Lover*. We have to rejoin the story in Chapter XXXVII: months after his near-calamitous encounter with Dickie, Maurice is spending a weekend with Clive and Anne at Penge. One night he throws open his bedroom window in a melodramatic attempt once more to become 'the outlaw', to cut through the 'rubbish' of his life and reach the reality of that wildwood, to connect with 'love − nobility − big spaces where passion clasped peace, spaces no science could reach'.

Through this window climbs Alec Scudder, under-gamekeeper on the Penge estate. 'Sir, was you calling out for me?' he says. 'Sir, I know . . . I know.'

The two enjoy a passionate night together, but the social and class differences between them seems to preclude the possibility of their developing a deeper relationship. Even as he sets up his happy ending, Forster remains surprisingly level-headed. Once we arrive there, he allows the realities of life in 'the wildwood' to speak for themselves: there is − and, he implies, there always would be − an uneasiness and inequality in Maurice's relationship with his chosen bit of rough:

> 'May I ask your name?' [Maurice] said awkwardly.
>   'I'm Scudder.'
>   'I know you're Scudder − I meant your other name.'
>   'Only Alec just.'

'Jolly name to have.'
'It's only my name.'
'I'm called Maurice.'[25]

It's propriety versus paganism, prose versus passion, nurture versus nature. Maurice is too cautious and, after the incident with Dickie, cannot trust himself to see Scudder again. Scudder, in turn, is only days away from emigrating to Argentina. Confusion and consternation – first at the British Museum, where they arrange to meet, but only argue; then on the deck of the SS *Normannia* in Southampton, where it is discovered that Scudder has not taken up his berth . . . Reunion and a tentative reconciliation take place back at Penge where the two men rediscover each other for that happy ending: 'Now we shan't be parted no more,' Scudder says, 'and that's finished.'

⟞⟞⟞

Re-read today, *Maurice* comes over as a complex and confused piece of work. Eschewing the complacency of *A Room with a View*, it is neither a 'trade' novel calculated to please the pre-Great War patrons of Boots' and Mudie's subscription libraries nor a tale raunchy enough to satisfy the tastes of a readership for whom, by the time of its eventual publication in 1971, the term 'trade' had taken on a whole new meaning. It should not, however, be lightly dismissed. The half-century gap between its composition and publication exactly matches the prolonged parturition and painful coming-of-age of the twentieth-century British homosexual. And the fact that – unlike, say, *The Loom of Youth* – it was not written for the market gives it a special value. It is a prison diary, an honest and only-recently-discovered account of 'how it was then'.

In the character of Maurice Hall it reveals the gulf which lay between what early twentieth-century society had lately come to expect of the upper middle-class (homosexual) man – 'indoors was his place and there he'd moulder, a respectable pillar of society who has never had the chance to misbehave' – and the secret 'outlaw' role which that same society's attitudes and his own 'inversion' forced him to adopt. Less successfully (largely, it has to be said, because of Forster's inability to create convincing working-class characters), it also examines the powerful appeal and inherent instability of inter-class relationships – and in doing so touches on a far wider issue.

'Only connect' was always Forster's message. He had made it explicit in his earlier novel *Howards End* (1910): 'Only connect, the prose and the passion'. Now he was descanting on the theme and improvising on the idea of a future – a 'Happier Year' – in which it would be possible to be true to oneself, complete, and enjoy a physical connection with the companion of one's choice which somehow went beyond Denton Welch's sex-*qua*-sex view of things and reached almost spiritual heights. In the penultimate chapter of *Maurice* the eponymous hero has *almost* got there; he is certainly in the foothills:

> His journey was nearly over. He was bound for his new home. He had brought out the man in Alec, and now it was Alec's turn to bring out the hero in him. He knew what the call was, and what his answer must be. They must live outside class, without relations or money; they must work and stick to each other till death. But England belonged to them. That, besides companionship, was their reward.[26]

If all this now sounds sentimentally unrealistic, it is because we have come a long way from the immediate post-Wildean world. There is no one alive now who was adult then; no one who can testify to the telling, if admittedly small-scale, Edwardian recrudescence of the open sexuality which had characterized the early 1890s and would not emerge again until the 1960s. In retrospect we can point to the emergence of Freud and Marie Stopes, and try to show how the climate of the times had emboldened D. H. Lawrence. We can search the autobiographies and private correspondence of the period, but (with the dubious exception of the flamboyantly heterosexual Frank Harris's) they are discreetly, legally anodyne.

Maurice remains a unique work in the homosexual canon because it attempts to capture and make concrete something that was never more than an under-tow. Like so many currents, however, it was mightily powerful. In literature it dragged at George Bernard Shaw and was eventually to shipwreck Lawrence on a reef of critical and legal controversy. Before it did so, however, it was Lawrence who, even more vividly than Forster, best brought it to life. Outwardly grounded in their author's ostensibly fecund heterosexuality (although this, like that of Ernest Hemingway, has latterly been the subject of some critical interest), Lawrence's novels too have a subtext. In *Women in Love* (1921) Gerald Critch and Birkin – broad heterosexual parallels of Maurice Hall and Scudder – 'normal' men, who also hail from separate social classes, come close to swearing their undying allegiance to each other in a platonic pact inspired by the working-class Birkin's somewhat unlikely enthusiasm for the 'obsolete' medieval German concept of *Blutbrüderschaft* ('blood-brotherhood'). 'We ought to swear to love each other, you and I, implicitly, and perfectly, finally, without any possibility of going back on it,' he tells Gerald. The latter is confused: 'He looked down at [Birkin], attracted, so deeply bondaged in fascinated attraction, that he was mistrustful, resenting the bondage, hating the attraction.' Later, however, but – tellingly – only after a bout of nude wrestling with Birkin, his thoughts crystallize and, quite literally, he levels with his social inferior: 'I've never felt it myself – not what I should call love. I've gone after women – and been keen enough over some of them. But I've never felt *love*. I don't believe I've ever felt as much *love* for a woman as I have for you – not *love*. You understand what I mean?'[27]

Writing out of impatience with a conservative status quo, Lawrence could say things at which the congenitally conservative Forster could only hint. Both, however, were responding to the rapidly changing mood of the times. As we have seen, sex, Love and *love* in all its forms were beginning to be mentioned. Even the act of writing *Maurice* was no accident. In the 'Terminal Note' which he left to be appended to the posthumously published 1971 edition of the novel, Forster described how it was written as the 'direct result' of his acquaintance-ship with the Whitmanesque seer and sexual pioneer Edward Carpenter and his 'comrade', George Merrill. One incident in the relationship had made a particular impression. Nearly half a century later Forster was able to recall how Merrill 'touched my backside – gently and just above the buttocks. I believe he touched most people's. The sensation was unusual and I still remember it, as I remember the position of a long vanished tooth. It was as much psychological as physical. It seemed to go straight through the small of my back into my ideas, without involving my thoughts.'[28]

———

It is too easy now to neglect or belittle Edward Carpenter's impact on the homosexual men left to fend for themselves in the post-Wildean vacuum. At the time, however, his influence was enormous. In the index of *Between the Acts*, a collection of the reminiscences of homosexual men covering the years between 1885 and 1967, there are six references to his name; there is only one to Wilde's.

Carpenter did more than expand the concept and vocabulary of Edwardian sexuality. Until very shortly before his death in 1929 he was a unique link between the then emerging British Modernism and the *avant-garde* of half a century earlier – the Fellowship of the New Life; H. G. Wells, Sidney and Beatrice Webb and the proto-socialist Fabian Society; William Morris and the Arts and Crafts movement. The fact that he was homosexual was almost incidental: his life story itself was almost emblematic.

Born in 1844 into a secure, pre-Darwinian world, by the age of twenty-three he had been ordained as an Anglican priest and appointed a clerical fellow at Trinity Hall, Cambridge. But academia did not suit him. He was bored by 'everlasting discussions of theories which never came anywhere near actual life'; new ideas were, quite literally, abroad. On a visit to America he had become a friend and disciple of Walt Whitman. 'Go out to nature – throw yourself in her arms – submit to her destinies,' Whitman had told him. It didn't take Carpenter long; by 1880 he had decided to 'go and make [his] life with the mass of the people and the manual workers'. There was one abiding reason for this. Carpenter later explained: 'My ideal of love is a powerful, strongly built man, of my own age or rather younger – preferably of the working class. Though having solid sense and character, he need not be specially intellectual.'[29]

At first Carpenter both made his life and found his ideal of love in the village of Totley, outside Sheffield. In 1883, however, he moved to an estate at nearby Millthorpe where, with Merrill, he created his own version of what was then called 'the Simple Life'. He espoused vegetarianism and pioneered the free, natural lifestyle which would come of age in the communes of the 1960s and 1970s. He spun rough, tweedy cloth from which he made his own clothes and spurned shoes entirely – 'leather coffins', he called them – preferring to wear his own home-made sandals. He and Merrill sunbathed whenever the weather was good enough – he was nicknamed 'hairy legs' – and swam naked in the nearby river. So too did their house-guests. And he, Carpenter, wrote – and wrote. The titles of just some of his more notable publications accurately sum up his preoccupations. There was *England's Ideal* and *Civilization, Its Cause and Cure*, and there were his later studies, *The Intermediate Sex* and *Love's Coming of Age*. His autobiography, *My Days and Dreams*, was published in 1916.

Carpenter was a maverick, but an important one. He was not a one-issue homo-political activist of the type with which we are familiar today. (He was, for instance, seemingly content for Merrill to be taken as his 'manservant'.) Rather, at Millthorpe and in his books he was reacting to a general feeling of unease, a panic which was well summed up by the popular novelist Sir Henry Rider Haggard (*King Solomon's Mines*) when he wrote, in 1899, that 'the great towns rob those who dwell and labour in them'. He was hardly alone in this. Within a very few years of the foundation of Millthorpe two 'progressive' New Schools had been established: Abbotsholme (1889), dedicated to the pursuit of 'the life of true freedom' – school hymn, 'The Love of Comrades'; compulsory nude bathing – was run by a one-time disciple of Carpenter's, Cecil Reddie; the more structured Bedales (1893) by J. H. Badley, who had been influenced by both Carpenter and Reddie.

In effect, then, Carpenter was a guru, *the* guru, for a generation of 'little men' – the Maurice Halls and Leonard Basts of Forster's fiction – who were also in quiet rebellion against what Forster called the 'vulgarity' of urban life. Forster, whose own yearnings for a 'Happier Year' happened to chime well with Carpenter's Uranianism, was to recall in 1960 that Carpenter had 'a prestige which cannot be understood today'. Half a lifetime on, those words are more true than ever. Forster went on:

> he was a rebel appropriate to his age. He was sentimental and a little sacramental [. . .] a socialist who ignored industrialism and a simple-lifer with an independent income and a Whitmannic poet whose nobility exceeded his strength [. . .] finally, he was a believer in the Love of Comrades, whom he sometimes called Uranians. It was this last aspect of him that attracted me in my loneliness.[30]

Finally, says Forster, 'he was a believer in the Love of Comrades' . . . And this is no idle taxonomy. Sex was never the centre of things at Millthorpe. 'I had never had to do with actual paederasty, so called,' Carpenter was to explain, in a particularly graceless piece of prose. 'My chief desire in love is bodily nearness or contact, as to sleep naked with a naked friend.' The opportunities for nude sunbathing and all that might follow from it were never the principal reasons for visiting him. Rather, a broad cross-section of the emerging intelligentsia of the Left headed north in search of 'a blessed physician for body, soul, and spirit' (as Reddie put it). D. H. Lawrence, George Bernard Shaw, Bertrand Russell and Rupert Brooke all arrived in the hope of enlightenment. But there *were*, not unnaturally, many homosexual men among the Millthorpe house-guests. 'Norman' was one such. Born, almost symbolically, in 1895, and at the time of his visit a sales assistant in a south London store, he had already discovered Carpenter's work and was seemingly seeking some reassurance in the post-Wilde vacuum:

I had read *The Intermediate Sex* by [about 1915]. I was also reading Compton Mackenzie, D. H. Lawrence, Dostoevsky, and oh my God, I was up there in the clouds, more brain than balls. I never read these new books about homosexuality now, [but] I read Carpenter at that time. These recent books that you see in the papers, I've never read. I like reading personal books. I read *Love's Coming of Age* and *Towards Democracy*. I had a copy when I was a soldier.[31]

Possessing, as he put it, 'more brain than balls', Norman knew – he had, after all, read the almost unreadable *Towards Democracy* – that the Uranianism of *The Intermediate Sex* and *Love's Coming of Age* was only a part of the Millthorpe milieu. Fascinatingly, what's more, for him it hardly mattered:

I saw Carpenter twice. Once in London, where he was staying in a boarding-house in Tavistock Square. I can remember going there. I must have liked the old man, because when I went north, for a time I thought I would go and see him again. *Of course, I didn't know that he was homosexual. I didn't even think of that.* He lived with George Merrill, who naturally I wasn't interested in. I thought he was the gardener. It was in the garden that Merrill kissed me. I must have been only twenty-one. Not good looking. I was rather shocked, owing to my loveless early life. I didn't know anything about kissing.[32]

We are back to *Maurice* – to the distinction between the platonic ideals of 'man-love' and the more physical pull of lust. In the novel Forster gropes his way towards bridging this gap: 'only connect'. He castigates a Cambridge in which the dons 'felt it right to spoil a love affair when they could'[33] and a world in which someone like Clive Durham is promoted as 'the ideal man – chaste with asceticism'[34] in his search for a greater, all-embracing honesty. And slowly, very slowly, he allows Maurice to find it. Gradually, insight of a distinctly Carpenterian kind dawns. Maurice

> would not – and this was the test – pretend to care about women when the only sex that attracted him was his own. He loved men and always had loved them. *He longed to embrace them and mingle his being with theirs.*[35]

> He could die for such a friend, he would allow such a friend to die for him; *they would make any sacrifice for each other, and count the world nothing, neither death nor distance nor crossness could part them,* because 'this is my friend'.[36]

But, unlike Carpenter, Forster was a realist, a pragmatist. Maurice is a convincing homosexual emblem precisely because his creator is no wide-eyed Candide. Forster's sense of irony suffuses the novel's subtext. 'The universe had been put in its place,' Maurice thinks, as he rushes to Penge for his reconciliation with Alec Scudder. But had it? Was sex – illicit, albeit consensual sex – enough to change not just the world order but the entire universe? Forster was far too aware of the realities of the life which was lived in the Britain of the first two decades of this century by men like him to give a simple answer. Instead, he hedged. But in doing so, perhaps unwittingly, in *Maurice* he identified the underlying, often unrecognized, hollowness of gay life over the next fifty years. Early on in the novel he had described how Maurice had 'remembered that Clive and he had only been together one day! And they had spent it careering about like fools – instead of in one another's arms! Maurice did not know that they had thus spent it perfectly – he was too young to detect the triviality of contact for contact's sake.'[37]

3

'I'm Awfully Proud to Think He's My Friend'

'SEX WAS, IT ALWAYS IS,/ The most enticing of mysteries', wrote W. H. Auden in a light-hearted squib of a poem looking back to the Edwardian certainties of his childhood.[1] Increasingly, however, during that same period sex in itself came to be seen as merely the beginning of something more serious; and the exigencies of the Great War only accelerated the process.

Writing in 1913–14, E. M. Forster had been more prescient than he could have imagined. After describing how Maurice Hall and Clive Durham had spent the majority of their time together 'careering about like fools – instead of in one another's arms!' he had gone on to remark, almost casually, that that was only because Maurice had been 'too young to detect the triviality of contact for contact's sake'.[2] If, for a moment, we allow the real world to impinge on the fictional, however, it is possible to flesh out that aside. We can imagine Maurice, called up only months after 'taking up' with Alec Scudder, ageing very rapidly; for the 'trouble in the Balkans' which precipitated a five-year pre-European conflagration had its implications for the British homosexual, too.

In the history books maps are rolled up and the lights go out all over Europe at this period. And, in consequence, little has been discovered or at any rate reported about the emotional, let alone the sexual, lives of 'our boys' on 'the Front'.[3] And they were just boys. It gives some sort of perspective to the tale of homosexual evolution to note that a boy born on the day of Oscar Wilde's conviction in May 1895 would have been nineteen, fresh out of public school perhaps, or already a work-hardened factory-hand or agricultural labourer, when, on 4 August 1914, Britain declared war on Germany. He would have been not quite twenty-one when Lloyd George's coalition government instituted the general conscription into the armed forces of all single men aged between eighteen and forty-one in March 1916.

Even the published works of such labile participants as Siegfried Sassoon and the Millthorpe-influenced Rupert Brooke are strangely silent about their feelings for their fellow-combatants: rare indeed are thoughts such as those of Stephen Spender who, on coming across the body of a boy shot dead in the Spanish Civil War, muses that 'He was a better target for a kiss'.[4] This is paradoxical, given the enforced propinquity of what memorialists were quick to dub 'the cream of the nation's manhood' in barracks, trenches and dug-outs and the devil-may-care attitude engendered by a situation in which odds on the survival of a front-line infantry officer were calculated in hours rather than days or weeks.

Tantalizing evidence exists, however, that some form of innocent intimacy was present, even on the front line. Ever since its first production in December 1928, *Journey's End*, R. C. Sherriff's ostensibly conventional play about trench life, has been widely praised for having caught 'the mood' and brought to the stage an accurate portrayal of How Things Seemed at the Time. A 1929 poster called it 'The Play That Is Sweeping the World' – but in all probability that was due more to the presence in the cast of a young Laurence Olivier than to the play's own verismo depiction of the way things were between 18 and 21 March 1918 (Sherriff is very specific about specifics) in a front-line dug-out at Saint-Quentin in central France.

Even today, the script is not without interest. It opens with a conversation between two middle-aged officers, Captain Hardy ('red-faced, cheerful-looking') and Osborne ('a fine head, with close-cropped, iron-grey hair. He looks about forty-five – physically as hard as nails'). They are 'old soldiers' and, over a tot of whisky, discuss the imminent arrival of a new young captain, Stanhope:

OSBORNE: There isn't a man to touch him as a commander of
   men. He'll command the battalion one day if –
HARDY: Yes, if! (*He laughs.*)
OSBORNE: You don't know him as I do; I love that fellow. I'd
   go to hell with him.

HARDY: Oh, you sweet, sentimental old darling!

OSBORNE: Come along. Finish handing over and stop blithering.

HARDY: There's nothing else to do.[5]

There is a relaxed bonhomie here; nothing in all the avuncularly –
even old-maidish – Edwardian bluster ('I love that fellow'; 'sentimental
old darling!'; 'stop blithering') betrays the slightest hint of a homosexual
under-tow. These are men forced by circumstances to 'rub along
together', who are contriving to do exactly that.

A member of the Oxfordshire and Buckinghamshire Light Infantry
remembered the camaraderie and affection which united those of the
regiment's officers and men who were forced to spend the Christmas
of 1916 in France:

> . . . our Company Officer used to get up at the front and say, 'Come
> on, Williams, give us a song, and keep the lads going.' Real bawdy
> songs they were, but it gave them a laugh and kept them going.
> Anyway at Christmas we'd all had plenty to drink and the lads had
> me on to sing. So I gave them a few of my specials. And they
> always wanted the apple song.
>
> > I once knew a fellow
> > his name was Ben,
> > He had nine of a family
> > (nearly ten!)
> > . . . Now all you gents
> > If you want any more,
> > I've an apple up me arse
> > And you can have the core!

And that wasn't the worst of it, by any means! I couldn't in all
decency repeat what came in the middle. But the lads liked it. They
all joined in, and after it was finished our sergeant came up and he
said, 'Williams, the Colonel wants to see you!' I thought, 'This is
it! Court martial for me.' So I went up to the table where all the
officers were, and Colonel Best's sitting there with his jacket
undone, smoking a cigar. He says, 'That was a good song, my lad.
Do you know any more like that?' I said, 'Well, just a few, Sir.'
So he said, 'Well, sing 'em, boy. Sing 'em!' And he gave me a
bottle of champagne![6]

Journey's End also hints, however − and it *is* no more than a hint − that there might have been a certain, repressed sexual tension behind all this. Quite reasonably, Sherriff implies that a khaki-clad version of more or less serious public-school 'pashes' and hero-worship, in which reluctant subalterns could well have been indulging only a matter of weeks before their call-up, continued in the trenches. He sets up a classically charged situation, confronting Captain Dennis Stanhope with the unexpected arrival of a one-time school friend, Raleigh.

Stanhope himself is 'no more than a boy; tall, slimly built, but broad-shouldered. His dark hair is carefully brushed; his uniform, though old and war-stained, is well cut and cared for. He is good looking, rather from attractive features than the healthy good looks of Raleigh.' Raleigh, too, is absurdly youthful: 'a well-built, healthy-looking boy of about eighteen'.[7] The decisive moment comes in the closing lines of Act II Scene 1. Cleverly, Sherriff keeps Raleigh off stage. Instead, he shows us Osborne and Stanhope censoring the letters home written by their men. One is from Raleigh:

OSBORNE (*reading*): He says: 'And now I come to the great news. I reported at Battalion Headquarters and the colonel looked in a little book, and said, 'You report to C Company − Captain Stanhope.' Can't you imagine what I felt? I was taken along some trenches and shown a dugout. There was an awfully nice officer there − quite old − with grey hair' − (OSBORNE *clears his throat*) − 'and then later Dennis came in. He looked tired, but that's because he works so frightfully hard, and because of the responsibility. Then I went on duty in the front line, and a sergeant told me all about Dennis. He said that Dennis is the finest officer in the battalion, and the men simply love him. He hardly ever sleeps in the dugout; he's always up in the front line with the men, cheering them on with jokes, and making them keen about things, like he did the kids at school. I'm awfully proud to think he's my friend.'
(*There is silence.* STANHOPE *has not moved while* OSBORNE *has read.*)
That's all. (*Pause.*) Shall I stick it down?
(STANHOPE *sits with lowered head. He murmurs something that sounds like* 'Yes, please'. *He rises heavily and crosses to the shadows*

by OSBORNE*'s bed. The sun is shining quite brightly in the trench outside.*)

THE CURTAIN FALLS[8]

As on stage, so on the page: from very different perspectives both Wilfred Owen and Michael Davidson also ruminated about the emotional the-men-simply-love-him ambiguity engendered by service life. Each was also a member of 'the officer class' and writing from direct experience. This is Owen, describing a Lieutenant (acting Captain) Sorrel in a letter he sent home from the Somme in the spring of 1917:

> He chokes filthiness as summarily as I ever heard a captain do, or try to do. He is himself an aesthete, and not virtuous according to English standards, perhaps, but no man swears in his presence, nor broaches those pleasantries which so amuse the English officer's mind.
>
> He seems to be one of the few young men who live up to my principle: that Amusement is never an excuse for 'immorality', but that Passion may be so.[9]

Quite what Owen means by describing Sorrel as 'an aesthete' and 'not virtuous according to English standards, perhaps' it is now as impossible to discover as the true import of the following paragraph. (But we might note that Owen's biographer Jon Stallworthy has established that, shortly after this letter was written, Sorrel was invalided home, suffering from shell-shock.) Lieutenant (acting Captain) Sorrel comes over, however, as a real-life Dennis Stanhope.

Sixty years on, Michael Davidson – something of a real-life Raleigh back in 1918 – was characteristically more candid when he came to write about the Great War in his autobiography:

> I was adjudged a 'good officer'; but I wasn't [. . .] I wasn't good for the men: I was too sorry for them, and shrank from 'checking' them or 'taking a name' or doing anything to add to their miseries and discomforts. I was 'familiar' with them – a disgracefully unofficer-like lapse in those days; and I made favourites; the pathetic elderly, homesick for their wives; the youngest and prettiest . . .[10]

Despite their comparative rarity, the first-hand recollections of the 'other ranks', of ordinary soldiers who had volunteered or were conscripted for service in the Great War, overwhelmingly bear out officers' mess accounts like these. Virtually all tell of a world of Tom Brown-ish affection and cold-shower purity. Even the memories of openly gay men in the main paint a picture of a service life whose wholesomeness would have appealed to Dr Arnold.

There are, seemingly, no official figures; so it is to this slim body of anecdotal evidence that we must turn to try to estimate the nature of prevalence of active homosexuality (or, more accurately, the lack of it) in the trenches; although we must be cautious in our examination of even this material. Obviously, relationships must have developed from time to time – just as there were isolated cases of desertion or (as the wartime General Orders put it) of 'misbehaving before the enemy in such a manner as to show cowardice'. That they were not officially noted, commented on in letters home or even specifically remembered by the great majority of survivors, however, is in itself important. For, just as the very word 'homosexual' was not in common currency at the time of the Great War, it seems at least distinctly possible that in working-class, non-metropolitan communities, rather than sophisticated, urban purlieus, there was no real notion that homosexual activity was 'wrong', abnormal or in any way unnatural – and it was from just such communities that the majority of the other ranks were drawn.

'Whereof we do not know, thereof we cannot speak', the philosopher Ludwig Wittgenstein was shortly to write. And one of the most telling features which the contributors to Kevin Porter and Jeffrey Weeks's anthology of homosexual recollections, *Between the Acts*, have in common is a certain *innocence*. There is little of the angst and isolation which fuels Forster's *Maurice*. Rather, Porter and Weeks's interviewees share a simplicity and matter-of-factness. 'Of course, I didn't know then that I was homosexual', is a common comment. Not infrequently, too, they describe how they virtually drifted into marriage.

'Fred' did – and remained married for the greater part of his adult life. 'I never went with a woman in my life, other than my own wife,' he says, while explaining that going with men meant playing by a different set of rules. It was somehow different, more natural:

I've always preferred a male's company to a female's company, and I do now today. I'd rather cuddle a man than I would a woman. Females never meant anything to me, really – although I always kept my vows. I was honest and I never went with another woman in my life other than my wife. But as regards sex with other men, well, I must openly confess that I wouldn't do it with every Tom, Dick and Harry. I have had sex with other men – and still do if it comes my way – and we agree, one with the other. I find a male's company is wonderful. There's something about your own sex. You're free and easy to talk and to give and to love. You're not bound to have sex, it's enough to love a person.

I used to keep the boar pigs, and I remember the first time I had it with a young farm labourer. He was eighteen and I was about twenty-six then. He brought the sow to the door and . . . have you ever seen a boar serving a sow? Well, it takes about half-an-hour. This particular time, the boar was serving the sow in the pen and this young farmer-kiddie says to me, 'Hey, don't you ever feel like a bit of sex when you see this going on?' 'Aye,' I says, 'how about it?' just like that. I didn't think no more. 'Oh,' he says, 'I will if you will.' And of course that did it. I was ready and he was ready.[11]

Read in the light of material like this the wartime experiences of the pseudonymous 'Norman' fall into a more convincing context. Caught up in the general conscription of 1916, he soon found himself in France – quite literally, an innocent abroad. Every bit as graphically as the officers', his memories explore the dichotomy between (physical) intimacy and true affection, as well as providing a textbook example of what a new breed of Freudian psychoanalysts was just beginning to describe as 'sublimation':

. . . I was completely withdrawn.

In the army I made only one friend. A little chap called Walter. There was nothing between us. I was quite innocent. We never talked about anything. I can't remember any talk about homosexuality during that army period, around 1916. The men would swear a lot, but I didn't hear any talk, surprisingly [. . .]

In France it was very primitive; all the soldiers were working-class men. A former barber, a former waiter, I got on very well with all of them. I got very friendly with a boy called David and I slept with him, because we had two blankets each, so we'd have one underneath and three on top. Of course, nothing happened. I mean I didn't want to sleep with him, but in the army they didn't bother about people sleeping together. It wasn't suspicious. People didn't even joke about homosexuality. I didn't realise I was homosexual. There were all these men and I saw them bathing and everything, but I was much more mental than sensual, and I think that's probably why I wasn't interested.[12]

'Gerald' (born in 1892) is another old soldier who describes this implicit code of chastity, but from a different and rather more interesting perspective. Albeit fleetingly – 'you got no chance for very much. It all had to be done in a moment' – he *had* had sex in the army. Although it is now impossible to know for certain, it seems likely that this occurred during training, before active service: 'I went in the army in 1914, and that was the first time I actually got seduced by a soldier, it was a sergeant. It was then I realised that I was that way. Ever since, my life has gone that way. That was the first contact I had with anybody, you know, from what they call, [to] put it bluntly, "bumming".' That incident notwithstanding, Gerald's testament is strikingly similar to Norman's: 'At that time [during the Great War] there was no talk about homosexuality. Not the slightest.'

Gerald goes further than Norman, however, and tries to explain this abstinence, at least in so far as he was concerned:

There was no sexual contact with anybody in the services. The simple reason [for me was], I got promoted to sergeant from corporal. As you're getting promotions, you couldn't take no chances. I had several chances, mind you, with two or three different private soldiers I knew. You can gauge 'em, but the point is, when you come to look at it you say to yourself – Well, is it mind over matter? You know, you say to yourself, No, I mustn't. You're jeopardising your chances, because if something happened you're going to get a court martial.[13]

The very real fear of exposure weighed on 'Fred', too. 'I was always scared,' he told Jeffrey Weeks in the late 1970s. A Welshman, born in 1894, he was aware of his sexual orientation before entering the army, and took great pains to conceal it. An episode which occurred one night shortly before his demobilization remained in his memory. He was at a barracks in Cardiff:

> . . . this young chap came in drunk. We'd practically all gone to bed, and we had the light on and he was singing there; and so he strips off in the nude, he did, and comes over to my bed. And, of course, when he came over to my bed he had a hard on, and he said, 'Come on, Fred bach, you've got to have this!' So I clutched hold of the clothes, and thought to myself, 'I'll learn him a lesson!' as he went to pull the clothes off. 'Hey! hang on a minute!' I said, 'on one condition.' He said, 'What's that?' I said, 'That I shag you first.' And, of course, his old boy went down just like that! And they all burst out laughing, made him look a fool. He never tried it on after.[14]

In his autobiography *The World, the Flesh and Myself*, Michael Davidson advanced another reason for the prevalence of his perhaps unexpected but still understandable self-denying ordinance. It is implicitly class-based and predicated on his own paedophile preferences (the book begins with the frank admission, 'This is the life-story of a lover of boys'). It is important, however, since Davidson's awareness and acceptance of his homosexuality occurred at almost exactly the same time as he was commissioned as an officer in the Machine Gun Corps. He was just eighteen – 'two years earlier', he remembered, 'I hadn't even reached puberty':

> Thompson [his middle-aged regimental batman] turned into a dumb, devoted friend: as one's Chinese or Malay factotum becomes. He spoke in sniffs and grunts, but his gentle presence was also a comfort; he looked after me with the objective care he gave to [Davidson's horse] Trixie. One of his tasks was to arrange hot water and my canvas bath; and somehow he got into the habit of drying me himself after I'd had it. We both enjoyed this, I think; though neither stepped over the purely ablutionary border (I never had anything 'to do' with my soldiers – I suppose they were too old for me; but I've been told it was often a part of trench life). Anyhow, sexuality at the front was for me generally quiescent, except as a casual, self-contained chore . . .[15]

In *Maurice* Forster had described how, as a schoolboy, Maurice Hall's 'chief indecencies were solitary' and 'brought him more fatigue than pleasure'. Now here is Davidson – a very different type of man – saying almost the same thing; writing about how 'quiescent' was the trench life of an otherwise priapic young man, how sexual expression became no more than a 'casual, self-contained chore'. It was almost as if service life not only perpetuated but concentrated the pariah status assigned to homosexuals at home before the outbreak of hostilities. Gerald's memories of the very real fear of courts martial are illustrative of a regime in which, understandably, one 'couldn't take no chances'. But ironically, and viewed in retrospect, they also point the way forward. Gerald goes on:

> I only met one other homosexual in the army. That was at Le Havre in 1917. We was [*sic*] on the boat coming home. I don't know how these things work, whether it's through the conversation, or whether it's the attitude of the individual concerned, but we seemed to come together, see. All of a sudden his arm was round my neck and this, that and the other; and then, of course, one thing led to another.[16]

The important words here are, 'We was on the boat coming home'. They barely contain the impatience and longing to be back in 'Blighty', which also found expression in the soldiers' songs of the period, whose bitter, ironic tone was much later to colour the Theatre Workshop musical *Oh, What a Lovely War!*:

> When this lousy war is over,
> No more soldiering for me,
> When I get my civvy clothes on,
> Oh, how happy I shall be!
> No more church parades on Sunday,
> No more putting in for leave,
> I shall kiss the sergeant-major,
> How I'll miss him, how he'll grieve!
> Amen.

There is, significantly and quite naturally, no lack of evidence for this atavistic yearning for home and Ivor Novello's home fires. Many of the songs reflect it. 'I want to go home,' moaned the most simplistic:

> . . . I want to go home,
> I don't want to go in the trenches no more,
> Where whizzbangs and shrapnel, they whistle and roar.
> Take me over the sea, where the alleyman can't get at me
> Oh my, I don't want to die, I want to go home.

It was another song, however, a parody of a contemporary music-hall hit, which unwittingly most accurately recorded the mood of returning servicemen like Gerald. Sung to the tune of 'I'll Make a Man of You', the squaddies' version had an urgency all of its own:

> I don't want to be a soldier,
> I don't want to go to war,
> I'd rather stay at home,
> Around the streets to roam,
> And live on the earnings of a lady typist.
> I don't want a bayonet in my belly,
> I don't want my bollocks shot away,
> I'd rather stay in England,
> In merry, merry England,
> And fornicate my bleeding life away.

Lines like 'live on the earnings of a lady typist' (even more than references to 'merry, merry England') exactly sum up the febrile excitement which the prospect of home leave, 'a Blighty one', eventual demobilization or, more rarely, a few days in Paris – 'Par-ee' – aroused just as much in serving homosexuals as in their home-and-hearth-loving or whore-hunting heterosexual comrades. 'The high-flying "spiritual" emotionalism of the last year or two [of the war] was replaced almost overnight by an insatiable hunger for downright carnal experience – a craving to *know* the physical secrets of as many boys as possible.'[17]

Gay or straight, for most single servicemen on home leave there was only one place they wanted to be – and, happily and conveniently, boat-trains from the Channel ports brought them right there, to Victoria and Charing Cross stations right in the heart of the West End of London. 'We was on the boat coming home' – Gerald's line is typical of many and seems to encapsulate not just relief at having survived, but also a determination to make up for lost time:

> On the arrival of the train there would be scores of young sailors tumbling out of the train, all it seemed in need of a good piss. They ran helter-skelter into the large lavatory on the platform, and pulling down the flap of their trousers pissed for all they were worth . . . if they happened to note some eager looker, they would exclaim, 'He's a beauty, isn't he? Like him up your bum, chum?' This sally would be followed by gales of laughter from all the other pissing fellows . . .[18]

It must have seemed like another world to men who only a couple of days earlier had been at Ypres or on the Somme, for unlike the Second World War, the Great War had comparatively little effect on the life of the capital. There were irregular Zeppelin attacks and air-raids (on 9 July 1917 *The Times* reported that 'at least twenty aeroplanes appeared over London. They hovered over London for a considerable time [. . .] Fortunately the casualties, though serious enough, were far fewer than in the [previous raid, in June], and the damage done was small when compared with the magnitude of the raid'). There were blackout restrictions, although these were not applied with anything like the severity of those in force during the Blitz. There was rationing too. But, again, this was nothing like as severe as that at the end of the Second World War. Complaints about it were little more than glum, long-suffering grumbles:

> My Tuesdays are meatless
> My Wednesdays are wheatless
> I'm getting more eatless each day.
> My home it is heatless
> My bed it is sheetless
> They're all sent to YMCA.
>
> My Club Rooms are treatless,
> My coffee is sweetless
> Each day I get poorer and wiser,
> My stockings are feetless,
> My trousers are seatless,
> My God, but I do hate the Kaiser![19]

Even this, however, should be seen in context. Mrs Anita Mostyn long remembered the evening her father, an army colonel, arrived back in London on home leave in 1918: 'Our cook had dinner all ready, laid out on the dining-room table, delicious roast beef and Yorkshire pudding which she'd made with two of our weekly rationed eggs. Father kept saying, "Goodness! I had no idea you could still eat as well as this in England." '[20]

In many respects, then, life continued as normal – all the more so in the West End, where social life went on regardless. For even a moderately moneyed member of what was then called 'the officer class', indeed, it must have seemed as if nothing had changed. Michael Davidson was no real 'toff', but every (public) moment when he was in London seems to have been spent in a round of society dining and partying in and around Duke Street which would not have disgraced an Edwardian lush. He found time, too, for haircuts at Truefitt ('who made George IV's wigs'), drinks at the Café Royal, the Carlton or Prince's in Piccadilly, and morning-after 'pick-me-ups' at Heppel's in the Haymarket. Beverley Nichols also had 'a good war'. Working as an instructor in the Officer Cadet Battalion at its headquarters in Cambridge and later in what he rather grandly called the 'Secret Service', he enjoyed extended periods of leave during 1917 and 1918 and moved in very much the same circles as Davidson. According to his biographer Bryan Connon, he too 'enjoyed non-stop meetings with friends in the setting of the Savile or the Bachelors' Club, the Ritz, the Carlton or the Café Royal'.

Assuredly, both Davidson and Nichols spent much of their precious time in town in 'sympathetic' company: one could hardly, at that time, arrive at the Café Royal with a boy in tow. But it is important to note that their gadding around was just an officers-only version of what was happening all over town. Even in the weeks before the Armistice, London's restaurants were still open and theatres were play-ing to full houses. Lillie Langtry was at the London Coliseum; there were revues with titles like *Bubbly, Tail-Up, Hullo, America!* and André Charlot's *Buzz-Buzz* playing in the Strand and on Shaftesbury Avenue. A farce called *A Little Bit of Fluff* was coming to the end of its run of over 1,200 performances at the Criterion Theatre, while the musical *Chu Chin Chow* was well on its way to notching up almost double that number at His Majesty's. There were prostitutes (of both sexes) plying their trade in Piccadilly and chorus girls waiting to 'make a man' of anyone in uniform at a score of stage doors.

Even for the more ordinary, other-ranks homosexual, then, the atmosphere of the capital in the years leading up to and immediately after the Armistice was charged and often positively electric. Although they date from a few years later, 'Roy's memories of the West End scene have the ring of authenticity:

> I took my aunt out one night to the theatre and we went to the gallery of the old Prince of Wales theatre. It's been tremendously altered now. We went to see *The Ghost Train*. We were in the gallery and I realised then, my instinct. Nobody told me. I kept on looking at the back and it was jet-black and crowded, crowded full of people standing, although there were a lot of empty seats. And that was, I think, my first realisation that this was a scene which I wanted to join in, I went back two or three days afterwards to see *The Ghost Train* and stood at the back and what was going on there was nobody's business!
>
> They were big meeting places. You did meet nice people in those days, something you don't do these days; and wealthy people too. They were not nasty people. They'd probably give you a whisky, which I thought was nice. Never occurred to me to take money. Just never occurred to them, I shouldn't think. It never occurred to anyone. I went round those theatres quite a lot.[21]

All in all, 'it was', as Michael Davidson recalled, 'a London where "Boat Race Night" rowdiness was the rule – everybody expected to be killed as soon as his leave was over, and there was no blackout or blitz to send one home.'[22]

Three-quarters of a century on, it is difficult to decide whether it was this determined rowdiness and *carpe diem* mentality which directly led to the emergence of a recognizably 'modern' homosexual underworld in London at this period, or whether it had always been around in a similar form and merely began to coalesce in the desperate, feverish mood of the wartime capital. On balance, the second sounds more likely (Davidson added that it was in 1917 that 'I deliberately began pursuing my secret wants. I didn't look for boys "on the game" – *I hardly knew there were any*' (my italics)).

Whichever, by the end of the war the 'scene' had developed into something appreciably different from the London which Wilde had known only a quarter of a century previously. That, as we have seen, had frequently been sordid and amateurish; Alfred Taylor's brothel and his maladroit attempts to pass himself off as a sort of upper-class pander cannot be described as anything else. But there had also been something dilettantish about it – what we might call the 'Savoy Hotel and cigarette cases' side of things.

Now, almost abruptly, things had got a great deal more 'professional' and codified. By 1917, for instance, when he was still only twenty, Michael Davidson was already adept at separating his public from his very much less modish private life. At a party that year a woman guest 'suddenly said: "There's something fishy about Michael – I think he's a woman-hater. I believe he likes little boys!" '

Davidson's reaction was wholly in period: 'Of course, I roared with laughter; *my double life had taken shape*.'[23]

Although there was no realistic alternative to such behaviour, Davidson seems to have revelled in the subterfuge and duplicity it involved: a dinner party one day, a furtive visit to 'some swimming baths which amply supplied the needs of the *voyeur* I was becoming, [where] generations of "dirty old men", apparently, had systematically bored peep-holes through the wooden partitions between every dressing-box', the next. It was all very much to his taste. His particular proclivities also led him to 'a strip of the Serpentine in Hyde Park [which] had been insulated by tradition and a surprisingly unprudish Board of Works for the bathing of "males only". There was a wonderful lot of juvenile nudity there,' he recalled. There were policemen too. One day, he wrote:

> I had taken my bathing-drawers and, aware of the notice 'bathers only', was sitting on the grass wondering how chilly the breeze blowing from the Marble Arch might be – besides, I had lent my slip to a boy who was shyer than most about going in with nothing on. All at once the delicious scene was harshly shivered: I was being astonishingly spoken to by a policeman, being ordered to 'go along' with him out of the bathing enclave; I was *in the hands of the Law.*

By not instantly undressing and plunging into the water, by dallying on the bank fully clad, I'd broken a Parks Regulation – that was all; yet walking away under police escort, I felt that each of those staring eyes was boring into my secret mind, that every man and boy discerned that I was 'like that' . . .[24]

It was his first – though hardly his last – brush with the law. His pathological attraction to 'feasting with partners' was several times to bring him to the attention of the police and, as we shall see, on one occasion lead him to prison during the next twenty years. In what is now almost routinely described as his 'courageous' autobiography *The World, the Flesh and Myself* (forgivably so, since it was first published as long ago as 1962, five years before the legalization of homosexuality) Davidson discusses all this and freely admits that by 1919 he had become an 'old hand'. He was

> conversant with the processes of 'picking up': as easy as winking at that time when a multitude of yearning faces, young and old, used – in Holbrook Jackson's words about Francis Thompson – to 'haunt the Embankment, the cavernous arches of Charing Cross, and the black and dusty colonnades of Covent Garden . . .' and one shameful night which still, 40 years later, puts me in a cold sweat when I think of it, I smuggled a boy into [our home in] Queen's Gate while my mother was asleep and smuggled him out with the dawn.[25]

There is more than a touch of braggadocio in these passages. Read in context, they are a sexual parallel to Davidson's account of his life as a raffish, often gin-soaked, foreign correspondent (criss-crossing continents to file stories for the *Observer*, risking his life to report on the war in Korea) which forms the core of the book. But the experiences they describe are not unique. In *his* more private off-duty moments Beverley Nichols chose to cruise the capital's Turkish baths, then more numerous than they are today. ('Uneventful night', he noted laconically in his diary after one such visit to the Russell Square baths.[26]) Indeed, it is hardly too fanciful to catch a refined echo of the tone of Davidson's (and Holbrook Jackson's) nostalgia for Charing Cross and Covent Garden in the start of a poem A. E. Housman chose to include in his *Last Poems*. It had been written before the turn of the century, but its inclusion in the 1922 collection is in itself significant:

> When first my way to fair I took
> Few pence in purse had I,
> And long I used to stand and look
> At things I could not buy.
>
> Now times are altered: if I care
> To buy a thing, I can;
> The pence are here and here's the fair,
> But where's the lost young man?[27]

Over and above the braggadocio, for the general reader, of course, another aspect of Davidson's book remains problematic. As a self-proclaimed 'lover of boys' (as against Housman's 'lads' or 'young men'), he is teetering at the very edge of what, even today, is seen as acceptable homosexual conduct. Because of this, perhaps, there is a truculence in his style, an insistence that we must share in everything which he experienced. Ordinarily, this would be welcome; frankness is all – but, particularly on matters sexual, he is too strident. Even the arrangement of the three nouns he uses in the title of the book is no accident – no more than is its nod towards the Book of Common Prayer's reference to 'the world, the flesh and the devil'. Davidson *wants* to be the very devil, but some of the book's key passages, smuggled in at unexpected moments, show him as someone very different, someone very much more sensitive. Perceptive as ever, Arthur Koestler recognized this when, in reviewing the book, he described it in part as the story of 'a courageous and lovable person's struggle to come to terms with his Grecian heresy'. Certainly, these personal animadversions of Davidson's put more lurid passages such as those quoted above into a more accurate context. For a moment, then, we must put aside any prejudice and allow one of these 'purple' passages to speak for itself:

> The moralists will execrate, the pundits doubtless pooh-pooh me. But here I'm stating, as far as I'm able, the truth about myself: my highest, most intense, pleasure or happiness is of the *mind*; and comes from seeing, being with, touching, looking into the mind of, a boy who, emotionally, mentally, rather than bodily, is *simpatico*;

and from visually absorbing the multiple delights of his nakedness. Any sexual *acts* which may, and generally do, accompany, follow or precede this mental joy are adjuncts – prologue or epilogue to the essential monograph of the mind.[28]

The italicization here is Davidson's own; but the longing and the loneliness which underpin the words is far more universal. 'Seeing, being with, touching, looking into the mind of' . . . the words not only go some way towards vitiating what might be perceived as the 'nastiness' of Davidson's more graphic effusions; they catch the mood which Forster had so presciently identified before war had even been declared, the realization of 'the triviality of contact for contact's sake' . . .

⤙

Unbidden, unconsciously, spontaneously, a new world was emerging. For all their brave words, seers and prophets such as Edward Carpenter (who lived until 1929) could only accept cups of tea or gin-and-Its and, like wise uncles, await news from the delivery room. For, just as the war brought men together, so too did the peace. Demobilization levelled the gap which had hitherto existed between 'officers' and 'other ranks' – 'men' – and in so doing established a curious, classless, interdependent confraternity of homosexual men which developed in Lloyd George's 'land fit for heroes to live in', and which, at least in essence, is still the paradigm for the vertiginous complexities of the contemporary gay scene.

In this respect, Roy's reminiscences of those evenings he spent at the Prince of Wales Theatre are especially important. In comparison with the likes of Michael Davidson and Beverley Nichols, Roy, born in 1908 and brought up in the south London suburb of Brixton, was a social nobody. And yet, at the theatre he met 'nice people', even 'wealthy people'. He wasn't there because he was 'on the game'; he wasn't a rent boy putting himself about to make money. Indeed, it never occurred to him to take money from another man; 'it never occurred to anyone', he says.

This is crucial, for what Roy was engaged in was a *social* rather than a commercial transaction – albeit one in which some form of sexual activity might or might not have played its part (the offer of tots of whisky suggests that it probably did). His story, indeed, is as perfect an encapsulation of the homosexual world as it was in around 1920 as Alfred Taylor's is of that same world in the 1890s. Implicitly, it hints at all the macrocosmic social and philanthropic aspirations of the post-war epoch. (Women over the age of thirty were given the right to vote in 1918.) Explicitly, and more importantly for our purposes, it exemplifies a world in which new liaisons were developing, relation-ships which crossed both class boundaries and social norms. 'Special friendships' which might or might not develop into something far more permanent were blossoming; 'things' which were completely different from the cynicism and commercialism so apparent in Alfred Taylor's world were happening. Less than a decade after he had dedi-cated *Maurice* to it, it was even possible to believe that E. M. Forster's 'better world' might be dawning.

It was possible, but . . . It was Housman, again, who put things into a more realistic perspective and, like one of his classical sages, waved a hortatory finger. One of the lesser of his *Last Poems* shrewdly pointed out that, however much men like Roy or Forster looked to a world in which 'two men should fall in love and remain in it for ever and ever', that world was not going to appear overnight. Nor, indeed, would it be any more comfortable – or, for that matter, necessarily any *better* – than the present:

> In the morning, in the morning,
> In the happy field of hay,
> Oh they looked at one another
> By the light of day.
>
> In the blue and silver morning
> On the haycock as they lay,
> Oh they looked at one another
> And then they looked away.[29]

~

At this point it is wholly fitting that we should return to Gerald, cold and lonely on the deck of the ship bringing him back from Le Havre in 1917. A man has come to stand beside him. He smiles and, later, slips an arm around Gerald's shoulder. His name is Phil, and – 'one thing leads to another' – very rapidly he and Gerald have fallen in love. It is the beginning of what Gerald later remembered as the 'affair I had for seven years'.

Things had changed.

They certainly hadn't gone according to plan where Gerald was concerned. Before meeting Phil he had believed that he would enter into a normal, heterosexual marriage, because that was 'the proper thing to do, although I had experience of the other side'. Now, a new scenario was presenting itself: 'When I come [sic] out of the army, we stuck together. I was living at the time in Ilford. I rejoined the army in 1920, then I went out to Germany. I was living with Phil at the same time and I saw him when I came home on leave and we kept a flat together.'

This is a virtually unique declaration. There had, of course, been homosexual couples before. The poet Algernon Charles Swinburne, for instance, had shared a Pooterish life with Theodore Watts-Dunton at No. 2 The Pines, Putney, for thirty years when he died in 1909. But even the Pooters had servants. Gerald's story is startling in its modernity:

> We had quite a happy life together. We done [sic] the housework between us. We shared everything fifty-fifty. If I saw the stove wanted cleaning I'd clean the stove. If he saw the chest of drawers [wanted] polishing he'd polish the chest of drawers. I used to go out about half-past eight in the morning, and he'd go out probably earlier, somewhere about half-past seven. On average, I was home about half-past five, he came home about half-past six. Whoever came home first made the meal. This was up to 1926, '27.[30]

The contemporary-sounding mundaneness of this account of what now seems a very ordinary partnership belies its importance. 'We shared everything fifty-fifty,' Gerald says. Except in hotels, Oscar Wilde never lived with Bosie, let alone made his evening meal; nor is it possible to picture Swinburne and Watts-Dunton sharing the cleaning and polishing in their Putney *ménage-à-deux*. Equally, it is difficult to believe that any of the young men paraded in the witness box in the Taylor–Wilde trials were by 1920 settling down to enjoy the beginnings of a peacefully domestic middle age.

For seven years Gerald and Phil were pioneering what was to come – the exclusive 'cosy' male–male relationship which had been anathema to Edward Carpenter and the turn-of-the-century socio-sexual radicals and had found no real place, even in the hugger-mugger of barracks and trenches, during the Great War. Gerald's account goes on, indeed, to delineate the decline and fall of what was, essentially, a *modern* relationship. If only to serve as a foretaste of what was to come, it is worth quoting at some length:

I don't think our friends or families knew [about our relationship], yet they had a very good suspicion. Phil and I often talked about it; only he said 'Well [. . .] as long as we love each other, what's it to do with other people?' And that was the true situation. We were faithful to each other. It wasn't a case of if he wanted to bring somebody home he'd bring 'em home; there was nothing like that. We'd probably have sex once a week, once a fortnight, all according to the mood we were in.

Then, we went out one night [to] the Quebec Club in Piccadilly. It was a gay club at that time. We hadn't been in there two minutes when, all of a sudden, up comes this other chap . . . They kiss each other and all that sort of business. I thought to myself, Well, I don't know, they're getting a bit too close together in their conversation and this, that and the other. I got a bit annoyed. One thing led to another, and this chap turned round. He said, 'Good gracious alive! Gerald darling, don't you know I knew Phil long before you knew her.' Well, of course, that aggravated it and then – bang, bang, bang! – all of a sudden there was that one climax. That was it. I left the flat. I left the flat to him.[31]

4 ∽

'Suivez-Moi, Jeune Homme'

TO THE MAJORITY OF ordinary homosexuals who were there, the 1920s might well have seemed just one more decade in which they were still commonly considered 'queers', 'nonces', 'poofters', 'benders', 'brown-noses', 'shirt-lifters' or 'nancy-boys'.[1] But fashionable London at least was beginning to embrace a new *gay* sensibility – in both senses of the world.[2] 'Gay' was one of the key words in its limited vocabulary. ('So', as in '*so* utterly', and 'too, *too* . . .' and '*simply*' were among the others, just as they had been among the Aesthetes.) But it is important to remember that the word 'gay' then still conveyed little more than notions of general innocence and frivolity – and continued to do so for the next quarter-century. As late as 1951 a musical by the (homosexual) Welsh composer and matinée idol Ivor Novello opened in London with the title *Gay's the Word*. There were no titters when the curtain went up; but, understandably, it is infrequently revived today.

The 'gayness' of the 1920s, however, made possible – if it didn't exactly bring about – the emergence in the West End of Novello, Noël Coward and Jack Buchanan; the appearance of fashionable new novelists such as Beverley Nichols, Hugh Walpole, Rafael Sabatini and Michael Arlen; the success of Harold Nicolson's 'funny new friend', the couturier Edward Molyneux (who continued to design costumes for Coward productions until 1966); the rise of Cecil Beaton; the very existence of his friends David and Stephen Tennant ('His lips are too magenta for my taste,' Lytton Strachey was to note of the latter); the discovery of a young actor called John Gielgud (when he played Romeo in 1924); and the glorious twilight of such wealthy, exotic dandies as Gerald Tyrwhitt, the fourteenth Lord Berners, and Ned, the fifth Earl of Lathom (who was to die from tuberculosis in 1930, as if to mark the end of an era).

It did not matter that both Buchanan and Arlen were (apparently) sturdily heterosexual; in the climate of the time they were *gay*. This was the 'Jazz Age', after all. Everyone was having a ball in a world which Arlen described as one of 'unseasonable delicacies, artichokes and asparagus, oysters and strawberries, plovers' eggs and grouse, caviare and cantaloup'.

There was Berners, a dilettante composer, writer and artist, high-spiritedly dyeing in pastel shades the doves which fluttered outside his house at Faringdon in Oxfordshire while making sure that everything inside was what Nichols called 'amusing': 'the feather flowers, the big bowls of pink sweets under pink geraniums, the Nottingham lace curtains in the ultra-modern bathrooms, the paper shrines, the copies of surrealistic magazines, etc.'. There was Arlen, originally an Armenian called Dikran Kouyoumdjian until he plucked a new English-sounding name from the pages of the London telephone directory, who – when he was not in the South of France – drove around London in a canary-yellow Rolls-Royce, the glamorous Atalanta, one of Britain's first 'trophy-wives', by his side. Everything had been paid for by the extraordinary success of his second novel, *The Green Hat*, which was first published in the summer of 1924. 'I'm every other inch a gentleman!' he gleefully told those real gentlemen who thought they, not he, went the full mile.

There was, too, the fabulously wealthy Lord Lathom. Always referred to in the gossip columns as 'that inveterate first-nighter', he insisted that his footmen heated incense in spoons to perfume either his London home in Cumberland Place or his country retreat in Yorkshire before guests arrived. His passions were orchids and the theatre. The former he banked in front of mirrors before every party; the latter he extravagantly bank-rolled. He financed West End shows and private productions of both his own, invariably unsuccessful plays (one was called *Wet Paint*) and shows which had been refused a public performance licence by the Lord Chamberlain. He mounted elaborate after-dinner masques for the entertainment of his friends, and subsid-ized the early careers of 'boys' such as Nichols, Novello and Coward whom he found 'amusing' to such an extent that by the end of the decade he was virtually penniless. Although he had absolutely no use for them, he bought two of Coward's earliest songs. Later, when Coward knew him rather better and approached him for a loan, he refused – but immediately gave him £200, a not-inconsiderable sum in 1921, as an outright gift. Far better, he said, than ruining a friendship . . .

There were the boys, too. Newcomers to the scene, if they didn't have the aristocratic background or the family money of Berners and Lathom, they were predominantly middle and upper middle class and – perhaps more importantly – young men born a decade or so after the Wilde trials and generally after Wilde's death. Jointly and severally, Noël Coward had the measure of them: in one of his slighter cabaret songs he listed them as 'Pretty boys, witty boys [. . .] Haughty boys, naughty boys [. . .] Faded boys, jaded boys, womankind's gift to a bulldog nation'.

Beaton, Novello, Nichols, Walpole, the designers Edward Moly-neux, Oliver Messel and Rex Whistler, the now-forgotten writers Collie Knox and Godfrey Winn and the slightly older Coward himself were *de facto* the neo-Aesthetes. Most were, like Coward and Novello, untainted by a university education and – another of the key words of the decades – splendidly *theatrical*.

Berners and Lathom and their likes (and there were many) almost too literally took them to their bosom. They introduced them to the delights of fine wine, good food and weekends in the country; and Lathom at least – who preferred a cologne aptly called 'Suivez-Moi, Jeune Homme' – rewarded their attentions with gifts of Cartier rings and cigarette cases for all the world as if Oscar Wilde had not been castigated for doing much the same.

The wealthy novelist and playwright Somerset Maugham took Godfrey Winn under his wing, even inviting him to stay for a month at the Villa Mauresque, his home at Cap Ferrat. For Winn this holiday with his 'literary god' was the first unsettling glimpse of a whole new world. 'I had no idea how much was to be added to my previously constricted knowledge of human emotions,' he wrote.

When I presented myself in the salon, before lunch, on the day of my arrival straight from the train, in my orthodox English grey flannel suit, my host took one look at me and gave me my first marching orders.

'No tie, no jacket, no socks. This is the South of France in

August, not Finals Day at Wimbledon.' When I returned from my
room for his reappraisal, he added, 'Gerald, take Godfrey into Nice
this afternoon and get him some linen slacks, shirts and espadrilles
at the Bon Marché, like yours.'

I glanced across at the man dressed in candy-pink beach-clothes,
who was handing round drinks, and instinctively something in me
revolted. *I don't want to look like you. To resemble you in any way,
ever.* [. . .]

Gerald Haxton, the man who had been Maugham's companion
on his extremely fruitful world travels, was, I suppose, at that time
in his late thirties. Already the signs of the dissipation that was
ultimately to destroy him were beginning to show on his face, and
in his increasingly bloodshot eyes [. . .] Only when he dived grace-
fully from the plank at one end of the pool, set high on the hillside
and surrounded by oleander bushes, did he capture and echo the
charm of his surroundings – although for myself that was cancelled
out by his insistence on always bathing naked, even when there
were women sunbathing on the yellow cushions along the marble
verge. I clung to my brief shorts throughout my visit. It wasn't so
much that I was prim, as that I was still unfledged.[3]

A new world was emerging, albeit a small and select one which was
centred on the West End of London and extended no further than a belt
of country houses in the Home Counties. Within it, however, a new
homosexual hedonism, which in many ways outdid the campness of
Wilde and the Aesthetes, evolved and flourished. Everyone knew everyone else – and felt safe in his company. By 1930, for example, Cecil
Beaton (then just twenty-six) was setting up home for himself at Ashcombe in Wiltshire – and doing so in some considerable style:

Summer 1930
. . . It happened that all my guests were painters and since the
weather was too inclement to tempt us out of doors, the Sunday
was dedicated to transforming my bedroom into a circus-room.
The room was to be painted in garish colours with niches filled
with circus performers, with baroque emblems, barley-sugar poles
and flowered mirrors. Each guest set to work on the white walls
to contribute his own panel. Rex Whistler painted a superb 'fat
woman', Lord Berners a Columbine with performing dogs (a very

ungainly mastiff was caught in the agonizing act of jumping through a paper hoop), Christopher Sykes painted a tumbler, upside down, balancing, among other objects, a goldfish bowl on his feet. Oliver Messel created a small negro, naked except for a pink flamingo ostrich feather worn on his head. Mme von Bismarck pictured an equestrienne on a flower-dappled circus pony, and her husband decided to portray 'the strong man of the Fair' with volute mustachios, tattoo marks, heavy ball-weights and chains. However, Yorck Bismarck eschewed the traditional circus manner of carefully finished realistic painting for the more modern slapdash strokes of the brush, and the next weekend Rex Whistler could not resist touching up the flowing chevelure and mustachios, the better to conform with the other murals.

'Please don't, Rex!' I pleaded. 'There'll be hell to pay if Yorck ever discovered you've touched a thing.'

But the temptation was too great. Rex was unable to resist repainting, meticulously and realistically, the crisply waving hair, the mustachios, then, of course, the column-like throat, the brawny chest, and so on down the whole over-muscular body.[4]

Unfortunately, no visual record of the fantastic, baroque *campness* – there is no other word – of the circus bedroom seems to have survived. However, as Beaton's diary entry implies, it is not the archness of having a 'weekender' where 'all my guests were painters' or even the notion of wanting a circus bedroom at all which should interest us. Rather, it is the fact that Lord Berners, a hereditary peer and by then approaching fifty, should so willingly have agreed to muck in with 'bright young things' scarcely half his age – even younger than Beaton, the painter and designer Rex Whistler turned twenty-five only in 1930 – and have continued to do so. The most famous photograph of Berners is a snap which Beaton took in 1937. It shows the peer at an elaborate Ashcombe *fête-champêtre*. He is wearing eighteenth-century court costume and a pig's head mask. He would have been around fifty-five years of age when it was taken.

As they said, though, it was all just a sign of the times. Five years later still, in 1942, Field Marshal Lord Wavell was to introduce Berners to friends with the phrase: 'He's a musician, and a saucy fellow.'[5]

Although he is perhaps less well known today than, say, Coward, Beaton or even Novello, Beverley Nichols uniquely personifies what we might call the 'society homosexual' of the twenties. Indeed, his life during the early part of the decade was in many ways the most typical.

At the end of the Great War he had criss-crossed America performing largely exiguous duties as the secretary of a British delegation charged with finding ways in which closer co-operation could be established between British and American universities. Formally demobilized in the first weeks of 1919, he returned to Oxford University to continue working towards the BA for which he had been reading when he was called up. But his heart was never in the work. Rather – like many an undergraduate before and since – he devoted days and whole weeks to the time-consuming business of becoming an Oxford 'character' and establishing what he called a 'suitable Platform' from which he could launch himself into a career of wealth and celebrity as soon as he came down.

He had to. Setting out to shock in the Oxford of the 1870s, Wilde and the Aesthetes had not needed to try very hard. Appalled, amused or just bewildered, their fellow-undergraduates were a captive audience, only too eager to record and relate every last *aperçu*, no matter how foolish, no matter how footling. (One acolyte saw Wilde drooling over a student athlete and wrote down what he heard. Hence, although Wilde's words on that occasion – 'His left leg is a Greek poem' – were hardly memorable, they have still gained a place in The Canon.[6]) Within a few decades, however, the narrow, trail-blazing path of this tiny, self-advertising clique had been crowded by a throng of fellow-travellers. Up at Trinity Hall, Cambridge, in 1909 there was the archly camp Ronald Firbank. A Max Beerbohm *de son jour*, he was later to make his name with novels whose very titles – *Concerning the Eccentricities of Cardinal Pirelli* (1926); *Prancing Nigger* (1924) – clearly intimated that they were not in the *Boys' Own Paper* – 'Sapper' – John Buchan mould.

Nor was Firbank:

In his room [at Cambridge] he would sit in curtained and shaded twilight, behind his head the yellow glimmer of candles set in carved and gilded candelabra. As he talked in his high-pitched voice, the silhouette of his face, large and fleshy, with low brow, aquiline nose, and full lips, would pass across the light. His hands, clasping his ankles or circling his head in frequent gestures, glinted with the sombre colours of his rings. Usually he wore a green jade Chinese ring, but occasionally he preferred the colour of some blue Egyptian rings, made of earthenware. In appearance, he always reminded A. C. Landsberg of the portraits of society women by Boldini . . .[7]

And that was at Cambridge, where *scientia* (or, as we shall see, Caesar's 'scientia atque usus militum') was traditionally rated as at least the equal of the *humanitas* of the Oxford Schools. At Balliol a decade and a half later Nichols saw the way that things were going and realized that he had no time to lose.

In the 1920s Oxford was fêting the arrival of such high-profile undergraduates as Harold Acton, Evelyn Waugh, John Betjeman, Anthony Powell, Brian Howard and, a little later, W. H. Auden and Stephen Spender. Along with a score or so of less literary contemporaries, these have subsequently been labelled 'the Brideshead Generation'[8] in deference to Waugh's novel, because of their camp, cavalier disregard of all traditional ideas of undergraduate decorum. But they were only the icing on the cake: in the 1920s the whole of what was then an overwhelming male university was, in Powell's words, 'indifferent to homosexuality'.

Indifferent to it himself, in his autobiographical writing Powell rather downplays what we might now almost describe as its prevalence. His suave irony belies the fact that, at least for Acton, Howard and 'the fast set' – among whom Powell counted himself – if it was not strictly *de rigueur*, homosexuality was certainly more than simply *comme il faut*. Like Powell, Waugh and Betjeman were also no more than dabblers (all were subsequently married and indeed fathered children). Auden, too – slightly younger and never a member of any set – ploughed his own furrow. But the effete and, it has to be said, privileged style of the Brideshead Generation permeated Oxford and was remarkably pervasive, trickling down indeed unto the third and fourth generation.

Waugh caught it well when he lampooned the Old Etonian Brian Howard – Brian Christian de Claiborne Howard, to give him his full name – in his novel *Brideshead Revisited*, which, we might pause to note, bears the now overlooked subtitle 'The Sacred and Profane

Memories of Captain Charles Ryder'. Thinly disguised, the friend whom Waugh once described as an 'incorrigible homosexual' there appears as Anthony Blanche. He is an ambivalent character, or at least one about whom his creator is ambivalent. He is, Waugh tells us, 'tall, slim, rather swarthy, with large saucy eyes [. . .] He had on a smooth chocolate-brown suit with loud white stripes, suède shoes, a large bow-tie and he drew off yellow, wash-leather gloves as he came into the room; part Gallic, part Yankee, part, perhaps Jew; wholly exotic.'[9]

Harold Acton needed no Waugh (although aspects of his character too are melded into the fictional character of Anthony Blanche). In his autobiography *Memoirs of an Aesthete*, published in 1948, he looked back with a certain cold eye on the licentious, even ludicrous excesses of his first years at Oxford:

Aquarium, my first volume of poems, was published during my second term [in 1923], and its red, black and yellow striped cover met me everywhere like a challenge. For a book of poems it had a prompt success. Since I was free from false modesty, as from everything false, and possessed of a resonant voice, I never faltered when I was asked to read them, but shouted them lustily down a megaphone. Nor would I tolerate interruptions. The megaphone could also be brandished as a weapon.

How many copies of *Aquarium* did I autograph with tender dedications! Where are they now, those witnesses of youthful passion? I think I know the answer. Not long ago I came across a copy in Charing Cross Road and purchased it – for three-pence. *Sic transit gloria* . . . At least it had been well-thumbed and nicely battered. The fly-leaf was torn out. Had it compromised the owner? My thoughts returned to the bygone loves to whom I had given copies, to blue eyes, green eyes, eyes like black diamonds, to gentle struggles and showers of burning kisses [. . .] I culled the *prémices*, and it is a subtle satisfaction, even in retrospect, to have kindled flames in Elgin marble breasts. After many years the breasts pretend to forget . . . Do they remember our ecstasies on the Thames and at Thame? Do they remember the poems they inspired? Let them blush as they read these words in their nuptial couches: I have not forgotten a single kiss.[10]

Poetry, *published* poetry, blue eyes, green eyes, eyes like black diamonds; gentle struggles; showers of burning kisses; Elgin marble breasts
... this was the milieu into which Nichols knowingly launched
himself. But, monomaniacal and fiercely ambitious, despite a somewhat precious, suede-shoed campness, unlike Acton, while at Oxford
Nichols seems to have had little interest in or contact with the physical
side of things. Instead of Elgin marble breasts he embraced the Oxford
student magazine *Isis* and various national periodicals in Britain and
America, bombarding them with his own poems as well as articles and
ideas, and finally achieved a long-held ambition when he was elected
President of the Union. That at least got him noticed, although it
is impossible now to determine whether apophthematism or irony
motivated the description of him which appeared in a lesser student
magazine during his final term:

> Jocular levity,
> Seasoned with brevity,
> Wisdom that's rare,
> Hark to our Beverley,
> Talking so cleverly,
> Young and so fair![11]

For a man of Nichols's pretension, however, even Oxford was a small
pond; even the presidency of the Union hardly satisfied his idea of a
'Platform'. What would – what *could*?

He came down with a mediocre degree and, as he was later – and
wholly characteristically – to write, 'a stack of unpaid bills from wine
merchants, florists and tailors'. He had no family estates to return to,
no family trusts to support him. In this respect he was an essentially
modern character: even Wilde, when he came down from Cambridge,
could expect as a last resort the support of his father, Sir William.
Nichols abandoned plans to read for the Bar and half-heartedly set
about trying to find some form of suitable employment. He advertised
his services in *The Times* and even persuaded friends to lobby the
former prime minister H. H. Asquith on his behalf. (Quoting Abraham
Lincoln, Asquith let him know that he could do nothing to help:
'There are more horses than oats.')

Almost inevitably, Nichols drifted into journalism. He had an
easy facility with words and, trading on his success with *Isis* and the

Oxford Union, was soon selling essays, feature pieces ('Have You Got Telephone Ear?') and theatre reviews to papers ranging from the *Sunday Times* to the *Daily Mirror*, as well as to the *New York Evening Post* and American periodicals such as *Outlook*. There was also a string of slight but generally well-received novels: *Prelude* (1920) was followed in quick succession by *Patchwork* (1921) and *Self* (1922).

If these and the many more which were to follow (by the end of his life he had published some sixty books on subjects ranging from politics to gardening and his beloved cats) are now forgotten, Nichols's theatrical career, which began rather more uncertainly at this time, is virtually unknown.

In 1921, largely due to the affection and influence of Ned Lathom, who thought him another Noël Coward, he managed to persuade the impresario André Charlot to include one of his songs, 'Eve', in the revue *A to Z* at the Prince of Wales Theatre – Charlot did not take too much persuading since Lathom was almost single-handedly backing *A to Z*. (Nor, given what we have already seen of the close-knit nature of 'gay' London at the time, does it come as any surprise to discover that Jack Buchanan was the star of the show and Ivor Novello among the other contributors.)

A decade later, after the failure of his drama *The Stag*, which ran for just six weeks at the Globe Theatre, Nichols was back in the West End, this time under the aegis of Charlot's rival, the producer C. B. Cochran (familiarly known as 'Cocky'). He was the composer and lyricist of three songs in *Cochran's 1930 Revue* ('The Little Things You Do', 'Since Eros Went Away' and 'Selection'). Inevitably, this too was virtually a 'gay' gang-show for, right through the twenties, as even Nichols's rather minor connection with it demonstrates, the theatre and in particular the musical theatre was central to the 'gayness' of London. It is difficult if not impossible now to gauge the importance of an open, acknowledged or even implicit *homosexuality* at the heart of it; but extracts from a couple of letters which Coward wrote in 1921 and 1922, shortly after Ned Lathom had introduced him, too, to Charlot (and which could as easily have been written by Nichols), vividly convey the mood of the West End at the time:

Darling, I've just played all the music to Charlot and he's delighted – he sat without a smile and then took me aside and said they were *all* good – so that's that. I now quite definitely enter the ranks of British Composers! [. . .] it will be very thrilling to hear all my songs done by a good orchestra, won't it? I am very excited as the music *is* good.

. . . You say you *expect* Ned is putting up money for the Revue – Certainly he is, *it's his solely and entirely*, Charlot is on a salary as Director! He is the usual taciturn manager – he's been charming to me and asked if I'd agree to let Clifton Webb play it *with* me (Clifton's salary is £80). I said of course providing that I was indisputably in the superior position! Aren't I a *dear*![12]

Inevitably, Nichols was very much at home in this milieu, and by the time that *Cochran's 1930 Revue* opened he was at the heart of things: Ivor Novello had also been involved in the writing; Berners had contributed a short ballet sequence; Oliver Messel and Rex Whistler were among the team of set and costume designers, while the cast was led by the magnificently camp Douglas Byng.

～

Witty, good-looking in a slightly effeminate way and something of a boulevardier, within a decade of coming down from Oxford, then, with a little help from well-placed friends, Nichols had secured for himself a position of sorts in London society. Indeed, after the success of Cochran's revue he was sounding downright complacent. In the spring of 1931 he wrote in his diary:

I have various memories – of a long line of chorus girls in smoke grey and black dresses singing 'The Little Things You Do' too enchantingly – of the opening number, the film, being greeted with a roar of 'ah' – of the numbers really holding the audience of the delighted Cocky – of supper at Lady Cunard's afterwards, everyone being a little weary and wondering whether they ought to patronize or gush, and myself not caring two hoots what they did – of some wonderfully good and wonderfully bad notices the next day – of Cocky at lunch asking me to write the next revue. So really what more could I want?[13]

Assiduously cultivated contemporaries such as Novello (five years his senior) and Coward (one year his junior), Somerset Maugham, as well as the veteran soprano Nellie Melba, and a legion of elderly, well-heeled homosexual 'patrons' happily captivated by Nichols's easy, drawing-room – others might say 'lounge-lizard' – charm, he now counted among his friends. By 1925 he felt that the world was ready for his autobiography.

And by and large it was. As his biographer Bryan Connon has demonstrated,[14] *Twenty-Five*, published when Nichols himself was just twenty-seven and largely composed of more or less fawning sketches of these friends – Maugham, Coward, Michael Arlen, fellow-novelist Elinor Glyn, and even Winston Churchill – attracted no less than sixty reviews. The *Morning Post* praised it; so too did the *Church of England Newspaper* and, even more bizarrely, the *Architects' Journal*. Friends such as Coward (in the *Daily Mail*) and P. G. Wodehouse (in the *Weekly Dispatch*) rallied round and delivered predictable 'puffs'. Jump-started by such self-perpetuating hype, many other papers named *Twenty-Five* as their 'Book of the Week'. A mere three – ironically, in the light of Nichols's subsequent career, one was in the *Gentlewoman* magazine – suggested that much of the book should never even have got as far as Nichols's editor's desk at the publishing firm of Jonathan Cape.

Their barbs did not matter, however. Like Coward and Novello, by the mid-1920s Nichols was 'launched'. He may have had to trim and accept a comfortable middle-brow 'platform' on the fringes of West End revue and the inside pages of middle-brow newspapers (although his continuing campaign for pacificism guaranteed him sporadic front-page coverage), but such incidentals as unpaid florists' and tailors' bills were things of the past. By 1924, indeed, he was in a position to leave the parental home in which he had intermittently lodged since the end of the war, and set up on his own.

He had to be in London, of course; and in the centre of London. That was what was so beguiling about the small house he found in Hasker Street, Knightsbridge, where he initially established himself as a bachelor-about-town. Merely the barest details – and a mind capable of imagining the stage sets for contemporary drawing-room plays by the likes of Coward (*The Vortex*, 1924), Frederick Lonsdale (*Aren't We All?*, 1923; *The Last of Mrs Cheyney*, 1925; *On Approval*, 1927) and the slightly younger Terence Rattigan – will bring everything to life. Much

of the house was furnished by a rather pathetically besotted Nellie
Melba, who gave Nichols (on what later transpired to be only permanent loan) a set of Queen Anne chairs, a Marie-Antoinette couch, an
Empire desk and several smaller items and paintings. A cleaning lady
came in every day to make sure that everything at Hasker Street was
fit and ready should any of Mr Nichols's famous friends – that Mr
Coward, say, or Rebecca West or Tallulah Bankhead – happen to
drop by.

Although there were a few setbacks and failures, the next ten years
were to be his salad days. Published extracts from the diary he kept
in the early months of 1934 show just how far he had come – and
how unlikely it would have been for any of his famous friends to have
found him at home, had they arrived unannounced:

20 February
Lunched today with Lady Mount Temple. The poor thing is in a
great state of agitation and told me in a stage whisper that her
husband had left her. 'He is a sadist,' she hissed. Next to me was
Lady Lymington whose husband has just resigned from the Tory
party. A nice woman, but unpardonably muddle-headed [. . .]

Dined with Catherine d'Erlanger. Catherine was in great form
and dinner was typical. Either she or her son-in-law Johnny were
[*sic*] at the telephone. Nobody was eating the same course at the
same time. One never does at Catherine's.

Went to Noël's *Conversation Piece* [. . .]

Back for a few minutes to Catherine's. How strange that great
home in Piccadilly is! . . .

21 February
Lunched with Mary Ridgely Carter at 41 Portman Square. Mary C.
is a tiresome American who ought to have been cast as a housemaid
and makes a very bad heiress. In love with me, apparently.

Dinner with Peter Spencer, now Lord Churchill. He ought to
play a large part in any autobiography I may write. He dined with
me at the Garrick . . .

23 February
Lunch at Claridge's with Mabel Corey, a rattling American who
had collected the King of Greece, the Duke of Marlborough, Lord

Elmleigh, Lady Birkenhead, Lady Alexander Haig and me. I sat next to Lady B. who told me she got £85 for saying she used Lyons Coffee Extract which she had never tasted.

5 March
Supper with Lady Colefax, Alfred Lunt, Lynn Fontanne, Victor Cazalet, H. G. Wells and Baroness Budberg (his lady love). I don't think H. G. Wells likes me. He said, 'You have made a profession of perpetual youth. Are you taking any measures to preserve it?' I replied, 'No, only measurements.'

6 March
John Gielgud to lunch. Very gay and charming. Told me he had just bought a country home for £1,000.

7 March
Lunch with Barbara Back [. . .] I am tired out as usual.

13 March
I dined with Victor Cazalet at the House of Commons . . .

14 March
Today I lunched at Claridge's with Alexander Korda, the Hungarian genius . . .

17 March
I spent the weekend with Gerald Berners at Faringdon, motoring Peter Churchill up. Nobody there except Lady Birkenhead, Olga Lynn and Robert Heber-Percy, generally known as 'the mad boy' – why mad, I do not know, for he struck me as merely rude. The main interest of a dull weekend was the character of our host which is a fluffy mixture of a great many talents without any basis of work or application.[15]

Sixty years on, much of this might strike us as Lord Berners struck Nichols that weekend, as downright 'fluffy' and superficial. It would be wrong, however, to see Nichols as being 'without any basis of work or application'. In spite of all the gadding about he remained prodigiously prolific throughout this period – and a darker side of his character was also emerging. While they revel in the snobbishly 'gay' side of things (it is hardly accidental that the entry describing the

Claridge's dinner on 23 February lists his fellow guests with a pedantic regard for social order) his diaries discreetly fail to mention another diversion which not infrequently kept Nichols away from the house in Hasker Street. Bryan Connon has established that in the mid-1920s he began renting a series of anonymous flats in and around Chelsea where he could more privately and conveniently entertain rough trade and guardsmen from the nearby barracks whose company he sought whenever his punishing public schedule allowed.

At this time, too – when he was still not quite thirty years of age – he made perhaps the definitive announcement of his arrival on the 'gay' scene by recruiting, in addition to his cleaning ladies, the first of a series of cook-valet-butler-companions who would look after him for most of the rest of his life. Gaskin, then just twenty-one, came highly recommended. But absolute discretion was obviously essential in such a post. Was Gaskin, well *you know* . . . ?

'Gay? He almost invented it!' a contemporary who knew both Nichols and Gaskin later recalled. And he was using the word in its contemporary sense.

⟐

Speaking more than twenty years ago in a television documentary, Gladys Calthrop, Noël Coward's long-time designer and factotum, gave graphic testimony to how cosy everything had been within the charmed Nichols-Coward-Lathom-Beaton circle during the 1920s:

> By chance Noël happened to be lunching with Michael Arlen, the Armenian novelist whose new book *The Green Hat* was a best-selling success in London that year. They were discussing their work, and Noël told him that [his play] *The Vortex* was in a ghastly mess because of the financial problem.
>
> 'How much do you need to put it on?' Michael asked.
>
> 'Oh, about £200,' Noël replied, and with that, Michael took out his cheque-book at the luncheon table, wrote out a cheque for £250, and handed it to him without so much as asking to read the play.[16]

Even as Calthrop told it, it all sounded so easy. Noël just happened to know newly wealthy, best-selling novelist Michael; they just happened to be lunching together and discussing their work . . . Today, it is quite impossible to decide whether in 1973 she was more absorbed by fond memories of an epoch even then long dead or by the social solecism which the egregious Arlen had committed by taking out his cheque book at a luncheon table. (Impossible to imagine the fifth Earl of Lathom doing that when *he* came to write Coward a cheque!) Quite possibly it was mixture of both. The Armenian-born − Calthrop effortlessly got that into the interview − Arlen certainly occupied a unique place in the literary world of the inter-war years.

If there was an element of sham and flim-flammery about him, however − something slightly shady, slightly bogus − it was reflected in the company he kept. It is as difficult now as it was then to make any moral differentiation between Arlen and the ambitious, acquiescent and − within their own circle − openly homosexual young men-about-town like Nichols, Novello, Walpole and Coward. Every bit as much as he was, they too were playing a game. For exactly the same reasons that Arlen felt it necessary to disguise his eastern European origins, they had no option but to publicly play down their sexual proclivities. Even in a world immeasurably more innocent and less prurient than our own, any suggestion of homosexuality in a 'man-about-town' such as Nichols, a major new personality or a gossip-column figure in the new firmament of stars would have been simply unimaginable. Happily for them, however, in the 1920s and 1930s the dissembling was easy enough. Looking back in 1957 (incidentally, in a letter to Beverley Nichols), Coward recalled that it took no more than 'appearing to be as blasé, world-weary and "jagged with sophistication" as we possibly could'. That, plus a stiff collar, the company of a complaisant female friend (Gladys Cooper was especially in demand) and, when the occasion demanded, a good dinner-suit armour-plated them from innuendo and the wrong sort of gossip.

They were unconditionally, if sometimes uncomprehendingly, 'taken up' on their own terms by society while still managing to pass as 'normal' in a wider world. It was, however, something of a schizophrenic existence. Somerset Maugham's double life was not atypical. An early leaver from one of Lady Emerald Cunard's exhausting late-night parties in the 1930s, he excused himself with the words 'I have to keep my youth' − only to have his disingenuous hostess ask, 'Then why didn't you bring him with you?' Happily for him, the denizens of Grosvenor Square were discreet in those days, and the fashionable young novelist and playwright could rest assured that his secret would remain hidden from the general public. To them, indeed, he was just another author: in a series of cigarette cards celebrating famous writers which was issued at around this time his portrait (as well as those of Arlen, Nichols and Hugh Walpole) appeared reassuringly alongside those of bluffer, more down-to-earth figures such as J. B. Priestley, 'Sapper' and Commander Stephen King-Hall.

More fundamentally, this necessary discretion was also to have unexpected and long-lasting consequences, for the subterfuge did much to temper the general public's image of the homosexual man. The matinée-idol carapace which Noël Coward built around himself in particular was to be especially enduring, not least because it appealed as much to women as it did to those who were members or putative members of his own circle. We might compare, for instance, the reactions to Coward of Ginette Spanier and the young John Gielgud when *The Vortex* finally opened in 1924. 'Noël Coward was the Beatles of our day,' Spanier once recalled, and went on:

> Do you realise that up till then nobody had ever called some-body 'darling' unless they were having a love affair with them? And the fact of everybody being so sophisticated and calling each other 'darling' was a habit started by Noël which has gone on till today. [. . .]
>
> I wanted to meet him so badly. I used to look round the corner in case he came down the street. And then after the war, it must have been 1945 or 1946, quite by chance we met in the South of France and in three minutes we became intimate, close and wonder-ful friends.[17]

Gielgud was similarly gushing. After visiting the one-time middle-class boy from an obscure London suburb in his dressing room following a performance of *The Vortex*, he wrote: 'I went to see Noël at the Royalty Theatre in Dean Street, very apprehensive of course, but very thrilled to meet him. His dressing-room was full of bottles of Chanel No. 5, with twenty dressing-gowns in the wardrobe.'[18]

Coward was to preserve this sexual ambivalence until the very end of his life. Enigmatic on-stage partnerships with Gertrude Lawrence as much as later 'friendships' with the young Princess Margaret and Marlene Dietrich effectively blurred the issue for decade after decade

– not least in the eyes of the 'adoring middle-aged women of Woking' who, at least in the years before what he himself called 'Dad's Renaissance', increasingly typified his audience. But if he can be criticized for maintaining the pretence far longer than was strictly necessary, it is important to remember that by the time he could have discreetly 'come out' he was trapped in a gilded cage every bit as secure as the one which had imprisoned his poor little rich girl: the image had long since taken over from reality.

Until very recently the 'sophisticated', Chanel-scented figure he particularly came to personify – cigarette-holder in one hand, gin-and-tonic or dry Martini in the other – somehow transcended sex and defused the whole idea of what we might call the physical side of homosexuality. Stories of men arrested in public lavatories, of erring clergymen or desperate businessmen caught with guardsmen still periodically made front-page headlines in the 1930s, but at the same time and at a deeper, almost unconscious, level, homosexuality was quickly becoming associated with the 'innocent' eccentricity of the members of his new *beau monde* whose lifestyle was far more frequently chronicled on the inside feature pages. By the 1930s, indeed, an effete, essentially harmless caricature 'queer' had emerged as the safe pocket-cartoon image of a 'certain type' of British man (think hairdresser, think antiques-dealer, think ballet-dancer). The '*darling*'s, the implicit off-stage presence of 'chorus boys', his predilection for cocktails and champagne, even whispers of such telltale signs of debauchery as his taste for black satin sheets all entered the national consciousness, but as props on a par with the labourer's cloth cap and Dennis the Menace's catapult.

The stereotype was to prove as harmless – and as useful – as it was enduring. Although Julian and his friend Sandy might (and frequently did) ape the camp excesses of the Coward era, no one was seriously affronted by their exploits on *Round the Horne*, the BBC radio comedy series which remained a popular Sunday lunchtime favourite as late as the mid-1960s. Similarly, at the same time as huge audiences were content to accept without comment the idea of Eric Morecambe and Ernie Wise apparently sharing a bed, the outrageous Mr Humphries ('I'm free!') was able to mince around the menswear floor of Grace

Brothers department store wholly free of any libidinous pre-life in the 1970s television series *Are You Being Served?*

It was as if there existed a tacit agreement between the homosexual and the wider community; as if, at some time in, say, the mid-1930s, a line had been drawn which neither side either cared or dared to cross. Thus Danny La Rue's outrageous drag and the innuendo-laden patter of Kenneth Williams and Larry Grayson were accepted at face value, and with exactly the same lack of prurient curiosity which had been afforded the Cowards and Nicholses of half a century earlier. Williams himself was struck by this, as he told Joe Orton in July 1967, only days after Parliament's decriminalization of male homosexual acts. Orton noted in his diary:

> He told me how he'd visited an East End pub. 'And all these young chaps were crowding round. One of them said to me, "Kaw! Ken, it's legal now, you know." And he started to pull his trousers down. And the landlady said, "Ernie! Now then! We'll have none of that." "But he's a celebrity, we've got to put on a show," Ernie said. "Not that kind of show," the landlady said. She was the disapproving type.'[19]

This comfortable, *acceptable* face of homosexuality – in his own account of the East End evening the normally fastidious Williams admitted he 'enjoyed it v. much' – persisted well into the 1980s because everyone played by rules which Coward (who died in 1973) would have understood. Grayson was able to talk about what his 'friend' Everard had done – but only because performer and audience alike knew that they would never see him doing it. In the same way, until AIDS forced their hands, performers such as Liberace and Freddie Mercury were able to enjoy huge international celebrity, trading on what amounted to parodies of the pre-war subfusc while still insisting on and – against all the evidence – convincing audiences of their own heterosexuality . . .

~

Superficially then, as late as the early 1980s it appeared as if nothing had changed for more than fifty years. It was still possible to imagine that, were it not for AIDS, nothing ever would – large numbers of the gay scene, indeed, believed exactly that. In clubs their loudest applause was reserved for drag entertainers who impersonated Judy Garland, Bette Davis, Marilyn Monroe, Carmen Miranda and other doyennes of what, rightly or wrongly, they still perceived as their own *belle époque*. It was as if they were desperate to perpetuate the safe (pre-AIDS) world of Coward and Nichols where the champagne always flowed; the world where every Julian had his Sandy (and money enough from somewhere to set himself up in an antique shop), where gay meant gay *per se*, the word 'queer' was a whispered term of endearment, and there were willing, uncomplicated boys on every street corner. Ironically, however, that very world was coming to an end even as Coward was scoring his first box-office success and a largely female readership was first discovering its taste for Nichols's sugary prose.

The late 1920s were the last years in which paternalistic, personal patronage, even in the rather etiolated form practised by the likes of Gerald Berners and Ned Lathom, had any real effect on the homosexual world (or, for that matter, any other). There were still – and of course there continue to be – relationships based on the Wilde-and-Bosie, older-man-and-young-attractive-partner model, but by the end of the decade a variety of circumstances had conspired to put paid to the full Medici style.

It was inevitable. The gay world of the twenties and thirties as we have previously seen it was no more immune to the vicissitudes of a wider fate than the more quotidian world of the straights:

> ... the day came when Britain went off the gold standard. This immensely rich country, which had been subsidising other nations and was the envy of Europe, suddenly, one morning in the autumn of 1931, found itself on the verge of bankruptcy [. . .] The atmosphere was that of wealthy people on the *Titanic*, whose sense of doom was aggravated by what they had to lose in addition to their lives.[20]

Quite simply, the economic and social mayhem which followed the Wall Street Crash, and the subsequent international depression, changed everything. For those subsisting on investment income or what had previously been called 'old money', the consequences were devastating. Few were able to weather the storm with the insouciance of the Bohemian socialite David Tennant who, with his then wife

Hermione Baddeley, managed to maintain something of the seigneurial style:

> With a private income of £15,000 a year, David did not have to worry about anything except fun. He bought a house in Wiltshire – not far away from Clouds [the home of his friend T. E. Lawrence] – and kept a fleet of cars and a Gypsy Moth aeroplane. He drove very fast down country lanes in racing cars of the latest model, or took his plane on trips to Paris. He filled his Wiltshire house with London friends and rarely saw 'the county' whom he referred to as 'the mug-wumps'.[21]

Much more typical were figures like Lathom, the fifth earl who, as we have already seen, was virtually penniless when he died in 1930.

'One can be poor when young, but never later on in life,' Cecil Beaton was later to note. Throughout his life he was almost pathologically worried about money: 'I am in the hopeless condition of knowing nothing about my own money affairs,' he was fretting as late as 1968. 'I rely on Eileen [Hose, his secretary] to be level headed enough to say when I am in a really serious jam. As it is, it is a battle to make money enough to pay the income tax.'[22] Everything was relative, however – 'In comparison with some, I suppose I am well off' – and always had been. Even when he was young, a rapidly acquired social éclat, bolstered by the appearance of Beaton's Book of Beauty, had kept real poverty from the door. Before he had turned thirty he was, as we have seen, already considering assuming the role of man of property – and rivalling Tennant in the patronizing manner in which he dealt with the mug-wumps of Wiltshire:

> I wrote to Mr Borley of Shaftesbury asking him if he would be willing to sell, or rent, the small house at Ashcombe. In order that I should not give the effect of affluence, I wrote on a small sheet of extremely thin tracing paper. Perhaps this created an effect of abject poverty: the note received no response. After a while I wrote again, this time on some rather pretentious stationery that I had ordered from Frank Smythson of Bond Street.[23]

Beaton was not alone in having this access to what we might call 'new money', money which he had earned rather than inherited. While Beverley Nichols and Gaskin the 'butler' were settling into

Hasker Street, Noël Coward too was facing what was almost literally an embarrassment of riches. As early as the mid-1930s, largely because of the huge popularity of his jingoistic epic *Cavalcade*, then playing at the Theatre Royal, Drury Lane, he was certainly financially secure. He had become his own master (if not quite yet The Master) and, according to his secretary and companion Cole Lesley, was already accustomed to living under the 'generous, though unthinking, assumption that everyone around him had enough money to do as they pleased'.[24] If he was not as wealthy as Ned Lathom had been a decade earlier – nor, by all accounts, as generous with his 'loans' – a steady flow of that new money allowed him, too, to mix with the best and buy virtually anything (or anyone) he wanted.

In retrospect it was a dangerous situation. Subtly, attitudes were shifting, and for no other reason than that the once obedient Bosies, the cravenly grateful 'boys', had grown up. 'Twenty-two, damn it! Hell take it,' Beaton wrote on his birthday in 1927. 'Or no! I do believe it is twenty-three! Yes, I was born in 1904. Good Lord, I'm twenty-three!' But he was not complaining. Socially, economically and not least sexually, he was well on his way to becoming, in a modern phrase, one of the masters of the universe.

So was Coward. Writing to his mother, again in 1927, he had boasted, 'I'm not the Empress Eugénie, I'm Napoleon!' At the time that might have been a slight exaggeration; within five years, however, it was to all intents and purposes true. By 1932 *Cavalcade* had been joined in the West End by his intimate revue *Words and Music*. Coward was emperor of all he surveyed – and, it is possible to argue, beginning to display a certain brash imperiousness.

Although the 'notices were terrible', *Words and Music* quickly settled into what was to become a respectable eight-month run largely because of the popularity of one song. 'Mad Dogs and Englishman' was to become indelibly associated with Coward for the rest of his life (he was still singing it in cabaret thirty years later). But more recently critics and biographers have shown greater interest in 'Mad About the Boy', another Coward standard which was first heard in the show.

Originally written to be sung by a woman, the song certainly presents contemporary audiences with much food for thought, not least because there does not appear to be a definitive version of the lyrics. Indeed, a whole 'new' verse full of supposedly homosexual and autobiographical references only emerged a decade or so after Coward's death. (So too did the story 'Mad About the Boy', that Coward had written while infatuated by James Cagney, with whom he had once enjoyed a 'rough and tumble [. . .] wrestling match on the floor'.)

There is no evidence that Coward ever sang this verse in public, or even wrote it down. It may well have been no more than a party squib, intended for purely private consumption; but phrases such as 'People I employ/ Have the impertinence to call me Myrna Loy,/ I rise above it,/ Frankly love it,/ Because I'm absolutely mad about the boy' seem to have been drawn from direct personal experience. If they were, they are unique – a contemporary allusion to changing times and a hubristic challenge to the world to do its worst.

Alone with his pastel-coloured doves at Faringdon, the middle-aged Lord Berners had once been thought of as the epitome of the 'saucy fellow'. But now? For obvious reasons, after a gap of half a century and more it is difficult to recreate with any accuracy the precise social and sexual dynamics of the relationships which existed between, say, Beverley Nichols and Gaskin or Coward and his 'companions'. Nichols's voluminous diaries have little to say on the subject (and are even less revealing about his Chelsea pick-ups). A similar reticence informs Beaton's and the autobiographies of Noël Coward; the apparently franker diaries of Hugh Walpole regrettably remain unpublished. However, it is possible to detect from other sources the beginnings at around this time of a more pragmatic attitude to sex; an earthier, more demotic version of the dinner-suited fumblings we have so far encountered.

'People I employ . . . I rise above it . . .' Contemporary or not, Coward's words suggest the existence of a hierarchy, a micro-economy of which he and his peers comprised only one stratum. To a large extent this was true. As we have seen in earlier chapters, even in the 1920s homosexual men did not exist only in and around Shaftesbury Avenue and Piccadilly, and not all of them wore dressing gowns. Away from the bright lights there were pocket Bernerses and Lathoms in every part of Britain. They might not have been titled, but neither were their protégés necessarily of the Coward, Nichols or Beaton class.

Rather, as 'Sam' graphically recalls, they were there 'to be had'. In the late 1920s he had opened a dance studio in Cambridge:

> I used to sometimes give tea dances on a Sunday afternoon at the studio, or perhaps a drag show. As a matter of fact my parties got quite well known and they used to come down from London. They used to call me Lady May Cambridge. They said, Lady May's putting on another do, and they all used to come down. Of course we had a wonderful time. We used to put on shows for ourselves and one or two of the pupils. A lot of my pupils *knew*, you know; and some very nice boys I had used to enter in the fun. I had [sex with] lots of my pupils; boy pupils. If I made a play for them they thought it was wonderful to be loved by a Principal at the school of dancing. I always used to 'do' them, of course.[25]

Wonderful it might have been; but, as always, there are two sides to the story – just as the phrase 'to be had' has two very different meanings.

'Bernard' looks back to very much the same time through wholly different eyes. Something of a drifter, he recollects a world in which it was fast becoming difficult to establish who was having who. His is a new, pragmatic homosexuality. He is not the pathetic 'unemployed gentleman's servant', the mendacious inadequate who appeared in the witness box in the Wilde trials; nor is he merely the precursor of the callous, scheming 'rent-boy', for all that he might have appeared as such to the 'Sam's he encountered:

> I was now about eighteen. One night at the Palladium I met a queer fellow whom I knew, and with him he had this man, quite an elderly man. Well, obviously, he was so old to me at the age of eighteen, that I couldn't possibly be interested. [But] the fellow he was with gave him my address. He came to see me the very next day. He was an Englishman. He's the only one I feel guilty about. He lived in Devon, was married and had two boys. He'd been in the Indian Army. He said, Well, what do you want to do? Well, to be honest I didn't really want to do anything. So he said, Would you like to go on the stage? So I said, Yes, I'd like to go on the stage, but I can't do anything. Well, he said, I'm going to teach you.
>
> He gave me enough money to live on, and my fees [for drama

school]. For about two years I didn't go! To this day I don't know where the Royal Academy of Dramatic Art is! I feel very bad about that now, although I didn't at the time [. . .]

In the end I met [an] American. Not only was he very rich but he was very generous. This great American was thirty-eight. Young, virile, loved the theatre, loved going to restaurants. Which I loved too [. . .] I was being taken to the Savoy Hotel and to a restaurant in Chelsea called The Queens. This American lived in Pall Mall. I thought this was wonderful. He said, go and take a house. So I said, All right. I took this studio in Chelsea.

When the Taunton fellow came back to London I confessed to him that I was leaving him. He wept and he said, You've let me down. Of course I didn't believe him. I didn't want to. And that was that. The American was a bastard. He was not exclusively homosexual. He used to mention the telephonist where he worked. She was a married woman. He mentioned her quite often. But I used to keep away from discussing that sort of thing. There wasn't any trouble. I kept out of people's normal lives, those people who had normal lives. He supported me. We had a housekeeper. I didn't look after the house. He used to go off to work, but I went to the races, to the dogs. We were together about seven years.[26]

Towards the end of his life Noël Coward noted that 'People were greedy and predatory, and if you gave them the chance they would steal unscrupulously the heart and soul out of you without really wanting to or even meaning to.' He was writing about the 1920s and 1930s but, as we shall see, he could have been referring to any of the subsequent decades.

5 ❦

'The Homintern'

AWAY FROM THE WEST END the 1930s were, in W. H. Auden's famous phrase, 'a low, dishonest decade'. But like most decades they had in fact begun before their time. (The sixties began in 1956 and were largely over by 1967.) The thirties had their origins in the economic depression of the late 1920s, the General Strike of May 1926 and the American Wall Street Crash of 1929, the ripples of which rapidly crossed the Atlantic. Unemployment was at (then) record levels and, perhaps even more importantly, there was a general feeling of queasiness as political power see-sawed between Labour, under Prime Minister Ramsay MacDonald, and Stanley Baldwin's Conservatives. 'Buddy Can You Spare a Dime?' was the popular song of the decade, just as a book like George Orwell's *The Road to Wigan Pier* (1937) now seems as redolent of the thirties as Michael Arlen's *The Green Hat* does of the 'roaring twenties' – certainly more so than the increasingly smug and self-satisfied effusions about gardening which Beverley Nichols had taken to producing by that time.

Politics rather than jazz, along with a certain doom-laden historicism, was in the air, as was exemplified by the voguish popularity of a rather dangerous proto-fascistic book by the German writer Oswald Spengler. *Untergang des Abendlandes* (1918–22) seemed exactly to sum up the *Zeitgeist* when it was published in English as *The Decline of the West* between 1926 and 1929.

That *Zeitgeist* or, more exactly, the mood on the streets had shifted palpably since the beginning of 1924 when, in a General Election, Britain elected its first Labour government and saw Ramsay Mac-Donald installed as its first Labour prime minister. Neither government nor prime minister lasted long, however. After it lost a vote of confidence in the November of that year the Labour Party went on to lose the second General Election of 1924, too. Baldwin and the Conservatives were back in office, but a corner had been turned – not least because the Liberal Party, last in power in 1918, was virtually wiped out in Parliament, and the whole country, and more particularly the House of Commons, divided into the broad Left–Right factions which have endured for seventy years.

Opinions only became more polarized eighteen months later when the Miners' Federation objected to a wage cut imposed by the owners of Britain's then privately managed coal mines and Baldwin declined to top up their pay-packets from the national coffers. On 4 May 1926 the country came to a stop when the Trades Union Congress called a General Strike in support of the miners. Not only was there no coal-mining; factories were closed, there were no trains, no trams, no lorries to make deliveries, no newspapers (apart from the government-published *British Gazette*) or postal collections. Practically all public services ground to a halt; even policemen virtually disappeared from the streets.

The strike lasted for just nine days. On 12 May the TUC was forced to concede defeat and, resentfully, those workers who still had jobs to go to made their way back to work. The ramifications of their action, however, were long-lasting. For a while the political divisions between Left and Right intensified into social warfare, or at least a period of deep mutual mistrust between 'the toffs' and the rest. Virginia Woolf, although instinctively a toff, was not alone in sensing that those nine days had irrevocably changed the nation, that the West really was in decline. On 12 May she noted in her diary: 'I saw this morning 5 or 6 armoured cars slowly going along Oxford Street; on each two soldiers sat in tin helmets, and one stood with his hand at the gun which was pointed straight ahead ready to fire. But I also noticed on one a policeman smoking a cigarette.'

Within less than a fortnight Britain had become a divided nation; and, although the superficial scars were quick to heal, it would remain so until Churchill's clarion calls to unite in 1940 effected some sort of rapprochement.

All this had a shattering impact on the intellectual life of the country. Beyond Woolf's Bloomsbury, there was a radical change of mood at its universities and particularly at Oxford, where, even within the collegiate community itself, things were falling apart.

A new generation of students had arrived in the mid-1920s and most of the likes of the Brideshead 'aesthetes' had already gone down. Something of their spirit lived on, however – 'The year must have been 1925 when still the tales of Harold Acton, Brian Howard and Cyril Connolly lingered . . .' John Betjeman was later to sigh. The freshmen gamely tried to live up to what they thought was expected of them, but the essential brio had evaporated, a casualty of more care-laden times.

This is sometimes difficult to believe, for there is a false jauntiness about the later memories of many of those who were there. 'We were the last generation of womanless Oxford. Men who liked women were apt to get sent down,' a characteristically elegiac Cyril Connolly claimed nearly half a century later.[1] Almost primly, Anthony Powell described a similar sexual climate: 'women [were] somewhat derided, homosexuality and autoeroticism approved'.[2] Post Acton, post Howard, however, even within their own set such homosexual activity as still survived at Oxford seems to have amounted to little more than a continuation of public-school larkiness. (Betjeman, who arrived at Magdalen College from Marlborough in 1925, wrote a long, 'very indecent and very vivid' poem called 'Bags in Dorm' at this time.) Certainly the frequently reported – and probably not entirely apocryphal – tales of the period which survive tell of little more than grown-up versions of dormitory fumbling – not least because virtually all the named participants were fundamentally heterosexual.

There is the story of how Evelyn Waugh (Lancing) and another, unnamed student were found prostrate and *in flagrante delicto* on a sofa in the predominantly gay Hypocrites' Club, Waugh's tongue deep inside the latter's mouth. There's the one about how W. H. Auden (Gresham's) was discovered by his college scout (bed-maker) in bed with Betjeman and had to pay the scout £5 to keep quiet: 'It wasn't worth it,' Auden later rather indelicately revealed. There's the 'fact' that Betjeman actually preferred the future Labour leader, Hugh Gait-skell (Winchester). 'Hugh,' he was once heard to ask him, 'may I stroke your bottom?' 'Oh, I suppose so,' said Gaitskell, 'if you *must*.'

All in all they do not amount to much. Seen in context, they are no more than tales of a would-be coterie desperately trying to perpetuate a suddenly alien past – and ending up, like Gaitskell and Betjeman, doing little more than rather frigidly going through the motions.

Oxford had changed. Socially and aesthetically in the years between, say, 1922 and 1927 the heart of the university skipped a beat – and, as it seems now, a generation. For the majority of undergraduates (and dons) life went on as it always had; but for the movers and shakers, the one-offs and true originals who define a generation, something fundamental had happened. In short, within no more than five years 'Brideshead' had all but ceded Balliol, University College and Christ Church ('The House') to Bolshevism.

In retrospect, there is a certain inevitability about this. For all their public-school upbringings, the 'Actonites' only *became* socialists during their time at Oxford;[3] concomitant upon the national political turmoil of 1924–6, like Gaitskell a small but significant number of those arriving at Oxford in the next few years *came up* as hardened socialists. They were uniquely politicized by their experiences of public school,[4] and had already caught the whiff of cordite. For them, the General Strike was the catalyst, and battle-lines were swiftly drawn between them and their fellow-students.

When the call to arms came in May 1926 the vast majority of undergraduates (or at least of those undergraduates who did anything at all) naturally nailed their colours somewhere below the Union Flag on Baldwin's mast and more or less seriously signed up as special constables, couriers, van drivers and chauffeurs. Faced by a General Strike, they were unequivocally on the government side, fighting for everything their class held dear: 'It was August 1914 all over again. The [government] volunteers saw themselves gallantly at war against the revolution. One of them said to me, "I wonder if I shall ever come back." The enrolment was Tom Brown's Last Stand.'

Only a small group of students rallied to the support of the TUC and the workers. Alan (later better-known as A. J. P.) Taylor – the author of the words quoted above – was one such, and a prominent member of the revolutionary band; others included Gaitskell, the stubbornly Marxist artist John Strachey (Lytton's nephew) and a more disparate group of fellow-travellers. Betjeman was amongst these; so, too, were his fellow poets W. H. Auden and Cecil Day-Lewis. It is difficult, however, to assess their true commitment to the cause. Although they were members of a uniquely politicized Oxford generation – future Labour cabinet members Richard Crossman, Michael Stewart, Anthony Greenwood, Patrick Gordon Walker and Barbara Castle (*née* Betts) were among their approximate contemporaries – many seem to have manned the barricades principally *pour épater les parents*. Betjeman was certainly there because he believed it would be a 'lark'. Stuffing envelopes, writing trades-union bulletins and driving cars for the TUC made a glamorous change from the more mundane routines of student life. Auden too was there primarily (and almost literally) for the ride. Driving a TUC car around London one day, he found himself near the Bloomsbury home of a female cousin and her husband. Much later he recalled: '. . . so I paid a call. The three of us were just sitting down to lunch when her husband asked me if I had come up to London to be a Special Constable. "No," I said, "I am driving a car for the TUC." Whereupon, to my utter astonishment, he ordered me to leave the house. It had never occurred to me that anyone took the General Strike seriously.'[5]

At the centre of this disparate cell of undergraduate revolt was the newly founded University Labour Club (ULC). By the early 1930s this had a paid-up membership (subscription 2/6*d*.) of around 500 despite the somewhat austere impression it made on outsiders. Even the young Harold Wilson (Jesus College, 1934–7) was mystified by the first few meetings he attended, finding them preoccupied with 'squabbling about tiffs with other sections of the Labour Party instead of getting down to something concrete'. He was quickly – if temporarily – disillusioned: 'Cole is speaking at the Labour Club tonight but I don't think I'll go,' he wrote home in 1934. 'I'll wait till next term for that sort of thing.'

It was almost inevitable that Wilson should have thought like this. Educated at a northern grammar school, he had little time for 'Marxist public school products rambling on about the exploited workers and the need for a socialist revolution': athletics were more to his taste ('If I could only get my cross-country really well up, I might get my half-blue next year'). For our present purposes, however, Wilson's reservations highlight an important point. Until the Labour Club lurched decisively to the Left and merged with the Communist-dominated October Club in 1935 to establish a 'popular front', Oxford socialism and the ULC itself were the upstart successors of 'Brides-head'.

Unlikely as it seems, Ben Pimlott has shown that, well before 1934, the Labour Club had become 'the crucible of fashion'. Reflecting this, even such previously apolitical students as Stephen Spender had ostentatiously begun sporting red ties, while the thirty-odd members of the Socialist Dons' Luncheon Club instituted a programme of weekly meetings. 'The student Left was as febrile, and as out of touch with reality, as ever it became in the course of a heady decade,' Pimlott observes – adding that 'it was fun to be a Communist at Oxford in the 1930s, if you had the money and the leisure to sustain the lifestyle.'[6] Comparatively few had – Wilson's early letters home are peppered with phrases such as 'It might pay to send butter (it is very dear here)' – but those who did found that there was indeed something for everybody in the people's party.

Surprisingly, perhaps, in the late twenties, in the era of Betjeman and Auden, this even seems to have included a tacit acceptance of homosexuality, or at least the abstract notion of homosexuality. There was, of course, nothing doctrinal about this. Rather, it was a matter of historical accident, a relic of the days when ULC meetings had been little more than smokers or *conversaziones*, informal gatherings held away from the university at the home in Holywell of G. D. H. Cole, a young reader in Economics (and the author of numerous detective stories) who was both openly socialist and at the very least homosexually inclined. No record of these early gatherings of what was then known merely as the 'Cole group' now exists, but it is possible to imagine discussion straying far beyond the minuted squabbling and rambling to which Harold Wilson was forced to listen when the ULC was formally established. It is possible, too, to see how Cole, a throw-back to the days of Edward Carpenter and E. M. Forster and temperamentally a Fabian rather than a freedom-fighter, influenced the lives of a whole generation of sexually and politically labile under-graduates.

Harold Wilson was, as we have seen, attracted by his socialism (and, we must assume, only by his socialism); so too was Hugh Gaitskell, who rapidly became Cole's unofficial lieutenant in that department. But in the light of Cole's homosexual sympathies, the appeal which he and the Labour Club held for a social and sexual dilettante such as

Betjeman, to say nothing of the homosexual but innately unclubbable Auden, also makes sense. 'Fashion' alone would have brought the former – who, by his own admission, had arrived at Oxford determined to become acquainted with 'the grand set' – into Cole's ambit soon enough. Auden's case is, however, more complicated. The poetry he was to publish only a few years later shows an almost hysterical revolutionary fervour:

> Financier, leaving your little room
> Where the money is made but not spent,
> You'll need your typist and your boy no more;
> The game is up for you and the others . . .[7]

We have seen, too, that he was, with whatever degree of sincerity, at least prepared to throw in his lot with the ULC activists during the General Strike. And yet, for all that his close (heterosexual) friend David Ayerst was also the ULC's student chairman, Auden never got round to forking out his 2/6d. and actually joining the party. It was as if the mere knowledge of the existence of a 'safe house' such as Cole's where forbidden subjects could be openly discussed had a reassuring appeal for the poet whose work was increasingly full of references to spies, mysterious outsiders and lonely agents; as if, too, the Labour Club satisfied a more basic need and brought him into contact, albeit vicarious contact, with the type of proletarian rough with whom he would later become better acquainted in Berlin . . .

Ultimately, of course, it is futile to speculate. In any case, another ULC non-joiner has left a further tantalizing hint of the sympathy felt by some elements of the Left towards the university's homosexual fraternity. In an attempt to explain why he had not joined the Labour Club, Tom Driberg implicitly confessed that he might have made a mistake: 'Maybe I would have been more interested if I had known that Cole, besides being one of the most brilliant and attractive of the younger dons, had homosexual tendencies.'[8]

❧

Thomas Edward Neil Driberg arrived at Christ Church, Oxford, in October 1924, already trailing the clouds of notoriety which were to dog his heels for the rest of his life. A few months earlier he had narrowly escaped expulsion from his public school (Lancing) when two boys 'betrayed' him to the headmaster after he had tried to seduce them in a dormitory. He was a roué, a Byronic – even Satanic – bucker of trends. 'With his dark hair and long nose', a friend was to note a few years later, 'he looked as though he had Indian blood – the son of a Maharajah.' More pertinently, he came up to 'The House' not as a mere socialist but as a full-blooded, card-carrying member of the Communist Party of Great Britain, albeit one with an apostate passion for the red brick and High Mass of Westminster Cathedral.

His life was always a mass of contradictions; a morass of inconsistencies. He was the Communist who was also a devout High Anglican; the Labour MP who had to all intents and purposes invented the modern gossip column (he was the *Daily Express*'s first William Hickey); the inveterate 'cottager' who lived in a Georgian country mansion; the one-time restaurant *plongeur* who ended his life as a member of the House of Lords. During his school days, when he had spent a summer holiday trying to sell copies of the *Daily Worker* for the Brighton branch of the Communist Party, it had been difficult enough to keep the disparate sides of his life apart: 'I was leading a triple life indeed. I had to conceal from my new comrades both the fact that I was being educated at a bourgeois public school and, still more, my ecclesiastical and sexual tastes. In its turn, the school must know nothing of the sex or the Party.'[9]

At Oxford, where the need for concealment and duplicity was considerably less pressing than it had been at Lancing, he simply threw caution to the winds. Unsurprisingly, academic work came very low on his list of priorities as he gave full vent to every aspect of his character. Like many an undergraduate before him, he was determined to get himself noticed. 'This was the period when "Oxford bags" were worn,' he wrote in his autobiography *Ruling Passions*, 'trousers very wide and flapping at the ankles, far wider than the Navy's bell-bottoms. In my first year at Oxford I got the widest pair I could find, at Hall Brothers in the High, and in an unusual colour – bright green.'[10] (He does not record whether he wore these on the frequent trips he made to London to see, among other things, performances by the Diaghilev Ballet.) He began writing for the undergraduate magazine *Cherwell* – 'probably the nearest I came to doing any sort of regular work while I was at Oxford' – and indulged his innate snobbery by cultivating every bit as assiduously as Betjeman the university's few remaining Actonites and anyone else who might conceivably have been a member of 'the grand set'.

Seemingly unaware of any possible conflict of interest, he also remained politically active. Impatient with the Labour Club because of what he called the 'moderation' of its stance, he set about establishing a university branch of the Communist Party. Despite help from national party organizers and his own considerable efforts, however, this never had anything like the popular appeal of the ULC. For much of the time he was associated with it, indeed, there were just two paid-up members – Driberg himself (president) and, when he finally extricated himself from the Labour Club, Alan Taylor.

Parallel with all this was inevitably the indulgence of his 'sexual tastes'. These were little short of gargantuan, and the typically forthright manner in which Driberg sought to assuage them is vividly illustrative of the difference between the attitudes of the decorous old guard and the new young turks. Evelyn Waugh might have been satisfied with passionate French-kissing, Betjeman with stroking Hugh Gaitskell's bottom, Harold Acton himself with 'kindling flames in Elgin marble breasts'; but, as we have seen, they were only dabblers. Driberg saw himself as a professional. For him sex was a passion; a 'ruling passion' indeed. And it was simply sex; neither love nor romance had any part in it. A quick fumble, an anonymous encounter in a public lavatory or, at the very most, a one-night stand in a cheap hotel with a bit of rough whom he had never met before and would never meet again – these were all that interested him.

There are copious examples of them all. Of how, at Alan Taylor's twenty-first birthday party, Driberg began pestering one of the waiters, causing the latter to complain to Taylor, 'I am a respectable married man and if that gentleman comes out to me again I shall go home.'[11] Of how, while 'cottaging' in one of Oxford's public lavatories, Driberg encountered a university don, with inevitable consequences (he 'looked far from donnish', Driberg explained). Of how any time, anywhere, almost any working-class youth could take his fancy . . .

In this last case, because of all that it says about Driberg and his attitudes at the time, it is worth quoting at some length – and in full graphic detail – the account he gave in *Ruling Passions* of one such pick-up. It took place during one of his long vacations from Oxford, when he was in London. After having tried his hand at prostitution ('harmless enough'), he was, bizarrely, attempting to earn money as a pavement artist with a 'pitch' on the Thames Embankment. But, in 'grey flannel trousers, a "sports" shirt and jacket', he was hardly dressed for the part. Then his eye lit upon one of the many shabbily dressed down-and-outs who then (as now) congregated in that area, 'a young man – perhaps twenty years old – with a face that was pale and thin and wistfully appealing'. The solution seemed obvious: 'I propositioned him: would he come and sleep the night with me at a cheap hotel and then, very early in the morning, change clothes with me?' This might now sound distinctly disingenuous; but the young man nevertheless 'accepted with alacrity' and Driberg led him off to a hotel he knew:

It was a warm night: we agreed to sleep naked, with only a sheet over us. He was reasonably clean (he had been to the public baths that day) and, to my relief, free of 'crabs' – the *Pediculi pubis* which were, and are, so often transmitted in such circumstances. Before getting into bed, we smoked a few cigarettes to drown the smell of his socks. No doubt as a result of prolonged under-feeding, his ribs were too prominent, but his body was well-proportioned, his skin delicate and fair. We spoke little; he smiled – again that wistful look which had first moved me. We turned to each other, and kissed: the alternate thrust and withdrawal of his tongue – soft but firm, warm, and slightly flavoured with peppermint chewing-gum – suggested experience. In view of his general condition, I had not expected a strong sexual response; but now, beating and throbbing against me, was a surprisingly thick, hard organ. Then, still without speaking, he showed what he really wanted, or thought that I did; for, after another kiss, he rolled over with his back towards me, his bottom pressing against my genitals. Sodomy does not happen to be my favourite sexual pastime; but I could hardly refuse so unassuming a charmer [. . .] The actual entry was, I fear I must say, suspiciously easy: this meant either that the orifice had been coated with Vaseline (or the rather better-class 'K.Y.') to facilitate previous entries, or that my bed-mate was suffering from diarrhoea, a common by-product of dietary impoverishment. The latter, alas, proved to be the case, as a saffron smear on the cheap cotton sheet testified. But before my withdrawal had brought about this regrettable result, he had already, suddenly, uncontrollably 'shot his load' of semen – and a pitiably thin, weak, liquid load it was (poverty, again), not sufficient in quantity to form on the sheet that other stain which chambermaids call a 'map of Ireland' [. . .]

We were up betimes and I (having given the boy almost all the money I had left) hastened to a pitch that I had thought promising in Russell Square.[12]

<hr>

One can easily imagine Driberg excitedly reporting all this to W. H. Auden when he got back to Oxford for the start of Michaelmas Term. The frank account of the sexual act, baldly stated and hitched to sociological detail ('diarrhoea, a common by-product of dietary impoverishment'), could almost have been devised to appeal to the 'clinical' mind of the man who, even before he attained the age of majority, had, according to Stephen Spender, 'an extensive knowledge of the theories of modern psychology' – the man whom contemporaries had even then taken to calling 'Uncle Wiz'.

Wystan Auden had arrived at Oxford – and by coincidence at Christ Church – a year behind Driberg, in October 1925. The two men soon met, and what Driberg described as a 'chaste' friendship certainly existed by the following summer, for it was at this time that Driberg introduced Auden to the work of T. S. Eliot. He showed him the first printed version of The Waste Land (which had appeared in the Criterion magazine some three years previously). 'Read it, at first, with incredulous hilarity (the Mrs Porter bit, for instance),' he told the unprepossessing fresher who would become the greatest English-born poet of his generation. 'Read it, again and again, with growing awe.' (Typically, Driberg dined out on this story for years afterwards, claiming it was he who had set the tone for the whole 'Audenesque' school of poetry.)

But the two men had a lot besides poetry in common. We have already seen that, like Driberg, at this period in his life Auden was seemingly coming to terms both with socialism and his own homosexuality. 'Seemingly' because, by refusing to write an autobiography and expressly (but ineffectively) forbidding any biography – he even asked his friends to burn all those of his letters which they retained after his death[13] – Auden left rather fewer clues to the true nature of his social and emotional development than many of his contemporaries. Enough remains, however, for us to see him as something of a minor-key Driberg – or, in his own cod-psychological terms, an introverted extrovert.

Spender's description of the man he first met at Oxford a couple of years later provides a convenient starting-point:

> He saw himself – as I then envisaged him – with certain potentialities and talents, certain desires, certain attitudes of mind, living within a community governed by certain rules and traditions, and consisting also of people with different potentialities, desires and attitudes. His aims were to fulfil his potentialities, obtain satisfaction for his desires, and maintain his attitudes without prejudice and without accepting any authority outside his own judgement.[14]

Spender was writing in 1951. Nearly half a century on, it is not difficult to deconstruct what he was trying to say. Auden had 'certain desires' but was 'living within a community governed by certain rules and [. . .] people with different [. . .] desires'. He wanted to 'obtain satisfaction for his desires' . . . Even in 1951 this must have been clear enough.

More recently, however, both the inevitable nature of Auden's 'desires' and the extent to which he managed to satisfy them have been explicitly delineated by Humphrey Carpenter in his biography of the poet.[15] He paints a picture of Auden explaining in Freudian terms that his sexual promiscuity had its roots in a 'complex' he had developed about the smallness of his penis. He has David Ayerst saying how Auden was always falling for unsuitable (i.e. heterosexual) undergraduates. He describes Auden finding some sort of solace in late-night walks around the back streets of Oxford (on a route which Cecil Day-Lewis remembered as taking in the canal tow-path and the city gas-works), and by picking up men on rail trips: 'Wystan could always, on the brief train journey to London, make a contact,' A. L. Rowse noticed.

Tellingly, Carpenter also describes how, even with a compliant fellow-student, Auden's 'wooing' was minimal. Completely un-abashed, he would simply walk into the understandably startled man's rooms and announce: 'You know what I've come for.' Like Driberg, at this period Auden saw sex (his preference, Carpenter reveals, was for fellatio) as just sex. Love did not come into it – *was not allowed to come into it.* According to Stanley Fisher, he believed that 'lust was an appetite and needed to be satisfied, but love was to be avoided as a snare.' Spender too seems to have been aware of this side of what he called Auden's 'amoral' nature. 'Self-knowledge,' he wrote, 'complete lack of inhibition and sense of guilt, and knowledge of others were essential to the fulfilment of his aims.'[16]

'Knowledge of others', the intimate knowledge of every aspect of his friends' personal and sexual lives, was especially important to Auden. But if there was a streak of prurience behind his attempts at omniscience it is important to remember that those friends – most notably Spender, Christopher Isherwood and Isherwood's 'closest heterosexual male friend', the novelist Edward Upward – almost literally beat a path to his door, so anxious were they to take the advice of Uncle Wiz. Isherwood has vividly described the experience. In his 1938 novel *Lions and Shadows* his young narrator visits an old school friend, 'Hugh Weston' (Auden's given names were Wystan Hugh):

> To several of us, including myself, he confided the first naughty stupendous breath-taking hints about the facts of sex. I remember him chiefly for his naughtiness, his insolence, his smirking tantalizing air of knowing disreputable and exciting secrets. With his hinted forbidden knowledge and stock of mispronounced scientific words, portentously uttered, he enjoyed among us, his semi-savage credulous schoolfellows, the status of a kind of witch-doctor [. . .]
>
> Weston's own attitude to sex, in its simplicity and utter lack of inhibition, fairly took my breath away. He was no Don Juan: he didn't run around hunting for his pleasures. But he took what came to him with a matter-of-factness and an appetite as hearty as that which he showed when sitting down to dinner. I don't think that, even in those days, he exaggerated much: certainly, his manner of describing these adventures bore all the hallmarks of truth. I found his shameless prosaic anecdotes only too hard to forget . . .[17]

Spender, too, has given a fictionalized but vividly realistic account of Auden's sexual socialism. *The Temple*, re-worked in 1988 from material he first wrote nearly sixty years previously, is the transparently autobiographical story of a young Oxford student-poet's infatuation with an uncaring heterosexual friend named Marston. Inevitably, Paul

Schoner (Spender) consults his friend Simon Wilmot (Auden) about the matter. Simon does not mince his words:

> Simon asked: 'By the way, are you a Verger?'
> 'A what?'
> 'A virgin?'
> Paul blushed furiously: 'I suppose so.'
> 'Well, you must know whether you are or you aren't.'
> 'I am then. Are you?'[18]

⌒

Virginal or not, this new Oxford sexuality, informed as it was by Freudian and other psychological influences – both Auden and the Cambridge-educated medical student Christopher Isherwood were attracted by the work of John Layard and the reputation of Dr Magnus Hirschfeld's *Institut Für Sexual-Wissenschaft* or Institute for Sexual Science in Germany – was symptomatic of the climate of the times. Homosexuality was no longer the solitary 'inversion' or 'perversion' it had been, even in Forster's (or Maurice's) day. Rather, it had become politicized.

This is not the place for detailed literary exegisis, but it would be perverse not to pause to consider what the two key 'thirties poets' were writing at this period. Perverse because, in much of the early published work of both Auden and Spender, the very *lexis* fuses the political with the implicitly homo-erotic. Ironically, individual poems take on something of the nature of Leni Riefenstahl's films of the Berlin Olympic Games. Spender thinks, wistfully, of 'the truly great' and 'great men' such as his friend 'Trigorin' ('This known great one')[19]; everything is a struggle, a battle for perfection in both the physical and the social sense. 'Oh young men oh young comrades', he implores, punctuation the first casualty of his struggle, 'it is too late now to stay in those houses . . .'

> Count rather those fabulous possessions
> which begin with your body and your burning soul
> the hairs on your skin the muscles extending
> in ranges with lakes across your limbs
>
> Count your eyes as jewels and your golden sex . . .

Count him, too; count Spender in; one of the comrades, one of the chosen, one of the few, who expects 'Thunder, fighting,/ Long struggles with men/ And climbing'.[20]

More assured, more certain of his place in the scheme of things, Auden too was seemingly melding his sexual feelings into a greater *Weltpolitik* at this time – and through the industry of his literary executor Edward Mendelson we can precisely chart the progress of his socio-sexual development. Thus we can date to the April of 1929 his poem beginning 'It was Easter . . .' (Easter Sunday fell on 31 March that year) with its echo of Keats: 'Season when lovers and writers find/ An altering speech for altering times'.[21] We can see too how at precisely that time those lovers and writers were being implicitly allied to his more characteristic dramatis personae of spies, agents, airmen, strangers and other loners and outsiders. Even then, each had

> . . . taught himself this balancing subterfuge
> Of the accosting profile, the erect carriage.

> The song, the varied action of the blood
> Would drown the warning from the iron wood
> Would cancel the inertia of the buried:

> Travelling by daylight on from house to house
> The longest way to the intrinsic peace,
> With love's fidelity and with love's weakness.[22]

In retrospect it is tempting to take the conflation of the outsider/ spy/socialist/homosexual too far; tempting to merge all the thirties archetypes into a single figure. To a greater extent than it did society as a whole, the process may have preoccupied the Oxford of the late 1920s and early 1930s but, as we have seen, for many reasons Oxford was a special case. Rather more typical in its reactions to changing times was Cambridge.

Traditionally more earth-bound than Matthew Arnold's 'home of lost causes', typically and illuminatingly as early as 1922 Cambridge had, for instance, had little time for the *angst*-ridden Cecil Beaton when he arrived as an undergraduate. 'I'm really a terrible, terrible homosexualist and try so hard not to be,' he had admitted to himself at around this time. 'I try so terribly hard to be good and not cheap and horrid.'[23] The university had found this difficult to believe. 'Wearing an evening jacket, red shoes, black-and-white trousers, and a huge blue cravat' whenever he ventured into the street from his rooms in St John's College, the precious Old Harrovian looked as though he was tittupping up Oxford's High to meet Harold Acton or Brian Howard. (More probably, he was on his way to the university's Amateur Dramatic Society where, by accident or design, he had been put in charge of 'dresses and scenery'.) It was a bad miscalculation, but it took Beaton some time to realize the fact: 'As the weather got chillier, he brightened the Cambridge scene with an outfit comprising fur gauntlet gloves, a cloth-of-gold tie, a scarlet jersey and Oxford bags.'[24]

By their own accounts at least, it was kindred spirits at Cambridge and the bracing, matter-of-fact ethos of the university itself which saved Beaton or at least limited the damage he could do to himself. George 'Dadie' Rylands noted: 'Oxford would have been very bad for Cecil. He would have gone straight down the Evelyn Waugh drain.' Cambridge was not like that, Rylands was implying – nor, he hoped, would it ever be. 'They [Waugh's Oxford set] drank champagne at eleven in the morning, while we drank beer at night – or occasionally Burgundy. We lived in a rather poverty-stricken, priggish way.'[25]

'Priggish' is perhaps a misleading way of putting it; 'conceited or didactic' (as the OED defines the word) hardly describes the Cambridge milieu and its homosexual demi-monde. 'Pragmatic' might better express the ethos in which scientia remained the muse, mind was paramount and things were more controlled than ever they were at Oxford. Just as there were no dreaming spires, so there were few drawling poets at Cambridge. Rather, its contemporaries of Oxford's neo-Aesthetes were, comparatively speaking, men of action. By the early 1930s Guy Burgess, Donald Maclean and Anthony Blunt at least already had one eye on the real world, the world beyond even the wide horizons of the Cambridgeshire Fens. Patricia Parry (later Lady Llewelyn-Davies) has recalled that 'The Spanish war was very real and many people [at Cambridge] thought that it was a rehearsal for a bigger war that was coming. If you have a lot of men who know there's a war coming then of course they will be interested in politics because

they know they will be the soldiers.'[26] Though hardly the most charis-
matic of the homosexual – or, in Maclean's case, bisexual – members
of the now notorious Cambridge Communist coterie, this was especially true of Blunt. Before he had even left public school, both politically
and sexually the broad course of his life had been set.

~

Even physically, Blunt was out of the ordinary. He stood 'a gangling
six feet two inches tall'; with his hang-dog, toothy face,[27] indeed, in
student snapshots he resembles nothing so much as a spectre at the
feast. But, variously described as 'clever, erudite and amusing', 'very
well read and cultured', 'patronising', 'always very supercilious' or just
coldly 'intellectual', he was viewed with something like awe by many
of his contemporaries, the majority of whom of course knew nothing
of his deeper preoccupations. Underneath everything, he was 'remote
and deeply serious', Patricia Parry concludes – hinting perhaps at
a single-minded ruthlessness which would only later make itself
apparent.

Nor was it only in this respect that the young Marxist seemed to
exemplify the Cambridge version of the Audenesque outsider. Crucially, although he had pitched up in the wealthy environment of
Trinity College (having matriculated from Marlborough, where he
had been a contemporary of John Betjeman), as the son of a clergyman
he did not have a traditional Trinity background. There was no family
wealth. He was quite literally an outsider; essentially no more than 'a
scholarship boy living on a limited income'. It rankled, and only served
to strengthen Blunt's single-minded pursuit of academic success. If he
was innately debarred from personifying the aesthetic ideal or, indeed,
from cutting any sort of dash as a sportsman, that was a field in which
he could – and did – dazzle spectacularly. He managed to win election
to the exclusive Apostles and, in 1930, having graduated with a First
in modern languages, he began working for a Trinity fellowship in
European art history.

But there was a cold single-mindedness about even this, as there
was about so many other aspects of Blunt's life – a belief that 'only
the best would do' which was to inform his taste in fine art, in food,
in the cigarettes he smoked, in the company he kept and, by no means
least, in the lovers he took. There, once again, only the best would

do: if he was not conventionally good-looking, they most certainly had to be.

At Cambridge the first of these, the son not of a mere clergyman but of a full major-general, was described by a mutual friend as being possessed of 'fair rather wavy hair and a broad forehead. He had quite a sensual mouth, a cleft chin and blue eyes'[28] – in other words he was the embodiment of the traditional aesthetic Ideal. A little later there was Virginia Woolf's nephew Julian Bell who, contemporary photographs suggest, fell into very much the same category and who was, pleasingly, 'completely and hopelessly infatuated' with Blunt. At some time, too, there was Guy Francis de Moncy Burgess.

Blunt seemingly first met Burgess in 1932, shortly after he had taken up his Trinity fellowship. Inevitably he was drawn to the brilliant, prize-winning Old Etonian: not only was he openly, flagrantly, recklessly homosexual, he was like a reincarnation of his first love. Cyril Connolly has recalled Burgess at that time as being 'tall-medium in height, with blue eyes, an inquisitive nose, sensual mouth, curly hair and alert fox-terrier expression [. . .] Despite his intelligence [he] was a round-faced, golden-pated Sancho Panza, extrovert, exhibitionist, manic, cynical and argumentative, avidly curious, yet sometimes vague and incompetent.'[29]

The two were for a time inseparable; despite Blunt's denials, it seems inconceivable that there was not a sexual element in their relationship. But there was another bond, too. Although coming from very different angles, Blunt and Burgess were at this time (1932–5) simultaneously moving closer and closer towards the Communist Party. For what it is worth – he was an arch-dissembler, and never more so than after his 'naming' in 1979 – Blunt has left a detailed account of his own conversion:

I became a Communist and more particularly a Marxist in 1935–36. The history of it is this: I had a sabbatical year from Cambridge in 1933–4 and when I came back in October 1934 I found that all my friends, an enormous number of my friends and almost all the intelligent and bright undergraduates who had come up to Cambridge had suddenly become Marxist under the impact of Hitler coming to power, and there was this very powerful group, very remarkable group of Communist intellectuals in Cambridge – Guy

Burgess was one, James Klugman was another, John Cornford was another [. . .] Guy put it to me that the best way to help anti-fascism, which was obviously the issue of the moment and which became much more acute with the Spanish Civil War in '36, was to help him in his work with the Russians.[30]

According to friend and fellow-traveller Goronwy Rees, however, Burgess had a typically more down-to-earth explanation for his friend's/lover's conversion. That they did not go to bed together, Rees insisted, was just a 'convenient falsehood' of Blunt's. Rees, who knew Burgess well at this period, remembered him constantly boasting of his 'conquests' – Blunt among them. Quite simply, Rees implied, Blunt had caught his Marxism in bed.

This is plausible enough; how Burgess acquired his, however, is a more difficult question. He left no autobiography or first-hand account and the writings about him divide into *pre-* and *ante-bellum* camps. Those written by his friends appeared long before Blunt's exposure – and, indeed, the 1967 decriminalization of male homosexuality (*The Missing Diplomats* by Cyril Connolly was rushed out in 1952, barely a year after Burgess's defection to Moscow with Donald Maclean; Tom Driberg's fuller, if hagiographical, *Guy Burgess: A Portrait with Background* was published in 1956) – and are thus discreet, even sometimes downright misleading. By contrast, books such as Andrew Boyle's *The Climate of Treason* (1979) and Barrie Penrose and Simon Freeman's *Conspiracy of Silence* (1987) try to tell the 'full' political story but rather marginalize Burgess's formative years.

From admittedly rather fragmentary evidence it is still possible to link Burgess's homosexuality with his espousal of Communism – indeed, in its essentials it is a story with which we are already familiar.

At Eton he had been academically formidable, winning both the Rosebery and Gladstone history prizes in 1929 as well as a Trinity scholarship. Even while he was there, however, he was always seen as something of an outsider, somehow 'odd'. (Not the least part of this oddness was that, after the sudden death of his father, he had been abruptly removed from the college and sent as a cadet to the Dartmouth Royal Naval College. But there his eyesight was found to be defective, and – almost uniquely – he was soon accepted back as an oppidan at Eton.) The college knew when it was, or thought it was, on to a good man, however: 'The great thing is that he really thinks for himself,' the headmaster noted at this time.

All the same, that perceived oddness and independent thinking, even then manifesting itself in an interest in socialism, in all probability combined to make him unpopular with the powerful Eton Collegers. He was 'quite a card' (we can only guess whether delicate euphemism lay behind those words), and basically 'too clever by half'. Thus when elections were held for membership of the exclusive Eton Society (familiarly known as 'Pop'), Burgess, who had expected to win easy entry into a position of privilege which would have allowed him his own fag, not to mention the right to wear gaudy waistcoats, was roundly defeated.

It was a shattering blow to his self-confidence, very possibly the single most wounding setback of his life.[31] Certainly he never forgot it. Or Eton. Even during the long years of his lonely exile in Moscow he continued to wear an Old Etonian bow-tie.

Psychology has taught us that such seemingly trivial slights can have dramatic, even catastrophic, consequences in later life. Along with his already apparent homosexuality, it seems to have hardened a streak of rebellion in Burgess: he was different; he wasn't good enough for them; *he'd show them!*

Viewed in this light, his behaviour when he went up to Cambridge – it was one of the dark ironies of fate which took him to Trinity and Blunt – makes a kind of sense. He made no particular secret of his homosexuality; indeed, he flaunted it. The bookshelves in his rooms in New Court contained 'an extraordinary array of explicit and extremely unpleasant pornographic literature', and he positively enjoyed the thrill of chasing any male undergraduate, no matter how demonstrably heterosexual, who took his fancy: '. . . we drank whisky together for a long time. At first [Burgess] made tentative amorous advances but quickly and cheerfully desisted when he discovered that I was as heterosexual as he was the opposite; he would have done the same to any young man, because sex to him was both a compulsion and a game which it was almost a duty to practise.'[32]

But at a deeper level even then there were essentially two Guy Burgesses. There was the good-looking, affable, extremely able Old Etonian – the soon-to-be Apostle, the man universally tipped for a history fellowship – who was a natural and active member of what

Andrew Boyle has called the 'vulgarly ostentatious' Pitt Club, and
who soon palled up with the young Victor Rothschild. But simultaneously, there was also the Burgess who was ploughing his way
through Lenin's *The State and Revolution* and other books with titles
such as *The XVIIIth Brumaire of Louis Bonaparte* and *Class Struggles in
France*; the Burgess who had joined the Anti-War Movement ('as
significant at Cambridge as the much-publicized "king-and-country"
debate at the Oxford Union');[33] and the Burgess who, in a most
un-Old Etonian manner, was collecting working-class friends.

Superficially, one could describe the most influential of these, an
ex-coal miner called Jim (or Jimmy) Lees, as a 'bit of rough'. But,
however convenient this might be – and there is no evidence that,
even at Cambridge, Burgess and Lees were ever more than friends –
the story is more complicated than that. 'Baldish and spectacled',
according to Tom Driberg, and a member of the Independent Labour
Party, Lees (who went on to become a lecturer at Nottingham University) was

> unlike anyone Guy had ever known before, [he] taught him a lot,
> and troubled his conscience. 'You', he would tell him, searingly,
> 'will get a First because your energies are not exhausted by life,
> because of the class-prejudices of the examiners, and because you
> got here easily and aren't frightened by it all. I don't have the
> brilliance of ignorance. I shall do ten times as much work as you
> – and get a good Second.'[34]

'He knew a great deal more than I did,' Burgess told Driberg (although
he omitted to mention that, far from getting the First which Lees had
predicted, he unexpectedly 'collapsed in tears during his finals' and,
equally unexpectedly, left Cambridge with only an *aegrotat* degree).
'He was interested in truth, I in brilliance. I made epigrams: he got
the right answers.'

Somehow Lees, with his first-hand stories of working-class pri-
vation, seems to have been able to prick Burgess's conscience. Month
by month under his tutelage, the one-time Pitt Club swell who in his
first year 'drank a bottle of Liebfraumilch '21 (at 3s.6d.!) every day at
luncheon' acquired a new seriousness. Politics became more than 'a
lark', even if his grass-roots left-wing activism today seems characteristically whimsical. He expended a great deal of energy in an (ultimately

successful) campaign to improve the working conditions of the hall waiters at Trinity. With other Cambridge students he turned out in support of the Jarrow Hunger Marchers in 1934, but walked with them only for the fifteen or so miles between Huntingdon and Cambridge; he caught a train to London in order to be present at their final rally in Hyde Park.

Two paths were converging, however. On one side there was the intellectual dialectic of Lees ('If you think like that, your place is in the Party . . .'), on the other the infinitely more seductive pleasures of the flesh which, like St Augustine, for the present he had no plans to forsake. Happily, they were to coincide one evening in the mid-1930s when Burgess first encountered Jack Hewit.

Seventeen years old at the time and the son of a Gateshead shipyard riveter, this 'half child and half warlock,/ with a truly feminine soul' (as W. H. Auden was later to describe him) then had a job in the chorus of a touring production of *No, No, Nanette*. That evening he was appearing at the south London Palace Theatre: 'Virtually the whole of the men's chorus was gay. Guy was waiting by the stage door for one of the boys. I saw him and asked my friend Douglas afterwards "Who was that, then?" and he said "A friend of mine who works in the BBC, and keep yer 'ands off it, dear." '[35]

But the attraction was reciprocal and that chance meeting meant as much to Burgess as it had to Hewit. Besides the luckless Douglas they had other friends in common and managed to keep in touch. Burgess finally seduced the young but not inexperienced Hewit in 1937 and, although there were to be many separations and infidelities on both sides – 'I think he invented promiscuity,' Hewit has recalled. 'He used to say, "Oh, anything from seventeen to seventy-five!" ' – the two were to remain notionally together until Burgess's abrupt flight to Russia in 1951.

Burgess and Hewit . . . The fastidious Blunt and his Aesthetic toy-boys . . . Driberg and his 'cottage' pick-ups . . . Auden and his late-night walks . . . the pattern is the same. It goes back to Maurice and Scudder; it goes back, indeed, a great deal farther than that. But there is an important difference. Essentially, Forster described how Maurice merely wanted experience of a 'bit of rough' – and we have already seen how that sort of *nostalgie de la boue* has always been central to the homosexual experience. Even today one has only to look at the models portrayed in gay magazines and the titles of gay telephone sex-lines to appreciate its continuing appeal. Photo-spreads of 'Bobby, 18, Farm-hand' or 'Christopher, 20, Construction Worker' and allegedly real-life confessional stories with titles like 'Builder Works His Erection', 'Fair-ground Lad Rides' and the blatant 'Rough and Ready' continue to pander to the fantasy.

In the 1930s, however, the emphasis was different. Threatened by the prospect of war in Spain and then on a wider European front (although not perhaps particularly worried by Patricia Parry's notion that they themselves might actually have to *fight* in it), Auden, Blunt, Burgess and the rest of their generation found themselves forced to confront a world suddenly bereft of the comfortable certainties to which they had been brought up. *Tempora mutantur, et nos mutamur in illis* – the times had changed, and they had no option but to change with them. 'Only connect', Forster had counselled. Now that was no longer enough.

Freshly down from Oxford or Cambridge – a fact which is often forgotten: in 1935, say, Burgess was just twenty-five, Auden, like Blunt, twenty-eight, and even Brian Howard only thirty – they were thrown on to their own devices. Some had starry Firsts, others (like Auden) heroic Thirds; more than one (Spender and Isherwood among them) no degrees at all. All were faced with the problem of establishing themselves both professionally and personally. ('Now it occurred to me that, at the age of twenty-nine, I might still become a poet and painter, as others had done.'[36]) Their left-wing beliefs would not allow anything which smacked of the exploitative, master-and-servant relationships which had characterized the previous generation. In their place, and particularly on a personal level, almost spontaneously there developed an *inclusiveness*, what Jack Hewit called a 'freemasonry', largely predicated on homosexuality. Outsiders all, they turned to one another for succour and support. Thus, at a New Year's Eve party in 1938 Auden could address Hewit in a specially composed piece of doggerel with the lines:

> If I could but penetrate time's vista
> And tell you your future, I would,

> But I only know you're my sister,
> I only know that you're good.[37]

Nine months later, infected by the prevailing mood of *Weltschmerz*, he was to elaborate on this theme and give it a wider public significance (and a resonance he was much later to repudiate) in his poem 'September 1, 1939':

> There is no such thing as the State
> And no one exists alone;
> Hunger allows no choice
> To the citizen or the police;
> We must love one another or die.[38]

Feeling somewhat excluded, both sexually and politically, Cyril Connolly dubbed this close-knit left-wing coterie 'the Homintern' after the then pan-European Communist International (the Comintern). Although friendly with most of its 'members' as individuals, he was temperamentally averse to the more lurid aspects of their lives, scandalous accounts of which were already beginning to circulate: 'the party didn't break up, in fact it got noisier, also more amorous, with male-female and also male-male and female-female couples quite openly embracing on cushions in corners'; 'there were two very tough working-class young men who had very obviously been picked up off the streets' . . .[39]

   In a strikingly effective simile, Hewit once described the Homintern as being 'like the five concentric circles in the Olympic emblem'. He went on: 'One person in one circle knew one in another and that's how people met. And people like me were passed around. I wasn't a trollop. Amoral perhaps, but not a trollop.'[40] This has the ring of truth, and Hewit's frankness suggests that, for all the obloquy which has been heaped on Burgess and, more latterly, Blunt, the Communist side of things was never really of any great importance. *Pace* Burgess and Blunt, no one ever really intended to bring about the 'radicalisation of the masses' for which the Communist International Congress had called as far back as 1928. Nor were they out to create a neo-Carpenterian Millthorpe, an introverted gay society, closed to all strangers. Rather, without ever consciously trying to, this rather heterogeneous group of Oxbridge *alumni*, their friends and, to be honest, more than a few of the 'very tough working-class young men' between them showed what could be achieved when homosexuality was regarded as nothing more – but nothing less – than a fact of life.

W. H. Auden again provides the most succinct statement of this. His New Year's Eve 1938 poem includes a stanza dedicated to Christopher Isherwood, with whom less than three weeks later he was to leave for the United States. It concludes:

> May your life in the States become better
> May you find lots of happiness there
> But my God if you ever turn heter
> I won't wish you a Happy New Year!

PART TWO

Ordinary People

6 ⌒

'I Had the Time of My Life'

FOR ANYONE BORN SINCE, say, the mid-fifties, pre-war London –
pre-war *Britain* indeed – is a fantasy land, two stages removed from
reality. Young Londoners now see only the accretions of the fifties
and sixties. They cannot remember the bomb-sites; still less can they
recall what once occupied them: the grand Odeon and Gaumont
cinemas; the terraces of back-to-back houses around the now vanished
docks; the decaying Pooterish semis; the grandly swaggering 'departmental stores' – Gamages, Arding and Hobbs, the *old* John Lewis's in
Oxford Street, Bon Marché in Brixton – with their uniformed door-
men and pinging mechanical or pneumatic cash-delivery systems; the
corner shops; the Lyons Corner Houses; the trams; the pubs which
were also 'commercial hotels' and, if they happened to be situated on
'arterial roads' like the A1, A4, A21 and A40 (the road to Oxford),
reckoned themselves 'road-houses'; the pubs in which social distinc-
tions still held sway:

> Those entering the Saloon Bar of 'The Midnight Bell' from the
> street came through a large door with a fancifully frosted glass pane,
> a handle like a dumb-bell, a brass inscription '*Saloon Bar and Lounge*',
> and a brass adjuration to Push. Anyone temperamentally so wilful,
> careless, or incredulous as to ignore this friendly admonition was
> instantly snubbed, for this door would only succumb to Pushing.
> Nevertheless hundreds of temperamental people nightly argued with
> this door and got the worst of it.
>
> Given proper treatment, however, it swung back in the most
> accomplished way, and announced you to the Saloon Bar with a
> welcoming creak. The Saloon Bar was narrow and about thirty feet

in length. On your right was the bar itself, in all its bottly glitter, and on your left was a row of tables set against a comfortable and continuous leather seat which went the whole length of the bar. At the far end the Saloon Bar opened out into the Saloon Lounge. This was a large, square room, filled with a dozen or so small, round, copper-covered tables. Around each table were three or four white wicker armchairs, and on each table there lay a large stone ash-tray supplied by a Whisky firm [. . .] This was no scene for the brawler, but rather for the principled and restrained drinker, with his wife. In here and in the Saloon Bar 'The Midnight Bell' did most of its business – the two other bars (the Public and the Private) being dreary, seatless, bareboarded structures wherein drunkenness was dispensed in coarser tumblers and at a cheaper rate to a mostly collarless and frankly downtrodden stratum of society. The Public Bar could nevertheless be glimpsed by a customer in the Saloon Bar . . .

This was the world – Patrick Hamilton's, J. B. Priestley's *News Chronicle*-reading, 'chessboard oil-cloth'-floored, 'gin-and-it'-drinking, Austin-, Morris- and Hillman-driving world – of London and Britain's other major cities in the immediate pre-war years. Class ruled; but, ensconced in one of the white wicker armchairs, or on the leather-covered banquettes in the sham-gentility of the Saloon Bar, the 'principled and restrained drinker' could still catch a glimpse of the 'collarless and frankly downtrodden' drinker in the Public. Tantalizing . . .

The journalist Michael Davidson was far from alone in making the most of it. He had first arrived in London in the mid-1920s; he was an old hand and knew the scene:

When I came to London I found a room at the top of Gower Street. It cost £1 a week, one-third of my income, but the house had one great advantage – the primary one sought, but so uneasily found, by every homosexual: it was what the Germans call *sturmfrei* – it was free of snoopers. It was the first abode of my *own* in the bottomless well of wickedness which I expected London to be [. . .] The high-flying 'spiritual' emotionalism of the [previous] year or two was replaced almost overnight by an insatiable hunger for downright carnal experience – a craving to *know* the physical secrets of as many boys as possible (this was the important delight, as it always had been: my own sensual enjoyment being of much smaller moment). In that decade after [the Great War] 'picking up' was easy: the Embankment and the furtive arches of Charing Cross were peopled with wanderers of every age, and under the colonnades of Covent Garden rows of homeless boys slept. In my restless search – the eternal search, I suppose, for Corvo's 'divine friend, much desired' – I even discovered a kind of hutment, put together with corrugated sheets in an alley by Savoy Hill, where boys sheltered at night; and sometimes I'd creep in there, to spend fevered, flea-bitten hours. Once, for the excitement, I paid a shilling for a bed in a common lodging-house across the river in the Borough.[2]

Picking up was easy in the 1920s, says Davidson. And, young as he was at the time, Jack Hewit remembers what could easily have been taken for a golden age as lasting well into the 1930s. Still a teenager (but for an accident of fate, the barely educated young Geordie might well have found himself living in Davidson's Savoy Hill 'hutment'), he soon became familiar with a network of relatively 'sturmfrei' cafés and bars in the West End of London. Most have long disappeared: there was Ward's Irish House in Piccadilly Circus, the Plough, the Swiss and the Fitzroy Tavern; the Cavour was in Leicester Square, the Standard Bar at the top of Coventry Street, only a few doors away from a particularly popular Lyons Corner House. 'Everybody in the gay set met up there on Sunday afternoons, queueing to get in,' Hewit recalls. 'The first floor was known as the Lily Pond. You went in, ordered your tea and toast, then table-hopped.'

Nor was there any lack of 'private' after-hours drinking clubs where half a crown would buy one annual – and not infrequently life – membership. Among many others there were the Sphinx, run by Muriel Belcher and Dolly Mayers, the Caravan, which provided drag entertainment both on and off the stage, the Festival and the Careless Stork,

. . . but the best was Le Boeuf sur le Toit; beautifully furnished, Leonard Blackett at the piano. Teddy Ashton owned it. He had an antiques shop underneath Jackson's, the grocers in Piccadilly. Dolly and Muriel opened another club together called the Music Box in Leicester Street which was a *howling* success during the war. Then after the war, Muriel opened the Colony and Dolly bought the Boeuf and changed its name to the Romilly Club which is where Guy [Burgess] fell down the stairs and had to go to hospital. Somebody pushed him, actually.[3]

Taken at face value, reminiscences such as these can easily give the impression that the Wilde trials and all the ensuing moral outrage of only thirty years previously had never occurred – that the living was easy. There is hard evidence, however, that it was not; facts and figures which prove that for the majority of homosexual men the golden age was yet to arrive and, for those living in provincial towns in particular, still a distant prospect. Chief amongst these are official records of the year-on-year percentage rise in the number of convictions for indictable sexual offences. These show that, in contrast with the period 1901–5 (when such figures were first recorded), homosexual offences had risen by 178 per cent in the years up to 1921, and by no less than 572 per cent at the outbreak of war in 1939. (By contrast, the increases for heterosexual offences over the same period were 155 per cent and 282 per cent respectively.)[4]

It is difficult to give any accurate interpretation of these statistics since specific details are no longer available. In all likelihood, however, the majority of the convictions recorded would have been for 'cottaging' or for cases of gross indecency brought after police raids on the type of clubs so enthusiastically frequented by Jack Hewit – and Quentin Crisp: 'The police thought of homosexuals as North American Indians thought of bison. They cast about for a way of exterminating them in herds [. . .] In a raid a hundred or more screaming, shrieking, fighting, kicking boys in feathered head-dresses and diamanté trains could be scooped, pushed or flung into vans by a relatively small squad of policemen.'[5]

Relatively unrevealing as they are, such statistics are as quoted above are not irrelevant to the present argument. Ironically, they confirm the more anecdotal evidence of the likes of Davidson and Hewit concerning the extent of homosexual activity. At the same time, they also suggest something of the determination with which society was still – according to Quentin Crisp again – 'stumbling about in search of a weapon with which to exterminate this monster [homosexuality] whose shape and size were not yet known or even guessed at'.[6]

In less inflammatory language we might say that 'concern' was being shown. Although the Love That Dare Not Speak Its Name itself might still have been tongue-tied except in the speak-easy atmosphere of its own clubs and bars, that name was more and more frequently on other tongues. Throughout the 1930s the *existence* – if not the tolerance – of homosexuality was increasingly acknowledged, at least among what we would now call the chattering classes. For 'free-thinkers', if not yet perhaps for 'opinion-formers', it had become a legitimate subject for discussion (and it is not too fanciful to suggest that its appearance on the agenda at this time began the process which would lead to an acceptance of the idea of its decriminalization thirty or more years later).

Inevitably perhaps, this new and increasingly informed curiosity is exemplified by the attitudes displayed by the surviving members of the Bloomsbury Group, most notably Virginia Woolf. Despite having come to maturity in the company of such notable homosexual men as Lytton Strachey, E. M. Forster and John Maynard Keynes in the early years of the century, and in an atmosphere where intellectual honesty was prized above everything else, only ten years previously, in 1925, she had talked of homosexuals in terms which must have seemed as caricatured in the mid-thirties as they do today:

> Have you any views on loving ones own sex? [she wrote in a letter to Jacques Raverat]. All the young men are so inclined, and I can't help finding it mildly foolish; though I have no particular reason. For one thing, all the young men tend to be pretty and ladylike, for some reason, at the moment. They paint and powder, which wasn't the style in our day at Cambridge [. . .] My cook said, 'Who was the lady in the drawing room? He has a voice like a girls, and a face like a persian cats, all white and serious, with large violet eyes and fluffy cheeks.' Well, you can't respect the amours of a creature like *that*.[7]

Within a very few years, however, Woolf's views more closely echoed what passed for 'enlightened opinion'. Among those for whom the phrase 'some of my best friends are queers' was becoming a badge of liberalism this had shifted significantly, and as early as 1930 homosexuality was being accorded a new seriousness. While there was still room for the publication that year of an alarmist book entitled

Degenerate Oxford?[8] (homosexuals, it averred, could be spotted by their
'gay suede shoes'), more considered attention was being paid to work
by more significant writers, and André Gide in particular. Something
of Parisian 'Bloomsberry' in his own right (and a long-standing friend
of Lytton Strachey), Gide had published *Corydon*, a neo-Socratic
defence of homosexuality in 1924, while his 1902 novel *L'Immoraliste*
first appeared in English translation in 1930.

It was at this time, too, that the publication and prosecution of Radclyffe-Hall's discreetly lesbian novel *The Well of Loneliness* was attracting
interest and controversy in equal measure – and nowhere more so than
around the dinner tables of Bloomsbury, as Woolf noted in her diary:

> Morgan [Forster] was here for the weekend; timid touchy, infinitely
> charming. One night we got drunk and talked of sodomy and
> sapphism, with emotion – so much so that next day he said he had
> been drunk. This was started by Radclyffe Hall and her meritorious
> dull book. They wrote articles [defending it] all day and got up
> petitions [. . .] Morgan said that Dr Head [Woolf's doctor] can
> convert the sodomites. 'Would you like to be converted?' Leonard
> [Woolf] asked. 'No', said Morgan, quite definitely.[9]

Frustratingly, neither here nor elsewhere in her diaries does Woolf give
specific details of exactly what late Bloomsbury thought of 'sodomy and
sapphism'. That she herself remained intrigued by the status of 'sods',
'queers' and 'Bugger Boys' (like many of her age and class, she routinely
and non-pejoratively employed such terms) is clear, however, from
the references to them which, as we shall see, occur in her diaries
from this time until shortly before her death in 1941. Thus, barely
more than five years after the *Well of Loneliness* trial – in which, despite
her reservations about the book, she had offered to appear as a defence
witness – we find the fifty-one-year-old novelist writing to her nephew
Quentin Bell in a reflective, almost Gidean mood. She was, she
implied, impatient with the conservatism, both literary and social, she
saw around her: 'How far can one say openly what is the relation of
a woman and a sod? In French, yes; but in Mr [John] Galsworthy's
English, no.'[10]

Inevitably, a younger generation of Woolf's 'Bugger Boys' had long shared this impatience. In comparison with 'abroad' and the forbidden fruit *everyone* knew to be available there, to them Britain still seemed cold, provincial and puritanical. For all the furtive pleasures which London offered, to their eyes somewhere like Germany was where the future lay. Alongside its Aryan culture of health, fitness and hiking, the post-war Weimar Republic had acquired a reputation for sexual tolerance, a reputation which continued even after Adolf Hitler came to power in 1933. Reports of the loucheness and 'divine decadence' of bars in Hamburg and Berlin were arriving almost daily. There were even rumours of a growing climate of homosexuality within elite corps of the German army. Certainly, Ernst Roehm, a close associate of Hitler and commander of the SA (*Sturmabteilung*), and many other officers in the so-called 'Brownshirts' were actively homosexual.

It all seemed too good to be true; and ultimately, of course, it was. Hitler had no time for homosexuality or any other manifestation of moral weakness. The Brownshirts were disbanded in 1934 and, on 15 November 1941, Heinrich Himmler decreed, in the name of the Führer, that any SS (*Schutzstaffel*) or police officer 'engaging in indecent behaviour with another man or allowing himself to be abused by him for indecent purposes will be condemned to death and executed'.[11] Outside the military, too, Hitler clamped down on homosexuals almost as ruthlessly as he did on gypsies and the Jews. In concentration camps they were identified by the pink triangle symbol which, a quarter of a century later, was adopted as an international symbol of gay pride. It has been estimated that some 60,000 were killed.

Had they only been able to read it, however, the likes of Christopher Isherwood and W. H. Auden, who had moved or (in Auden's case) seasonally migrated to Germany during the previous decade, would have been confirmed in the radicalism of their beliefs by an internal Hitler Youth report on a 'swing' festival which was held in Hamburg as late as February 1940:

The dance music was all English and American [. . .] The participants accompanied the dances and songs, without exception, by singing the English words. Indeed, throughout the evening they attempted only to speak English; at some tables even French.

The dancers were an appalling sight. None of the couples danced normally [. . .] they all 'jitterbugged' on the stage like wild creatures. Several boys could be observed dancing together, always with two cigarettes in the mouth, one in each corner.[12]

Isherwood was later to leave no one in any doubt about his motives for moving to Germany: in his third-person autobiography *Christopher and His Kind* he states explicitly that 'To Christopher, Berlin meant Boys'.[13] John Lehmann, too, was drawn there at this period and rapidly found himself 'in a daze, my head swimming with pretty boys' inviting smiles and inviting thighs'.[14] Even Stephen Spender took the plunge and began exploring the hitherto unimaginable sexual freedom available in Berlin and on Rügen Island.

But Spender's is a complex story – and brings us back to London. Aware of but temperamentally quite unsuited to the wholly un-English mores of the Kit Kat Club, he was never really a part of the promiscuous world of Auden and Isherwood. Rather, the Spender of this period (roughly from 1931 until his precipitate first marriage at the end of 1936) was in many respects the epitome of a new, post-Wildean and specifically English homosexuality.

He was tall, fresh-faced and articulate in a diffident kind of way. He seemed as at home, or equally ill-at-ease, in a Berlin *Lokal* as he was in any Bloomsbury drawing room – and inevitably, as an ambitious young writer, he soon came to know a good number of these. Lady Colefax and Lady Ottoline Morrell, as well as the indefatigable Virginia Woolf and the other society hostesses of the day, enthusiastically 'took him up'. For them, he represented a 'good catch', a decorative addition to the guest-lists of their weekly 'at homes' and a novel alternative to the likes of, say, Hugh Walpole or Beverley Nichols.

For Woolf, however, Spender was rather more than that. In her candid and occasionally caustic comments about him there is the suggestion that she found him not quite 'one of us'; but she was intrigued. Like another of her protégés, the preternaturally good-looking John Lehmann, he was a generation younger and fundamentally different in attitude to the likes of Forster and Strachey. He was a 'sod' unlike any she had previously encountered and, at least to begin with, she observed him with forensic detachment.

He was 'a rattle headed bolt eyed young man, raw bones, loose jointed', she noted. He thought himself the greatest poet of all time

('I daresay he is – it's not a subject that interests me enormously at the moment')[15] – but she and her husband Leonard still thought it worth inviting him to a succession of lunches and dinners, the better to get to know him. Informal by their standards – 'Don't change of course; I expect we shall be alone,' she was wont to write in her terse notes of invitation – these were nevertheless a terrifying ordeal for a stammering, blushing poet then still only in his mid-twenties – half the age of his host and hostess.

We should be grateful that they happened at all, however, since Woolf's recollections provide a unique outsider's eye view of the fast-evolving homosexual community. Here, for instance, she is writing the day after Spender had been to dinner one night in December 1933. It was no Berlin she was describing, but for the normally far-from-narrow-minded Woolfs it might just as well have been:

> I see being young as hellish. One wants to cut a figure. [Spender] is writing about Henry James and has tea alone with Ottoline and is married to a Sergeant in the Guards. They [the new generation of homosexual writers] have set up a new quarter in Maida Vale; I propose to call them the Lilies of the Valley. Theres William Plomer, with his policemen; then Stephen [Spender], then Auden and Joe Ackerly [sic] all lodged in Maida Vale, and wearing different coloured Lilies. Their great sorrow at the moment is Siegfried Sassoon's defection; he's gone and married a woman.[16]

Writing about the same period, Spender himself is characteristically more restrained – nowhere more so than in his 1951 autobiography *World Within World*, in which his relationship with that 'Sergeant in the Guards' is discreetly down-played. He wasn't, for a start, a sergeant, or even in the Guards; that seems to have been a flight of Woolf's imagination. Rather, the man Spender calls Jimmy Younger in *World Within World* (a pseudonym maintained by Isherwood in *Christopher and His Kind*) was no more than an ordinary ex-serviceman. Tony Hyndman had been born in a working-class district of Cardiff and seemingly received nothing more than an elementary school education. He was, in short, a pick-up, a bit of rough, the sort of man with whom an Oxford-educated would-be poet, already the supper-time pet of hostesses such as Virginia Woolf and Lady Ottoline Morrell, would ostensibly have had nothing in common.

But, as must have become clear by now, things were not as simple as that, for Spender or anyone else. Politics and the economic situation had changed the essential dynamic of the homosexual world as fundamentally as they had changed everything else. The old, almost seigneurial relationship between the Wildean buck and the cowed, compliant servant-boy was evolving into something more formal, more commercial but ironically rather less exploitative. As 'John', a Tynesider born in 1917, tries to explain, life for young men like him – and the slightly older Tony Hyndman – had become a business:

During the thirties the whole of the queer world was divided into castes, right. There were the boys on the game, there were the boys who weren't on the game but who were amenable (pick someone up, and go and have dinner with them, go to bed with them), and there were the 'kept' boys. And then, of course, there were the 'steamers' or punters themselves. That's the old-fashioned term for them. I first heard it when I was about thirteen and somebody said, 'Oh, he's a steamer, he'll give you half a crown, you see.' They tended to be older and better off and, of course, in high society.

You weren't just taken out because you were pretty; you were taken out because you were a pretty face in the first place, but you weren't taken out the second time because you were just a pretty face. What a lot of people do is, they find a boy they like and then they try to remodel him. Which is stupid.[17]

Spender seemingly met Tony while out 'cruising' in the West End of London. He was on the crest of a wave. He was a published poet, he had received an advance for his book on Henry James (published as *The Destructive Element* in 1935) and was generally enjoying life *in medias res*. 'I spend most of my evenings in the Amusement Park near Marble Arch or the Haymarket,' he told Isherwood at around this time, knowing that Isherwood would know what he meant. He went on:

London seems much improved. The other day a cissy friend of [his brother] Humphrey's got off a bus, and as he alighted the conductor smirked & said, 'What a short ride you've been,' so Eddy said, 'Never mind, I'll come a longer one next time.' Two days ago I went to Sadler's Wells with my sister. I did not know whether we were in the right tube for Angel [station], so I held out our tickets to the collector and said, 'Angel?' in a querying voice. 'I am,' he replied with an enticing smile.[18]

Something of a 'steamer'[19], then, Spender found the apparently good-looking, good-natured if rather argumentative Jimmy Younger/ Tony Hyndman rather more than a one-night stand: 'I did not want to live alone and I did not consider marrying. I was in the mood when people advertise for a companion in the newspapers. I used to enquire of my friends of their friends in case they knew anyone suitable. So when by chance I met a young man who was unemployed, called Jimmy Younger, I asked him to live in my flat and work for me.'[20]

There is something breathtakingly audacious even in this euphemistic account. However, 'John' 's memories suggest that the almost casual 'asked him to live in my flat' was merely *comme il faut* for someone of Spender's class and persuasion – and Virginia Woolf's ironic, possibly even sarcastic, description of Spender as 'married' to Tony only serves to emphasize the 'normality' of the situation. It was undoubtedly only one among many – there was 'Plomer, with his policemen', of course – and, as these things went, one of the more pedestrian. ('There were gay marriages going on, too. One would get into drag as a bride and somebody would marry them and [they would] have a party.'[21]) But the wealth of detail available – sanitized and selective though it undoubtedly is – makes the Spender–Tony relationship a useful archetype.

We have already seen that it was based on a chance encounter; Spender himself has admitted that asking Tony to 'work for me' made no economic sense at all. By his own account he was earning a bare £3 a week from hack journalism at this time. He was hardly in the Beverley Nichols league, and he had neither the means nor the need for a 'secretary', the grace-and-favour role which Tony was assigned. Nevertheless, although the periphrasis fooled no one, least of all Virginia Woolf, for some time the relationship seemed to work: 'We painted our Maida Vale flat, Jimmy cooked, I worked, we entertained and were entertained. Occasionally we quarrelled, largely because I was furious with him for having so little to do – then I repented because I realized that there really was very little he could do.' Soon,

however, the strains in this inter-class 'marriage' began to show.
Spender realized that 'the pressure was greater on him than on me.
For it was he who was living my life, not I his.'

So, hadn't it all been a big, liberal, left-wing mistake? 'I sometimes
asked myself whether I shouldn't be doing him more good by turning
him out, than by keeping him with me. In ordinary circumstances it
would certainly have been better to force him to stand on his own
feet. But the question was made rather theoretical by the fact that if
he had left me he would simply have been thrown amongst the millions
of the unemployed.'[22]

～

Spender and Tony stayed together – Spender adopting increasingly
desperate strategies to keep them so – for around three years. Their
emotional fandango, however, was symptomatic of the age. That we
know so much about it is also significant since it is from about this
period – the years leading up to the outbreak of war in 1939 – that
we can begin to turn to the written and oral records of other, more
ordinary, men who were there. Freed from the fear of prosecution by
the decriminalization of homosexuality in 1967, books were published
and already-old men faced microphones to leave us a vivid, first-hand
picture of the homosexual world as it existed in the late 1930s. The
following amalgam of their individual experiences tells a story which
is greater than the sum of its parts:

> As I wandered along Piccadilly or Shaftesbury Avenue, I passed
> young men standing at the street corners who said, 'Isn't it terrible
> tonight, dear? No men about. The Dilly's not what it used to be.'
> Though the Indian boy at school had once amazed us all with the
> information that in Birmingham there were male prostitutes, I had
> never believed that I would actually see one. Here they were for
> all the world to recognize – or almost all the world. A passer-by
> would have to be very innocent indeed not to catch the meaning
> of the mannequin walk and the stance in which the hip was only
> prevented from total dislocation by the hand placed upon it.[23]

> . . . we sat huddled together in a café called the Black Cat. (We
> were not putting up with any such nonsense as 'Au Chat Noir'
> which was written over the window.) This was in Old Compton

Street. It looked like a dozen other cafés in Soho. It had a horseshoe bar of occasionally scrubbed wood, black and white check linoleum on the floor and mirrors everywhere. The deafening glass boxes in which nowadays customers sit and eat with their ankles on view to the public had not then been built. In that happier time all was squalor and a silence spangled only with the swish of knives and the tinkle of glass as the windows of the Black Cat got pushed in.[24]

I used to belong to all the clubs, it was half a crown a year to be a member. They were mostly around Soho, there were a couple in Mayfair, but it was mostly around Soho – Dean Street, Romilly Street. Mostly only a room up a staircase. Usually run by a woman for homosexual customers. That's how one used to meet people. You had to show a card, and she got to know you eventually. You got a membership through another member or you were taken and made a member. The famous one, of course, was a club in Panton Street, and also the Music Box.[25]

Day after uneventful day, night after loveless night, we sat in this café buying each other cups of tea, combing each other's hair and trying on each other's lipsticks. We were waited on with indulgent contempt by an elderly gentleman, who later achieved a fame that we would have then thought quite beyond him, by being involved in a murder case. Had the denizens of the Black Cat known he was such a desperate character, they would doubtless have done much more to provoke him. As it was we only bored him by making, with ladylike sips, each cup of tea last as long as a four-course meal. From time to time he threw us out. When this happened we waltzed round the neighbouring streets in search of love or money or both.[26]

In the café there was a lot of stylized cattiness, but this was never unkindly meant. Nothing at all was meant by it. It was a formal game of innuendoes about other people being older than they said, about their teeth being false and their hair being a wig. Such conversation was thought to be smart and so very feminine.[27]

. . . one day I'd been stopped in the street by a good-looking man whom I didn't know, who said, 'What a lovely day.' And I agreed, it was a beautiful spring day. And he said, 'I like the look of you.'

'Mutual, I like the look of you, too.' He said, 'Would you like to come to my birthday party on Saturday,' and I hesitated, then said, 'Yes, I'd love to.' And went, and it proved to be – to my surprise, I must say – a party entirely of men in a private house. Roughly about fifteen men of all sorts, tall and short, and dark and fair, and some shy and some quite outgoing. And I realised this was what probably went on in small groups of people meeting ostensibly for birthday parties, very secret. It was all male.[28]

I used to give parties like mad. When we were living in rooms we used to have pay parties. Or people would bring cut sandwiches so thick nobody would eat them, and would bring a bottle. Have bottle parties. There was always a party somewhere.[29]

. . . Duncan plied me with more drink – it was a very strong cup with white wine and gin in it – and then, deciding that I was not likely to resist any more, whispered: 'I'm going to take you back to my studio now.' That night was the first happy sexual experience I had in my life. Duncan was a good, if rather lazy lover [. . .] While we looked into one another's eyes, smiling happily, as I lay on top of him after we had come, and he ruffled my hair, he said suddenly: 'You take me just as if I were a woman, you know.' I was startled, and in some curious way pleased. All I could find to say was: 'Let's do it again.' 'In the morning,' whispered Duncan, and gave me a long kiss. We woke up late. My eye opened on a large untidy studio with a north light in the roof which hadn't been cleaned for a long time, a large table covered with paints and brushes, a few books, a copy of the *New Statesman*, and a half empty bottle of wine.[30]

The clubs didn't close and the partying didn't obediently end when, on 3 September 1939, Neville Chamberlain, the Prime Minister, announced that 'this country is at war with Germany'. But nor did war come immediately on that bright Sunday morning. In fact, for month after month, very little *did* come. In London and other major cities there was a mandatory night-time blackout; but for most adult males, homosexual and heterosexual, the greatest imposition was already a fact of life. In April 1939 – in the post-Munich lull which nominally passed for peace – the government had introduced a limited form of conscription. Approved by Parliament and given royal assent the following month, the Military Training Act compelled all men aged twenty and twenty-one to undergo six months of basic square-bashing. Within thirty-six hours of Chamberlain's declaration of war, however, this had been superseded by the emergency National Service (Armed Forces) Act. Thenceforth – at least for what was even then becoming known as 'the duration' – *all* men aged between eighteen and forty-one, saving only those deemed exempt by a 1938 Schedule of Reserved Occupations, were made liable to conscription.

Soon, official envelopes were dropping through tens of thousands of letter boxes summoning men, regardless of their class or sexual orientation, to hastily opened recruitment offices.

> I went and volunteered [recalled 'Trevor'], and that's a funny little story, too. I went to this office and gave my name and address. And [the recruiting officer] said, 'Well, have you any particular preference for which service you want to go into?' And I said, 'Yes, I'd like to go into the Navy.' Because I'd heard things about the Navy! And he said, 'Have you any special reason?' And – I was joking – I said, very American, 'Sure, I think Navy blue and my blue eyes would look fine together.' He was furious. He said, 'Listen mister, there's a war on, no bloody nonsense.'[31]

Gay or straight, not every prospective conscript displayed such sang-froid when faced by the call-up board. A period of enforced military service threatened to destroy the whole tenor of their lives. Basic training was underscored by a sense of dull foreboding and undertaken with the numbed quietude which Stephen Spender found among the men who, like him, were directed to the Auxiliary Fire Service: 'They wore dungarees like rompers, were made to obey humiliating and often ridiculous orders given to them by officers whom they sometimes considered to be their inferiors, and were robbed of the little dignity which they had attained in civilian life.'[32] For gay men in particular the hugger-mugger that was service life, the rigours of basic training and even their appearance before a medical board posed particular problems. To have admitted their homosexuality then and there would have resulted in the threat of later prosecution, and very few found themselves turned down for active service purely because of their sexual proclivities. Only extreme cases like Quentin Crisp – who at the time of his medical examination had dyed crimson hair worn at 'hooligan length' – were granted a complete and immediate exemption:

> I was fully prepared to march at the head of my men, an occupation in which I had had considerable practice, but the authorities were not having any of that [. . .] 'You'll never be wanted,' [the doctor] said and thrust at me a smaller piece of paper. This described me as being incapable of being in grades A, B, etc. because I suffered from sexual perversion.[33]

The majority of homosexual men had no option but to make the best of things. 'Neil', untypically perhaps, determined to play the system at its own game and looked forward to service life with 'a sense of adventure':

> I knew I was one hundred per cent homosexual, and I knew that homosexuality was absolutely forbidden in the armed forces and that there were horrendous sanctions against it – but I fully intended to continue leading an active homosexual life. I realised it was going to be dangerous, but I went into it quite deliberately, with my eyes wide open.
>
> As part of my medical examination I was seen by a psychiatrist who asked me whether I was homosexual. So I just looked shocked and said, 'No!'[34]

'Neil' had a 'good war' and remained in the services after 1945. Others, too, found service life unexpectedly congenial, or at least not nearly as bad as they had imagined it would be. Spender found that life in his fire station billet 'brought out the warmth, good nature and humour of the men [. . .] character, which might have been unsympathetic in other circumstances, was made sociable by our tolerance of each other'.[35] Seconded to Intelligence, Beverley Nichols, too, found his days in uniform unexpectedly congenial. 'I had the time of my life,' he recalled.

～

Inspired by the qualified success of a similar campaign in the United States, in the mid-1990s British gay and lesbian pressure groups led by

Stonewall and Rank Outsiders intensified their long-running campaign to overturn a ban on lesbian and gay men serving in the British armed forces. While legal battles raged at the High Court in London and questions were repeatedly raised in Parliament, the issue briefly became the subject of national debate. Current affairs programmes on radio and television preferred to rehearse the contemporary civil liberties side of the argument, but a different, parallel case for the reversal of the ban emerged in the correspondence columns of broadsheet newspapers. Unexpectedly perhaps, letters from heterosexual ex-servicemen highlighted both the role which homosexual fighting men played in the services from the Second World War until the present day and – despite Ministry of Defence statistics purporting to show deep-seated resistance to their presence – the broad-minded toleration with which they were generally accepted:

> In 1943 I had a Divisional Officer, a captain of Marines, who was overtly gay. He was also a heavily decorated hero. He was the first of many gay servicemen and women I met during four years in the navy and later the R.A.F. I did not see or hear of any trouble [or] loss of discipline . . .

> Dear Sir,
> I served in the army as a band boy in the late Forties [rising] to Sergeant in 1959. During this period I was aware that I was serving with some homosexuals and can confirm that it was not a problem. A simple rule was observed by both heterosexuals and homosexuals – no sexual activity within the confines of the barracks or elsewhere on duty.[36]

Fascinatingly, impartial and unsolicited recollections such as these corroborate a tantalizingly small archive of first-hand reminiscences by the homosexual men who served in any of the three services during the Second World War. Fearful as many were that military life would be 'like school or even Oxford' all over again, the majority of those who have recalled the experience look back with a mixture of relief, nostalgia and affection. A sentence like 'I was six years and a hundred-and-twelve days in the army, and ravishing it was too!' echoes a commonly held feeling. Overall – although 'homophobia, jokes about nancy-boys and aggression were still part of the atmosphere' and 'you had to be so bloody careful!' – the memories of soldiers, sailors, airmen and prisoners of war evoke an atmosphere of what almost amounted to official and private forbearance. There is also more than a suggestion that in extenuating circumstances normal rules did not necessarily apply; that no one was going to blame even ostensibly heterosexual – and not infrequently married – men for finding what sexual relief they could in a stressful, all-male environment:

> When people are getting blown up all around you by a bomb or something or other you only care about the moment. You know, every man during the war thought every night could be his last, so of course he was determined to go out with a bang – and very often I was that bang.[37]

> 'Clara' [a transvestite internee] was quite liked and approved of. She used to go down to the mangrove swamp and was available for a quick blow-job if anybody was interested. The army often turned a blind eye to people's little eccentricities.[38]

> The attitude to homosexuality in the army was protective. They used to send me up like mad; but if any stranger did it he used to be kicked to death, you know? I was regarded as rather strange. I have never been particularly 'femme', but my turn of phrase and attitude was regarded as rather strange. I was a sort of Evelyn Home to the boys – you know, comfort for the troops![39]

> In the early years of my captivity [in Singapore] I'd been given a sarong. I was wearing this one day when I went out to the latrines, and on my way back I heard through the straw sides of our hut somebody saying they reckoned that [I] was a nancy-boy. Then immediately a butch Cockney boy said, Oh no he wasn't; he was terribly brave in action. This amused me – the idea that you couldn't be brave and gay.[40]

Permanent and semi-permanent sexual relationships inevitably developed, both between men in barracks at home and those on active service abroad. Many men recalling that 'it was very easy to pick up other servicemen' and that 'there used to be a lot [of sex] to be had' allude to relationships which were very much more meaningful than a desperate, anonymous 'bang' or a quick blow-job from 'Clara'.

Several, too, mention the etiquette which surrounded these, the discretion with which they were embarked upon and the series of ad hoc rules and conventions which governed their progress. 'David', for instance, attempts to draw a line between a fully sexual relationship and an intense but chaste 'comradeship' which flourished in the Guards:

Strange to say, although I did have sex relations with three separate guardsmen, the chap that I really liked – you could say loved in a way, because I had quite an emotional feeling [for him] – wouldn't have sex with me. He was a heterosexual type. He reciprocated on the level of comradeship. This is very important. Comradeship was permitted, and in the regiment there were pairs. I mean it was understood by everyone that so-and-so was the personal friend of so-and-so. Comradeship was allowed – on the understanding, of course, that there was no sexual relationship; no sex.

You could have sex with a fellow guardsman just like that, very easily, given the appropriate circumstances. You'd got to be alone in the guard room. You'd got to be gay yourself and the other chap'd got to be gay. Given that situation it happened just like that. These were not extensive or deep or even very close relationships, really. With one man, I think I had sex twice. On another occasion perhaps three times. In the third case there was something like a relationship. I mean we used to go out to the cinema together, so that there was a relationship apart from just sex.[41]

Inevitably, these relationships reflected the social dynamics of the wider society from which the armed forces were drawn. Rank broadly paralleled but never completely overrode class distinction. Thus 'Neil', soon commissioned in the RAF, 'made it a point of principle never, never, never to have sex with an N.C.O. or an Other Rank' and is quite candid in explaining why:

If I had sex with another officer, that was no big deal; but if I had sex with a sergeant or a corporal, he might feel that he would like to brag to his colleagues about it. And, although if [the authorities] were running an investigation, I could not be intimidated by rank, he would very likely be intimidated and make a confession. Thus, N.C.O.s and Other Ranks were highly dangerous as partners; more vulnerable and less reliable.[42]

Significantly, however, although he came from the same starting-point (and implicitly shared the same class values) as 'Neil', 'Cecil', a naval commander, found that the very constraints which rank imposed actually validated precisely the sort of modern, guilt-free relationship he seems to have despaired of finding in the civilian world:

> Up until [I joined the navy] I had thought that homosexuality, or the indulgence in homosexual sex, was something between you and – well, I hate to say so, but I suppose what I mean is – inferior people. Not necessarily socially inferior, because during the war I was having affairs with sergeants of the army or air mechanics from the navy, and there was no social implication there. So that experience was an extremely valuable one. It opened up to my eyes the idea that *there could be homosexual relationships with your equals* which could have, what seemed to me then, a really elevated nature.[43]

Back at home manners and morals were, if anything, in an even greater state of flux. In London, 'Neil' remembers, the streets and parks 'were humming with all kinds of sex, with *every* kind of sex'. 'This was the season of farewells to the young who were being prepared for their role in the armed might that was steadily being built up,' John Lehmann was later to write. 'An atmosphere of heightened emotion dominated; kisses were exchanged with those one would never in normal times have reached the point of kissing.'[44] And then there was – officially at least – the blackout: 'I wouldn't say there were blackouts, because you had blue lights everywhere and everybody carried a torch with a bit of tissue paper on it. I don't know how much went on in door-ways';[45] 'The blackout may have been a curse, but to people like us it was a boon. The 'trade' was there for the asking and I took full advantage of it.'[46]

Unexpectedly, the blackout was to do more for the homosexual men who, for one reason or another, found themselves in London or one of Britain's other major cities than any other event until the decriminalization of homosexuality more than twenty years later. Chaos reigned, as the historian Angus Calder has pointed out: '. . . to make one's way from back street or suburb to the city centre was a

LEFT Oscar Wilde and Lord Alfred Douglas, 1895 A studio portrait, taken shortly before Wilde appeared at the Old Bailey, which emphasizes both Wilde's commanding presence and the youthful beauty of 'Bosie'.

BELOW Oscar Wilde in his 'Aesthetic' lecturing costume, *c.* 1880. Long before his infatuation with Bosie brought his sexual predilections to public notice, Wilde had cultivated the public persona which later generations would recognize as camp.

Edward Carpenter, *c.* 1900. The beard and rough tweeds so characteristic of the earthy 'manlove' espoused by the sexual pioneer at his commune in Milthorpe survive in this studio photograph.

A. E. Housman, *c.* 1900. By contrast, the donnish Housman, yearning for a nostalgic Shropshire 'ladslove', maintains a more conservative appearance.

E. M. Forster, *c.* 1900. Caught in 'the Valley of the Shadow of Life', the novelist created Maurice Hall – 'handsome, healthy, bodily attractive, mentally torpid, not a bad business man' – as his own antithesis . . . and the 'ideal' homosexual.

'JAGGED WITH SOPHISTICATION'

Noel Coward's phrase aptly sums up the lifestyle of his friend Cecil Beaton in the inter-war years. The designer and photographer cut a dash wherever he went:

BELOW Cecil Beaton at Leicester Races, 1925, with Miss Peggy Broadbent and Miss Joyce Greig.

ABOVE Cecil Beaton *en fête* in the studio: a 1937 portrait by Gordon Anthony.

BELOW Cecil Beaton relaxing at home: *left to right* – Mr J. Lutro, Princess Paley, Lady Charles Cavendish, Mrs Harcourt Smith, Cecil Beaton.

HAPPY IN THE CLOSET

Like the majority of more ordinary homosexual men, many prominent individuals kept their sexual tastes very private.

Somerset Maugham, photographed (and heavily retouched) by Sasha, c. 1924.

Beverley Nichols, tight-lipped in 1930.

KEEPING THINGS UNDER HIS HAT

Lord Berners, writer, composer, socialite.

RIGHT Cutting a Hitchcockian dash.

BELOW Playing the country squire on the lawns of Faringdon with (*left*) Gertrude Stein.

'O YOUNG MEN,
O YOUNG COMRADES'

A new generation of post-Wildean
gay men came on the scene in the
early 1930s.

John Lehmann,
popular for his
'mesmeric' good
looks, popularizer
of guardsmen.

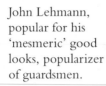

Christopher Isherwood (*left*) and W. H. Auden, in London in 1938 – well after each had
discovered that 'Berlin meant boys'.

Angus Wilson, 1952
As discreet in life as he was
in his novels and short stories,
in the 'police state'
of the 1950s Wilson was
not alone in keeping an eye
on what was happening
behind his back.

Tom Driberg, 1971
The elder statesman of the Labour Party
was not quite the patrician figure he wanted
to appear.

Sir John Wolfenden
The unlikely patron saint of gay
liberation was Vice-Chancellor of
Reading University when he
was appointed the chairman of
a government committee on
sexual offences.

A BIT OF ROUGH

A homosexual *nostalgie de la boue*, first discovered by the public in the late nineteenth century, re-emerged in the 1960s.

Joe Orton, 'the Oscar Wilde of Welfare State gentility', brought 'the language of the tribe' to the West End stage before he was battered to death by his lover Kenneth Halliwell in 1967.

Ronnie Kray (right, with twin brother Reggie), 1966. The East End gang-leaders quickly caught the lizard eyes of Tom Driberg and the Conservative MP Bob Boothby.

CARRYING ON

The decriminalization of most homosexual acts in 1967 freed gay men to be themselves. But . . .

Kenneth Williams, as one half of radio's 'Julian and Sandy' and, later, a television personality, embodied ideas first made acceptable fifty years earlier.

Ian McKellan in 1979 – years before coming out and receiving a knighthood – displays the defiance of the gay man of an earlier era (see picture of Beaton at the races in 1925).

prospect fraught with depression and even danger. In September 1939 the total [number] of people killed in road accidents increased by nearly one hundred per cent. This excludes others who walked into canals, fell down steps, plunged through glass roofs and toppled from railway platforms.'[47] Once again a *carpe diem* attitude resurfaced. No one knew what might happen that night, that week, that month – and with some reason ('Careless talk costs lives!'). No figures were released at the time; but it is now possible to say that, between the outbreak of war in September 1939 and the end of 1942, more civilians on the Home Front were killed as a result of enemy action than servicemen on active service overseas. The Blitz alone caused some 44,000 fatalities in London and ports and cities such as Hull, Coventry and Portsmouth, among them 818 officers of the London Fire Service.

Chaos reigned, anything went – and men like John Lehmann and Quentin Crisp were having the time of their lives. The Yanks (and the Canadians) were coming and in the perilous darkness the phrase 'Over here' took on wholly new connotations:

> For most of 1940 London by night was like one of those dimly-lit parties that their hosts hope are slightly wicked. In a cosy gloom young men and women strolled arm in arm along Piccadilly murmuring, 'It's not as bad tonight as last night, is it?' Policemen allowed themselves a certain skittishness. 'Don't care, huh?' they cried as I passed them sheltering in doorways. Taxi-drivers unbent so far as to take one part of the way home free of charge. As soon as the bombs started to fall, the city because like a paved double bed. Voices whispered suggestively to you as you walked along; hands reached out if you stood still and in dimly lit trains people carried on as they had once behaved only in taxis [. . .]
>
> Once, when I emerged from Leicester Square Underground station, the outline of the buildings on the opposite side of the road looked so unfamiliar that I thought I must have taken the wrong exit. When I asked an invisible passer-by where I was, he kissed me on the lips, told me I was in Newport Street and walked on.[48]

And then, of course, there were the much-fabled guardsmen, 'so renowned', as John Lehmann puts it, 'for their deeds of valour and also for their uninhibited, if venal, attention to the needs of older and perhaps lonely inverts in London and other cities where they happen to be stationed'. Lehmann (born in 1907) evidently viewed himself as one such, and had a wealth of experience to pass on where guardsmen were concerned. Initially, he believed, they were best approached in pubs:

> One would gradually edge one's way, in as unremarkable a manner as possible, towards a likely lad one had spotted somewhere round the bar, and with whom one had perhaps exchanged a quick glance. One would stand beside him for a few moments, testing as it were with one's antennae whether he was waiting for one to make a move. This would be followed by a casual remark about the weather, or some sporting event of the day. If the response appeared friendly, one went on to offer him a drink. 'Don't mind if I do, mild and bitter, please.' Thus launched, the relationship developed with desultory conversation (it must be remembered that English-men never mind silences), gradually moving closer to the young man's own life, his regimental duties, and so on. It might become animated, he might show an eager wish to unburden himself, and one might drop a few hints oneself about where one lived, and one's bachelor state; but nothing like an out-and-out proposal. More drinks followed; the situation, if all was going well, relaxed. Then, as closing time approached – one never departed too early – the crucial suggestion was made: 'Why not come and have another drink with me at home?' 'Thanks very much.' 'My car is just round the corner.' And out one went . . .[49]

If all this today sounds trite and hackneyed, it certainly seems to have worked for Lehmann himself. There is no reason to doubt the claim he makes in his autobiographical novel *In the Purely Pagan Sense* that he (or his alter ego, the book's Jack Marlowe) enjoyed a brief relation-ship with 'Jim Walker, of the 3rd Battalion, Grenadier Guards' and later

> took up with a young trumpeter from the Household Cavalry. About Jim's height he was slimmer, with long and well-shaped thighs, and a body as smooth but not so hard as Jim's. His name was Fred. I knew I was only one of his many clients, but he had a captivating abandon which appealed very strongly to me, and he made me feel that in his eyes no one else mattered as long as he

was with me. After dinner, we would put on a gramophone record, *Tiger Rag* or *There's a Small Hotel* perhaps, and slip into bed. He never said 'Ouch!' or appeared anything but satisfied when I pushed my cock into him; and yet I am certain he was not queer, or rather would not turn out to be queer when he grew older.[50]

We should be careful, however, about taking too literally Lehmann's suggestion that virtually every guardsman, regardless of his own sexuality, was as easily picked up and as meekly – and busily – compliant as Fred. Certainly 'David', the one-time guardsman we have previously encountered, did not think so: 'I think the reputation for male prostitution in the Guards has been blown up and exaggerated a bit. I mean, it just wasn't true that all guardsmen were male prostitutes [. . .] Some were, but I would say perhaps the sort of percentage that you would find in civilian society anyway.'[51]

With or without the active participation of each and every guardsman, lubriciousness added unfamiliar thrills and undreamed-of opportunities to life on the Home Front. 'Oh, what went on was no one's business!' recalled 'David', who might reasonably have been expected to have seen and done everything during a pre-war career in the theatre. Anything went; Lehmann's small hotel had never had it so good. Even in the wider, heterosexual world there had been a surge in the number of weddings celebrated in the months after the declaration of war; now to the strains of the 1939 hit 'Hands, Knees and Boomps-a-Daisy' and Cole Porter's 'Let's Do It (Let's Fall in Love)' the whole pace had quickened. Numerous tales of British girls 'getting involved with' American GIs and even 'getting into trouble' for the sake of a pair of nylons, a bar of chocolate or a packet of chewing-gum date from this period.

Sex was in the air, and as he was moved from one posting to another in different parts of Britain 'Roy' could hardly catch his breath:

I got on very well in the army; I loved it, you know. Went to Edinburgh – the place was a riot, a riot!

And even London. I was on leave. I was passing through London. Bloody bombs falling all over the place, and there was a Canadian, a little Canadian, and he said, 'Where do I go?' And I took him to the Salvation Army and they shut the door in his face because he was drunk. I said, 'What do you mean, the bombs are falling, the shells, the shrapnel!' 'Can't help it.' So, I had a booking for the Union Jack Club across the road in Waterloo, and took him across there. I said, 'You follow me.' So he slept with me that night. He was willing; he was TBH. I knew a lot of married men; I used to have married men.

Yes, Edinburgh was a tremendous city. It was so full of sailors and quite easy; quite, quite easy. The place was as if the world had gone mad because it was so easy.[52]

And then peace broke out . . .

7 ~

'The Horrors of Peace Were Many'

QUENTIN CRISP CHOSE his words carefully and knew exactly what he meant when, in a portentous, single-sentence paragraph, he wrote: 'Peace broke out.'

VE Day, proclaimed by Prime Minister Winston Churchill on 8 May 1945, had been marked by a spontaneous outburst of national rejoicing. Members of Parliament held a special Thanksgiving Service. 'We must have looked like a picture by Giovanni Bellini as we filed, 500 strong, into St Margaret's [the parliamentary church in Westminster],' the Conservative MP Henry 'Chips' Channon wrote, setting a grandly jubilant note. In towns and villages across the country, too, church bells rang, Union flags were waved, bunting fluttered and, in the burnt and gutted East End, street parties feasted on whatever rationed food they could get their hands on.

And then, as night fell, all the lights came on. 'The curtains were left undrawn because a community spirit is abroad and everyone wants to share in everyone else's rejoicings,' George Beardmore recorded in his diary.[1] 'All the searchlights shone in the sky, the office girls and [Mr] Gates went up to Town to join the vast crowds in front of Buckingham Palace.' Churchill stood alongside the King and Queen on the balcony there, cheered by tens of thousands of people who thronged the Mall – among them, anonymously, the young Princesses Elizabeth and Margaret Rose. 'There were Americans and young ATS girls making whoopee,' Naomi Mitchison noted, adding: 'I have seldom seen so many ATS so much drunk on so little!'[2]

It was a genuinely joyous occasion, with the whole nation giddily poised between wartime necessity and a bright new future. In the *Observer* the following Sunday advertisements for a pamphlet entitled

'Golden Rules for Patching' (by Mrs Sew-and-Sew) and the Ministry of Fuel and Power's bulletin 'Practical Ideas for Better Steam Usage' jostled with upbeat prognostications of a coming consumerist peace. Forty London theatres were advertising shows (everything from Ivor Novello in *Perchance to Dream* at the Hippodrome to *The Duchess of Malfi* at the Haymarket). Pringle were advertising clothes; Clarks were offering a new range of shoes, and Telephone Rentals Ltd a service which would let 'key men contact each other on the instant'.[3]

Only Quentin Crisp, it seemed, was truly aware of what the coming of peace really meant. 'The American soldiers were still with us then, which made London very beautiful and exciting,' he admitted, remembering VE Day. But all in all that was small consolation. To him, the celebrations that evening marked the end of an era, a staging-post in his life and, indirectly, in that of every other homosexual man. In *The Naked Civil Servant* he noted: 'The lights were all on for the first time in four years which was rather a shame since I preferred it when the lights were off. I actually found the war very exciting with the sky pink with doom, the docks burning and the streets rattling with anti-aircraft fire. Suddenly all that came to an end and we went back to being our dreary selves.'[4] Nearly twenty years later, in 1995, the private catastrophe that was VE night was still haunting him:

On that terrible evening, as I was weaving my way through the West End with a prolonged 'grand chain' movement as though I were doing the lancers with the whole world, my name was called. I heard it above the shouting, laughing, singing that went on all night. Turning, I saw in a doorway the man who had put up with my airs and graces all those long horrible months in Baron's Court when I had first come to London fourteen years earlier.

I paused questioningly in front of him. He said, 'You look terrible.' The horrors of peace were many.[5]

It was not as if he had enjoyed a particularly 'good war'. The black-out gave some protection, the sheer availability of servicemen offered extra opportunities, but not even Crisp could be wholly above the law:

Outside the Hippodrome Theatre I met by chance a certain part-time hooligan called Mr Palmer. I slapped onto his plate his ration of eternal wisdom for the day and turned into Coventry Street. Almost immediately I was stopped by the same two men [plain-clothed policemen who had earlier interviewed him in the street]. 'Just a minute, you,' they said. 'We are taking you in for soliciting.'[6]

Crisp was arrested, taken to Savile Row police station, charged, and bailed to appear the next day in a police court. He had been in such places before: 'When I knew the Irish and Scottish boys, I was often in the police courts to act as chorus to them or their friends and to cry "Woe unto Ilium" if an unfair verdict was given.' Now, however, he found himself in the dock – but, happily for him, it was a hopeless, vainglorious case which the police had brought:

Various kind people gave evidence as to the irreproachability of my character and, to my relief, Mr Palmer went into the witness box to declare that he had spoken to me the previous afternoon because he knew me [. . .] Everyone who spoke on my behalf was asked by the magistrate's clerk if he knew that I was homosexual and replied that he did. This question was in each case followed immediately by the words, uttered in a voice hoarse with incredulity, 'And yet you describe him as respectable?' All said, 'Yes'.

When the magistrate tired of this recital of my praises he said that the evidence against me was insufficient to convict me. I was dismissed.[7]

Convictions for soliciting and other, more serious offences including the inevitable 'gross indecency' had continued throughout the war; indeed, aided by the special circumstances of the blackout, they actually increased. The war years saw the beginning of a dramatic, almost exponential, year-on-year increase in the number of reported indictable homosexual offences which was to peak in 1963 (see graph) at a level twenty-four times higher than it had been in the early years of the century. But, in a curious sense, as long as hostilities continued it was as if they did not matter or were no more than a distraction, a tiresome irrelevance to the business of the moment.

Rates of change in the increase in indictable offences 1900–1963
[Average 1900–1905 = 100]

	1921	1938	1948	1961	1963
Homosexual offences	178	572	1405	2513	2437
Heterosexual offences	155	282	588	1218	1248
Indictable crimes (males aged 15–19)	115	130	135	131	130

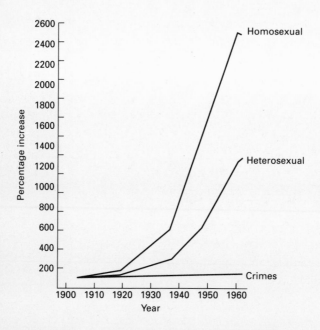

From: A. H. Halsey (ed.), *Trends in British Society Since 1900*, Macmillan, 1972, p. 533.

With the coming of peace, however, as Quentin Crisp suggests, everything changed – or seemed to change. Among homosexual men there was a palpable sense of vulnerability: now that the lights had come on again, they felt exposed.

In the straitened, utilitarian peace, they were. In the popular demonology of the day they were hardly differentiated from the spivs who, with their silk shirts, flashy ties and sharp five-guinea suits, epitomized the 'selfishness' which was hobbling the establishment of a genuine welfare state – the spivs who, as David Hughes was to point out, were themselves 'almost feminine' and full of 'pansy braggadocio'.[8] They were aberrants, and – such was the mood of the times – a 'social problem'. Even such a deeply unsympathetic figure as the Bishop of Southwark could tell the House of Lords in 1954 that 'Behind an immense number of these cases of homosexuality there still lie unsatisfactory or broken homes.'

There were differences, however. While the nation could take the spiv (or at least the variety performer Arthur English, who billed himself as 'The Prince of the Wide Boys') to its heart, the homosexual did not fare so well. The liberal aspirations of the authors of the 1948 Criminal Justice Bill, which proposed an end to flogging and hard labour and a massive expansion of the probation service, were not shared by the country at large. More normal was an impatience with 'enlightened' ideas and a rejection of the very notion of a 'cushy' welfare state culture which could even countenance 'excusing' homosexuality. A few years later, in 1961, this was to be well caught in the ground-breaking film *Victim*. Although primarily concerned with a well-connected barrister (Dirk Bogarde) and his attempt to expose a blackmail ring, its script (by Janet Green and John McCormick) also offered an almost-too-schematic insight into the 'lower orders' ' attitude to 'the problem':

– I don't know how you can stand them.
– Who?
– Eddie and Phip and the rest of them. All the same, the whole bloomin' lot.
– I thought they amused you.
– They're good for a laugh, all right. Very witty at times. Generous too. But I hate their bloody guts!
– Hey!
– Don't look at me like that.
– They're just not quite normal, dear. What's that matter to you? If they had gammy legs or something, you'd be sorry for them.
– Sorry for them? Not me. It's always excuses. Every newspaper you pick up, it's excuses – environment; too much love as kids; too little love as kids; they can't help it; it's part of nature. Well, to my mind it's a weak, rotten part of nature, and if they ever make it legal they may as well license every other perversion.

Nor were such attitudes wholly confined to the likes of the barman and the 'model' featured in the film. 'A tolerance which is prepared to take no notice of that which is essentially evil and wicked is not at all the sort of tolerance we want,' Earl Jowitt had fulminated in the House of Lords in 1954.[9] His insight into the origins of that evil and wickedness notwithstanding, the Bishop of Southwark could only agree. The whole subject of homosexuality was 'intensely repugnant', he told their lordships. Whatever brought it about, it raised 'intense moral indignation in many minds, and perhaps some kind of primitive radical horror. Society – our society, at any rate – reacts very violently against it, because it feels that such practices are injecting poison into the bloodstream.'[10]

Further echoes of this mood were not hard to find. Rabidly homophobic books were being published, as often as not with their true intent masked by pseudo-scholarship. *Society and the Homosexual* (1952) and *Homosexuality* (1955) were followed by *They Stand Apart: A Critical Survey of Homosexuality* (1955), which was 'critical' in every sense, talking of 'potential evil', 'corroding practices' and the homosexual's 'filthy errand'. More recently, Sir Dirk Bogarde has recalled that the lawyer responsible for clearing the script of *Victim*, 'said he saw nothing libellous in it at all, but he wished he hadn't read it and he was now going to wash out his mouth and wash his hands'.[11]

Demoralized by an explosion in the overall crime rate – 266,265 indictable offences had been committed in 1937; in 1948 there were 522,684 – police forces in every part of the country took the lead in this flight from liberalism and adopted a more than usually rebarbative approach. At the height of the Cold War homosexuals on the streets of London came to fear a tap on the shoulder from 'Mavis *Polizei*'[12] every bit as much as their counterparts in Berlin had done a decade earlier:

Bernard was startled [. . .] by a firmly enunciating, slightly Cockney voice, 'Excuse me, I'm a police officer. We're charging this young man with importuning. I have had occasion to notice that he approached you a few minutes ago. I should be glad to know if you wish to offer further evidence against him.' Bernard's eyes were riveted upon the face of the young man with the long dark hair. His underlip was trembling, his eyes – over-large with terror – were on the point of tears.[13]

For the majority of men, this was a fear more real and more visceral than that of the blackmailer. 'The police *were* after me,' the poet James Kirkup was convinced. 'I felt guilty because I was "queer" and therefore a criminal,' the novelist Paul Bailey remembered. 'It was a very unpleasant time to live in,' the writer Colin Spencer has recalled:

> I can remember people sending me letters which had little bits of sticky paper on the back to show if they had been opened or not [. . .] They were terrified of the knock on the door in the early morning or late at night; the idea that the bed sheets might be inspected for semen stains – which was something that actually happened! There was suddenly a police state in England in the Fifties.[14]

Police spies were everywhere, or so it was believed; walls had ears (sometimes quite literally so – the first authorized use of telephone tapping in Scotland had been to acquire evidence of a suspect's homosexuality). Wherever he went, the 'queer' had perpetually to be on his guard:

> . . . one of the most frightening episodes, in retrospect, started in the charmless toilet standing at the top of the main street in Chippenham. Here I picked up an elderly, rubicund gent, and as we stood there weighing each other up and keeping a sharp ear open for a policeman's ominous tread, we exchanged the usual pleasantries: 'Do you come here often?' 'Got anywhere to go?' 'Is this the only cottage in town?' 'Do you do Greek?' ('Ancient or Modern?' was my reply to this never very hopeful query as to whether I accepted anal intercourse – a regretful negative was my answer.) 'Got the time on you?' 'Got a light?' 'What about a bit of French?', etc. etc. These very predictable conversations were of the utmost boredom, like those I usually had years later with the Japanese, though in very different circumstances.
>
> It transpired that my gent had to catch a bus to Bath, the one that passes through Corsham, so we got the same bus and went upstairs, where there were many empty seats, and indulged in mutual masturbation all the way to my stop. I had an orgasm round about Pickwick, and it was only then that I noticed our local plain-clothes officer was sitting on the opposite side of the bus, a few seats in

front of us. We had covered ourselves carefully with coats when the conductor came upstairs to take our fares, and tried to cover our passion with stony faces and nonchalant cigarettes.[15]

———

It was a time of bluff and counter-bluff, of spies, duplicity and Reds under the bed. It was the time of missing diplomats, McCarthyism, *The Third Man* (Graham Greene/Carol Reed, 1949), squalid bedsits and fly-blown terraces in the early fiction of Muriel Spark and Angus Wilson and the *angst*-filled existentialism of Martin Heidegger and Jean-Paul Sartre (the latter's *Roads to Freedom* trilogy had first appeared in an English Penguin edition in 1947). Inevitably, and in common with many other homosexual men of the period, Peter Wildeblood too felt he had no choice but to dissemble: 'It was necessary for me to watch every word I spoke, and every gesture that I made, in case I gave myself away. When jokes were made about "queers" I had to laugh with the rest, and when the talk was about women I had to invent conquests of my own. I hated myself at such moments, but there seemed nothing else that I could do.'[16]

It was a grubby game, and fittingly one played with a wholly contemporary mixture of seriousness and innocence. For if 'queers' were terrified of discovery, it is not at all clear whether, other than the police and the practised blackmailers of the prominent, their putative discoverers would even have recognized them. (Paul Bailey recalls a book published at the time which revealed that male homosexuals always urinated on to the side of the toilet bowl, never directly into the water – a somewhat recherché tip.) In an age which had yet to absorb the camp archetypes provided on television by Larry Grayson and *Are You Being Served?*'s Mr Humphries (or even to confront Julian and his friend Sandy on radio's *Round the Horne*), for the most part homosexuals – *real* homosexuals – went almost unnoticed. 'Outwardly respectable,' wrote Peter Wildeblood, 'discreetly dressed, careful in their behaviour [they were] the last people ever to be suspected by that legendary character, the man-in-the-street.'[17] 'Richard', who was a teacher at the time, looks back laconically at this world of ingenuous atavism and tells a story of prep school life which would make tabloid headlines were it to happen today:

I was into 'chickens' [under-age boys] in those days. I got a charge out of teaching; I taught best when there was someone in the class whom I fancied a bit.

There was one school I was at, a progressive school, vegetarian in fact, and run along the lines of A. S. Neill, where there was a lad I was attracted to; basically straight, but a very sexual young man. I got him to help me around the school, and on one school camp – at the headmaster's suggestion! – he shared my tent for a fortnight without anyone thinking anything of it. That's how naive people were in those days![18]

In the purlieus of society – or, more typically perhaps, in the crush bars of West End theatres – there was a 'gay scene' (and one which, if only in the pages of Angus Wilson, even then knew itself as such[19]). But it was precious and intensely introspective:

'Terence', he said, 'is battling at the bar. It suits him to the ground. Pure Barkers' sales. Bless his little Kensington heart. Bernard, my dear, you look tired.' And as Bernard was about to speak, 'Oh I know, bitching me! Tired equals old. You must make him rest, dear,' he said to Eric; 'you know, feet up and forty winks. Not that I should think you'd be much good at making people rest', he stared Eric up and down; 'you look a proper little fidget to me.'

Eric, despite all he had heard from Bernard, was obviously being lulled into cosiness by Sherman's conventionally malicious chatter. Bernard awaited uneasily the three or four brutal thrusts with which Sherman usually followed such a softening-up process when he was 'among friends'.[20]

Understandably, it was rare for any man who was fortunate enough to be among such 'friends' voluntarily to break cover, although it sometimes happened – in their very different ways Guy Burgess and Quentin Crisp both escaped the normal consequences of displaying flamboyant behaviour precisely *because* of the way they flaunted their differentness. In a very few cases there were also otherwise ordinary men who, for one reason or another, felt it imperative to 'come out' (although that is a term they would not have understood). He did not give names or dates, but in 1955 Peter Wildeblood recalled 'a surgeon, respected and discreet, who threw away his good name in order to remain, night and day, at the bedside of his friend who was dying in hospital'.[21]

Caught in the midst of this world of secrecy, guilt and suspicion were many young but fundamentally homosexual men who had grown up during the war years. Theirs was a peculiar and unique predicament. Literature and the media were unable (or at least unwilling) to provide them with positive role models, as Kenneth Williams was to remark:

The author may have his homosexual commit suicide (or cause himself to be killed) because –

a he wishes to show that the man decides that his position as abnormal is incompatible with his position in society, and therefore takes his own life;

b he wishes to show that the frustration involved with abnormality is so great that the human spirit cannot bear the strain, & so kills himself;

c he wishes to show that the homosexual believes his desire to be wicked, and decides to kill his own wicked self;

d he wishes to show that the homosexual, believing his desires would horrify those he loves, sacrifices himself in order to spare their feelings.[22]

Equally important, their elders, understandably preoccupied with their own survival, were disinclined to discharge their once-traditional, Ned Lathom function as 'patrons' or 'uncles'. Matters had simply been taken out of their hands: 'It's absolutely beastly, I know, but there's nothing one can do,' an old queen was to lament in Angus Wilson's novel *Hemlock and After* (1952). 'It's so frightening, frightening for oneself, I mean.'[23]

In retrospect all this was to have important consequences, for it was to be this immediate post-war generation with its vivid and unparalleled memories of fear and loneliness which was to be the primary catalyst of the legal and social upheavals which would immeasurably better the lot of the homosexual in succeeding decades. At the time, however, these men were forced to cope as best they could: 'The people everyone assumed to be gay were not my type. They were too camp, too effeminate; they just weren't the kind of people I was attracted to. I rather wanted to get to know them, though simply because *I wanted to meet some gay people*.'[24]

It was men such as this who would later describe how they had had to look up works like 'homosexual' and 'perversion' in dictionaries and encyclopaedias to reassure themselves that they were not unique. 'Nicholas', born in 1934 and educated at a single-sex boarding school, certainly preserved an almost unbelievable innocence and naivety:

There were one or two boys [at school] I felt sexually attracted to. One of them, a really nice-looking boy, was actually pursuing me, but I didn't recognize sexual invitations for what they were in those days. He used to say extremely come-hither-ish things such as 'What wonderful legs you've got.' But it never crossed my mind that he was attracted to me! This went on until I went up to Cambridge in 1953. There I met an incredibly attractive boy, who was blond and butch and masculine and sporty – all those things which I am attracted to – and he made advances to me; but I didn't recognize *them* for what they were. He said, for instance, 'Why don't you come out and sunbathe with me? I love sunbathing in the nude.' Then he asked me to stay with him at his home over the holidays – 'I've only got a single bed, but . . .' – and *still* I didn't think to myself, 'He's trying to proposition me.' It just never occurred to me!²⁵

There was as yet no homosexual community, no meeting-place, no common ground. 'Nicholas' remained an outsider – not necessarily shut out, just wholly ignorant of the existence of the door. Nor was he by any means unique. Even the young Joe Orton (who had grown up in the working-class suburbs of Leicester) was seemingly something of an innocent abroad during his first few weeks as a drama student in London. This at any rate is the impression given by a gnomic diary he began at the time:

15 *May 1951*: Started at R.A.D.A. O bliss! [. . .]
18 *May*: Digs in Gower Street. Such fun.
19 *May*: Oh the larks.

MEMO
Someone in the other class keeps looking at me.

20 *May*: Did nothing.

21 May: Mr Constable's special movement [class]. Was eyed. [. . .]
25 May: Met Ken and John at Charing Cross Road.

MEMO
I don't quite understand Ken. [. . .]

1 June: Met Ken and John again. This time with Rex Butler.
2 June: Flo rang Ken.

MEMO
Am beginning to understand Ken.

3 June: Did nothing.
4 June: Mr Constable's movement. Well! [. . .]
8 June: Met Ken. He invites us to live with him.
9 June: Went to the pictures.

MEMO
I am puzzled.

10 June: Did nothing.
11 June: Must leave our digs.
12 June: Ken offers to share flat again.
13 June: I say no.
14 June: Ken offers again.
15 June: We accept because we must.
16 June: Move into Ken's flat.
17 June: Well!
18 June: Well!!
19 June: Well!!![26]

⁓

Seen today, *Victim* is a period-piece, stagier than many other black-and-white films of its period and dated in both dialogue and diction. It also remains an 'issue' film and, as such, limited. To a contemporary audience, indeed, it completely misses the point: its concentration on the relatively peripheral problem of the blackmail of homosexuals bizarrely overshadows any real engagement with the wider questions posed by the continuing illegality of homosexuality itself. Instead, largely because of the demands of the plot, it goes so far as to characterize those in the upper reaches of the Metropolitan Police as sympathizers, or at least as being possessed of a restraining, avuncular liberalism:

— If only these unfortunate devils [the blackmailers' homosexual victims] would come to us in the first place . . .
— If only they led normal lives they wouldn't need to come at all.
— If the law punished every abnormality we'd be kept pretty busy, Sergeant.
— Even so, sir, this law was made for a very good reason. If it were changed other weaknesses would follow.
— I see you're a true Puritan, Bridie.
— There's nothing wrong with that, sir.
— Of course not. But there was a time when *that* was against the law.

It is doubtful whether, to the majority of homosexuals, it seemed that way at the time; for, in London at least, the years immediately preceding the film's release in 1961 were marked by an officially sanctioned intensification of the police harassment which had developed since the end of the war. Partly in response to public 'concern' when scant but sufficient details of the lifestyles of Guy Burgess and Donald Maclean became known after their defection in May 1951, all manifestations of homosexuality had been included in a crackdown on law and order instituted by Sir David Maxwell Fyfe, a prosecutor at the Nuremberg trials who became Home Secretary that year.

The writer Francis Wheen has aptly described as 'neanderthal' the qualities which he brought to the Home Office – a reference, perhaps, to that fact that it was Maxwell Fyfe who sanctioned the controversial hangings of both Derek Bentley and Timothy Evans. But less remarked upon – although hardly less splenetic – was his treatment of homosexuals. He was certainly behind the enforced resignation from the House of Commons of William Field after the Labour MP was found guilty of 'soliciting or importuning for immoral purposes' and fined £15 in January 1953. It is difficult to believe, too, that the prosecutions of Rupert Croft-Cooke and the actor John Gielgud on minor indecency charges at around this time would have been brought without his imprimatur.

If these cases made the headlines, however, the impact of Maxwell

Fyfe's zeal was equally profound on homosexuals in more normal walks of life. 'I went for a walk in a park', recalls one,

> and in the gents I met the brother of a friend. We were simply talking, when two plain-clothes policemen charged in, waving torches and shouting, 'gotcha, gotcha' [. . .] I had made enemies among some of the more conventional and conservative officials like the town clerk and the chief constable. We were charged with a 'serious offence'. I still find it distressing to talk about it because not only did it wreck my career, but it was a situation that clearly illustrated the gross unfairness of the law then . . .[27]

The range and scale — and indeed the unfairness — of this activity is further demonstrated by a more detailed examination of the statistics. We have already seen that the total number of prosecutions for alleged homosexual offences had been increasing year by year since 1939. Yet even this tells only half the story; more is revealed by a breakdown of the global figures. Thus, in 1952, the first full year after Maxwell Fyfe's appointment, there were 670 prosecutions for sodomy and besti-ality, 3,087 for the 'serious offences' of attempted sodomy and indecent assault, and 1,686 for gross indecency; by contrast, the figures for 1939 had been, respectively, 134 and a mere 822 and 320. This explosion, particularly in the number of prosecutions for relatively minor offences, can largely be explained by the intimidatory and hitherto unheard-of tactics employed by the police:

> I lived in the West Country, in a very conservative seaside town. At that time obviously being gay was totally illegal, and one particular member of our gay community was caught 'cottaging' by the police. They threatened him with ten years in prison if he didn't tell them the names of all the gay men who lived in the area. So he went round in a police car to everywhere we worked or lived and a dozen of us ended up at the Quarter Sessions in Exeter Assizes. I was charged at the great age of fifteen with gross indecency and buggery.
>
> When it came to the sentencing it was rather frightening for myself and another young chap of nineteen. They were sending people down — to prison — for four to six years. We were just shaking

in our shoes wondering what was going to happen. Fortunately, we were put on probation.[28]

Inevitably, it was in London – where Maxwell Fyfe's lead was enthusiastically endorsed by a newly appointed commissioner of the Metropolitan Police, Sir John Nott-Bower – rather than the provinces that the new police offensive against homosexuals was most apparent. Previously tolerated, nominally 'private' clubs, most of them little more than afternoon drinking dens, were selected for special attention. For those like Bobbie's, a 'rather dingy little room' near Dean Street in Soho which was largely frequented by spivs and the *demi-monde*, police raids and prosecutions for licensing irregularities had always been an occupational hazard. Now they also became facts of life for more established venues such as the Mousehole coffee bar and the venerable Rockingham Club – 'piss-elegant and full of queens who thought they were in the Athenaeum'[29] – where Tom Driberg, E. M. Forster and J. R. Ackerley were occasionally to be observed among the regular clientele. One such raid, at the Mousehole, was instituted after a plain-clothes policeman on an unannounced visit reported that another man had complimented him on his hairstyle and then placed a hand on his knee.

Outraged by the vicious randomness of this particular 'unnecessary interference in people's private lives', Ackerley and Forster planned to write a letter of protest to a national newspaper. Forster even drafted the letter. 'I have occasionally drawn a cup of coffee in the Mousehole myself,' he wrote, 'little knowing of my peril, or that a policeman might be observing me and might demand my name and address because my taste in clothes differed from his.'[30] Prudently, perhaps, the letter was never sent. Other regulars had no option but to remain more phlegmatic. Their names having been solemnly written down in a policeman's notebook – intimidating enough, but generally the end of the matter – they merely moved on to another pub or club until the heat died down and old haunts re-opened. There was a regular transhumance up and down Rathbone Place, off Oxford Street, among traditionally tolerant, 'bohemian' pubs, including the Black Horse, the Wheatsheaf, the Marquis of Granby and the nearby Bricklayers' Arms, during this period.

Nor were police activities confined to this superficial level of harassment and intimidation. An altogether more sinister side of their campaign against homosexuals was reported by a newspaper in, of all places, Sydney, Australia:

> For many years past the [London] police had turned a blind eye to male vice. They made arrests only when definite complaints were made from innocent people, or where homosexuality had encouraged other crimes.
>
> They knew the names of thousands of perverts – many of high social position and some world-famous – but they took no action. Now, meeting Sir John [Nott-Bower]'s demands, they are making it a priority job to increase the number of arrests [. . .]
>
> The Special Branch began compiling a 'Black Book' of known perverts in influential Government jobs [in 1951] after the disappearance of the diplomats Donald Maclean and Guy Burgess, who were known to have pervert associates. Now comes the difficult task of side-tracking these men into less-important jobs – or of putting them behind bars.[31]

Not surprisingly, in the face of all this 'Nicholas' recalls that at the time he 'was terrified of the law, and frightened of being had up in court'. Down at his isolated prep school, 'Richard' might have been able to get away with things; people there didn't know what they were looking for, if indeed they were looking at all. In London things were different; the police did know, and they *were* looking:

> I was terrified of imprisonment, and at the back of my mind I knew it [homosexuality] was against the law. I remember once, I was on a Tube train in about 1958 and sitting next to me was a most attractive man. I asked him if he had the time and he began to move up to me and 'give me the old eye'. I knew, this time, what was going on. He said, 'Won't you come with me?' And I was *so tempted*, but there was this little voice inside me saying, 'No! no! get out of here!' I could already see trials and prison and all the publicity. I was so frightened! [. . .]
>
> And then my mother guessed – she'd had an uncle who was gay – because she noticed I was very sad after [a close friend] had been to stay with us. She said, 'Well, tell me, is it against the law, this thing that you're worried about?' That was the only thing that she

was concerned about. She wasn't shocked at all; her only concern was that I would get into trouble. [. . .]

I didn't do National Service, but I did do Basic Training – twice, in 1954 and 1955 for a month or six weeks each time. This was at the time of the Montagu trial. It was endlessly talked about at the camp. It was all the soldiers could talk about. And of course, that reinforced the fear that I had of being caught.[32]

It had been more than half a century since the Wilde trials when what 'Nicholas' refers to as 'the Montagu trial' was mounted in Winchester. But, with its tantalizing mixture of aristocracy and 'male vice', it too seemed primed irrevocably to change the moral climate. Nothing, as the judge had prophesied in 1895, would be quite the same as it had been before.

Born in 1921, and a 'professional' rent-boy on the West End scene since 1938, 'Tony' might well have been considered too fly to have been overly worried by it. ('Only once [was I] ever in a club when the police raided, but they only took names.') He 'never saw myself as anything like the street boys', and anyway harboured secret ambitions to give up prostitution altogether and go on the stage. There were only two bars he used: 'one in Piccadilly you went straight into, and one in Leicester Square called the Cavour. It went in for an awful lot of chorus boys, and that's really why I went, because I thought I might land a job.' Nevertheless, even he was shocked when the young Lord Montagu of Beaulieu (who had succeeded to the baronetcy in 1929, at the age of three), his second cousin Michael Pitt-Rivers, his friend the writer and journalist Peter Wildeblood and two other men were arrested in January 1953:

One was aware of the law. I used to see those 'Piccadilly Boys', as we used to call them, sometimes getting arrested and being taken away in black marias. I used to think in terms [of], 'Well, that will never happen to me, because I don't do that sort of thing.' It never occurred to me that there might be detectives undercover in a club. I used to think of it as it is now – perfectly legal provided you mind your own business. I don't think I was made fully aware of the law until years later, when the Montagu case came up. Then

you realised that you could be had up for something that had
happened three years before.[33]

Shocked, too, and if anything more convulsively, was the journalist
Michael Davidson. Not only was he a friend of Edward Montagu's;
before the war he had himself served a short term in prison for homosexual offences. Now he found himself pitched practically and emo-
tionally into the centre of an even greater drama. In the summer of
1953 the novelist Robin Maugham (nephew of Somerset) had invited
him to share a house in Dorset for a month's holiday. The weather
was glorious, it was Coronation year and they had been asked to go
on board HMS *Adamant* to watch the commemorative naval review.

The night before the Review we went over to Beaulieu to dine
with Edward Montagu; and the next day drove into Portsmouth.
Adamant was lying next to the aircraft carrier allotted to members
of both houses of parliament, so Montagu, being a peer, boarded
her [. . .] That evening we met Edward in a Portsmouth bar; luckily
we had a driver to take us back.

It wasn't long after returning from Dorset to my Bayswater home
that the telephone woke me up one midnight. The call came from
Beaulieu, from a friend staying there: Edward Montagu, he said,
was being charged with 'a certain offence' and so was another man;
would I instantly go round to that other man's flat and tell him
what was happening? I went round to his mews flat, banged the
poor fellow up, and gave him the confounding news; nobody could
know better than I how he then felt: I suppose there is no knowledge
so *shocking*, in the same physical way, as the knowledge (whether
one's innocent or guilty) that the whole ghastly trail of police-court,
trial, and perhaps prison, lies ahead; it affects one's *bodily* health as
well as one's mind's. One's transported in a flash from a real world
of ordinary things like bus-stops, tobacconists' shops and sitting in
cinemas beside ordinary people to whom policemen are men who
will tell them the time – to a nightmare world, a city of dreadful
night where the *knowledge* gnaws at one's mind like a rat. Punishment begins long before judicial punishment can be imposed. For
a little time after this I was running errands in connection with the
defence, seeing Edward and the others while they were on bail and
so on; and then, in August, Robin proposed that we should go to

Ischia for a holiday, offering in his generous way to stand me the fare. So it was on that island weeks later, that I read one morning in a Naples paper the dumbfounding news that a brand new charge had been brought against Edward; and that this time Michael Pitt-Rivers was implicated. The police had been out to 'get' poor hunted Edward; and in doing so had triumphantly scooped up two other men as well.[34]

Davidson, as his own account suggests, had only become involved in the affair *in medias res*. As the full story unfolded in court, 'the Montagu Case' was seen to have had its origins in events which took place well before the Coronation.

In the summer of 1952 Lord Montagu had offered Peter Wildeblood the use of a 'Spartan' beach hut near Beaulieu. Wildeblood wanted to get on with some writing, but 'did not want to be alone all the time, and it seemed quite a good idea to take Eddie McNally along'. McNally, whom he had met in Piccadilly Circus some months previously, was a twenty-three-year-old RAF corporal. He asked whether he could bring his friend, another RAF serviceman called John Reynolds. Wildeblood agreed, unaware at this time that both men were experienced operators on 'the game', and the three made their way down to the Hampshire beach hut.

> The holiday began more or less according to plan. Lord Montagu was spending that weekend at Beaulieu with a large house-party, and when McNally and I arrived by train from London he met us at the station, took us into Lymington to buy provisions, and deposited us at the beach hut. Reynolds had been delayed, but arrived later that evening and was brought down to the hut by Edward with some of his house-guests. Some sandwiches and a few bottles of beer were also brought down, by way of supper.
>
> The party which followed has achieved more notoriety than any other since the days of Nero, but I feel bound to confess that it was, in fact, extremely dull.[35]

'There was', Wildeblood insists, 'no dancing between males and no activities [*sic*] which could be described as improper.' During the course of the evening, however, he met Michael Pitt-Rivers and it was agreed that he and the two airmen should continue their holiday at Larmer Tree, a house on the Pitt-Rivers family estate. Everyone enjoyed himself; and Wildeblood, though still intermittently seeing and writing to McNally, had to all intents and purposes forgotten about the holiday when, in the autumn of 1953, Edward Montagu and another friend were charged with indecent assault on a party of Boy Scouts who had also been staying at the beach hut.

That charge was thrown out, but – in an ironic parody of the Wilde trials – Montagu was subjected to a re-trial on a lesser, but related, count. Meanwhile, some of Wildeblood's letters to McNally had been passed to the police, and Wildeblood, then the diplomatic correspondent of the *Daily Mail*, was roused early in the morning of 8 January 1953:

> . . . there was a thunderous knocking at the door. I ran downstairs in pyjamas and dressing-gown and opened it. Three men were standing outside, wearing mackintoshes and trilby hats. One of them said: 'Are you Mr Wildeblood?' I told him that I was. He said: 'We are police officers from the Hampshire Constabulary and from New Scotland Yard. We have come to arrest you, Wildeblood, for offences arising out of your association with Edward McNally and John Reynolds in the summer of 1952.'
>
> It was a bitterly cold morning, and when I heard these words, so incongruous in their stilted language, I felt as though I was drowning in an icy sea.[36]

A little later, Wildeblood had composed himself. There is a certain – and unattractively self-serving – braggadocio in his suggestion that if the arresting officers had 'really wanted a list of homosexuals from me I would [have been] happy to oblige, beginning with judges, policemen and members of the Government'; but, given his subsequent actions, no reason to disbelieve his later decision that 'Far from incriminating Edward Montagu and Michael Pitt-Rivers, as [the police] hoped, I would simply tell the truth about myself. I had no illusions about the amount of publicity which would be involved. I would be the first homosexual to tell what it felt like to be an exile in one's own country. I might destroy myself, but perhaps I could help others.'[37]

Many fascinating – and shameful – parallels can be found between the trials of Montagu, Wildeblood and Pitt-Rivers in 1953 and those of Oscar Wilde and Alfred Taylor in 1895. Not the least of these is the way in which class came to play as implicit a role in the proceedings of the Montagu trial at Winchester as it had done when Wilde stood in the dock at the Old Bailey. Michael Pitt-Rivers's counsel made great play of this in his closing speech.

> Foreigners think we are a nation of snobs, [he told the jury]. Well, I think we are. But you must have got some pretty basic snobbery in this case. It is now said that, because on a sunshiny holiday, with chaps in beach clothes down in a beach hut – in those circumstances when they are all calling one another by their Christian names, [when] you let them call you by your Christian name – that is a badge of some indecent association. Really! Did ever snobbery put forward a more greasy exterior than that [put forward] by the prosecution in this case?

Commenting on this side of things, Peter Wildeblood was later to write: 'The real crime of Lord Montagu, for example, in the eyes of some "Society" people, was that he became acquainted – on no matter what basis – with a man who (to quote the prosecuting counsel) was "infinitely his social inferior".'[38]

By all accounts, there was some truth in that. Behind the prosecution there were echoes of Wilde's 'feasting with panthers' and 'Tony' 's precise pigeon-holing of the different types of male prostitute. There was also the suggestion that, as well as a 'security'-inspired passion for rooting out homosexuals in high places, there was perhaps another, socio-political motive behind Sir David Maxwell Fyfe's homophobia. In his 1955 book *Against the Law* Wildeblood reported that in a 'recent' survey of 321 criminal cases involving homosexuality the accused men fell into the following social categories:

Shop and clerical workers	16%
Artisans (factory workers)	15%
Transport and Post Office workers	11%
Unskilled labourers	10%
Hotel workers and domestic servants	7%
Students, trainees and schoolboys	6%

Schoolmasters	4%
Agricultural workers	4%
Clergymen	2%
The mentally deficient	2%
Of independent means	2%
Unclassified	11%[39]

The taxonomy is archaic, but the table is a vivid illustration of the legal and social reality facing homosexuals in the Britain of the 1950s. As the Victorian music-hall song had it, despite the dreadful lessons learnt in the aftermath of the Burgess and Maclean defection, it was still 'the rich what gets the pleasure, the poor what gets the blame'. Simple mental arithmetic shows that, of the 321 cases brought, some 189 (59 per cent) were against lower middle- and working-class men, predominantly 'artisans', unskilled labourers and (a fast-disappearing category) domestic servants. By contrast, just seven were launched against 'gentlemen' (or at least those 'of independent means'); even adding in the mysterious 'unclassified' category, that total still reaches no more than 42 (13 per cent).

We should, then, give at least some credence to Michael Davidson's suggestion that Lord Montagu's arrest – together with the unexpected scoopings-up of Wildeblood and Pitt-Rivers – was, to policemen more accustomed to detaining wretched members of the lower orders, quite a coup. They might or might not have been expressly out to 'get' him, as Wildeblood suggests; his name might or might not have been in the Special Branch's 'Black Book' (it has never been produced, let alone opened) – but now they had him and they were not lightly going to let him go.

Thus, along with Wildeblood and Pitt-Rivers, the twenty-seven-year-old peer faced a committal hearing in front of magistrates at Lymington, near Beaulieu, charged with more than twenty separate offences against the infamous Labouchère amendment to the 1886 Criminal Law Amendment Act. McNally and Reynolds, whom even the prosecution described as 'men of the lowest possible moral character', had turned Queen's evidence and told the court that what Wildeblood was to describe as a 'Spartan' beach hut was in fact 'a gilded den of vice in which all-male orgies went on till dawn'.[40]

Amidst much publicity, the three defendants were committed for trial. But, as far as Peter Wildeblood was concerned, the damage had already been done: 'From now on, Edward Montagu's name would be indelibly connected in the public mind – and therefore in the minds of the twelve men who would later try him – not only with Boy Scouts, but with all-male parties and champagne orgies.'

The hearing finally began on 15 March 1954 when, in the lofty surroundings of the Great Hall of Winchester Castle, the defendants each pleaded 'Not Guilty' to all of the nineteen charges on which they were finally indicted. The ensuing trial ran for over a week, accounts of it not infrequently jostling reports of the latest Mau Mau atrocities in Kenya from the front pages of tabloid newspapers. Again and again, it sounded as if all concerned were merely re-enacting the Wilde trials. Wildeblood's counsel, Peter (later Lord) Rawlinson, in particular, had something of Sir Edward Carson's forensic irony – 'Is that an *ordinary* letter?' – when he came to cross-examine McNally:

> During 1952 and 1953 were you what you would describe as 'in love' with Peter Wildeblood? – Yes, sir.
>
> And when you wrote him those letters of which we have heard, did you mean the expressions of sentiment which you expressed? – Yes, sir.
>
> Let us remind ourselves of them. In December 1953 you said, 'As for me, well, I never change.' Did you mean that? – Yes, sir.
>
> When you wrote, 'I'm still very much in love', did you mean that? – Yes, sir.
>
> And the letters you wrote were quite sincere letters? – Yes, sir.

It did no good, however. After retiring for little more than four hours, the jury returned with their verdict. Throughout the trial the journalists covering it had run a book – as journalists everywhere tend to do – on the likely outcome. Having heard the counsels' closing speeches they were offering odds of eleven-to-two on an acquittal. The defendants were not so sanguine, and their fears were confirmed when the jury foreman rose to give their decisions as count after count was read out. 'Guilty . . . Guilty . . . Guilty . . . Not Guilty.' Wildeblood listened, he was to recall, with a 'dull curiosity' – '*Guilty . . . Guilty . . . Guilty*' – bleakly aware of the power of the judge: 'He could put me in prison for fifteen years if he felt so disposed.'

He didn't, but neither could he overlook the jury's verdict. In the circumstances, though – and in marked contrast to Mr Justice Wills's peroration against Wilde – when he came to sentence Montagu, Pitt-Rivers and Wildeblood the judge was considered and almost humane in his remarks:

> You have all three been found guilty of serious offences. You, Montagu, of less serious offences than the other two. I have paid the greatest attention to everything that has been said on your behalf, and particular attention, Wildeblood, to the difficulties which you have, no doubt, encountered. But, of course, it is quite impossible for these offences to be passed over. I am dealing with you in the most lenient way that I possibly can. You, Wildeblood, will go to prison for eighteen months; you, Montagu, for twelve months; and you, Pitt-Rivers, for eighteen months.[41]

Waiting for the jury to reach their verdict, Peter Wildeblood had given a friendly journalist, Peter Drake of the *Daily Express*, a message to pass on to his mother, who had supported him throughout the protracted legal proceedings. In part, it read: 'Whatever they decide, I do not want you to be ashamed of anything I have done. Be glad, rather, that at last a little light has been cast on this dark territory in which, through no fault of their own, many thousands of other men are condemned to live, in loneliness and fear.'[42] It was a prescient remark. Obscurely – Wildeblood was among the first to notice it – a little light *had* been cast by the trial.

The whole issue of homosexuality had once again been brought to the forefront of public attention and, to-ing and fro-ing between the hotel in which he was staying and the courtroom, Wildeblood was repeatedly exposed to the reactions to it of the men and women of Winchester. On one occasion a woman spat at him: 'She was a respectable-looking, middle-aged, tweedy person wearing a sensible felt hat. She was standing on the pavement as the car went by. I saw her suck in her cheeks, and the next moment a big blob of spit was running down the windscreen.'[43] More often, however, there were spontaneous expressions of support and a new understanding which genuinely surprised him: 'Undaunted by exploding flashbulbs and curious faces peering through the window, [a taxi driver] remarked: "Personally, and speaking man-to-man, I think it's a lot of bleeding nonsense. If two chaps carry on like that and don't do no harm to no one, what business is it of anybody else's?" '[44]

This continued after the sentences were announced and chimed well with the journalists' predictions and the underlying tenor of the judge's words. As the defendants made their way out of the castle – and prepared to climb into the veteran Rolls-Royce which was to take them off to prison – Wildeblood noticed a group of men and women surrounding the car. It might have been the car itself which had excited their interest, but

> then one of the women said, in a loud, toneless voice: 'Which is Lord Montagu? Ah, there he is!' I thought: Please don't let them do any more to him. They've had their pound of flesh. And then the crowd began to press round us, shouting. It was some moments before I realised that they were not shouting insults, but words of encouragement. They tried to pat us on the back and told us to 'Keep smiling', and when the doors were shut they went on talking through the windows and gave the thumbs-up sign and clapped their hands.[45]

Farther away, too, attitudes were subtly altering. If the onlookers outside Winchester Castle were unwitting bell-wethers, ten years after the end of the war others were beginning to follow their lead. Almost imperceptibly, a sense of reason was beginning to supplant neanderthal prejudice, albeit only in certain quarters. Thus we find the novelist Patrick Hamilton writing to his brother Bruce at around this time:

> The police love to victimise anyone well known. Press and public too. Here you have a perfectly ordinary young man (with a liking, no doubt, for Boy Scouts, Airmen, and other male whores) being fantastically pilloried – and convicted *on the word of the male whores*.
>
> In my tolerance for homosexuality I personally go further than the average civilised person, who is often heard saying that it is all right provided 'they don't corrupt the *young*'. I don't see this. I don't think the young *are* corruptible. I think that homosexuality is something constitutional – you either have it or not – I myself have had passes made at me as a boy, but they just didn't 'take'.

And although, at Westminster [School] I could (I now know) have satisfied these leanings in the case of one boy in particular – *still*, I'm sure I'd never have acquired the habit.[46]

8 ～

'The Ray of Hope'

'HOMOSEXUALS IN GENERAL are exhibitionists and proselytisers and are a danger to others, especially the young,' Sir David Maxwell Fyfe told the House of Commons on 3 December 1953. And he went on: 'So long as I hold the office of Home Secretary I shall give no countenance to the view that they should not be prevented from being such a danger.'

Even the legalistic double negative failed to cloak the minister's own deep antipathy towards any possible change in the law. Nevertheless, of all people it was that same David Maxwell Fyfe who went back to the House of Commons a mere nine months later to announce that the government had decided to set up a departmental committee to enquire into all aspects of the law as it related to homosexuality and prostitution. (Once again there were parallels with the Wilde case; the Criminal Law Amendment Act had, of course, begun its life as a bill designed to protect the rights of vulnerable young girls.)

The committee – the Wolfenden Committee, as it was known, after its chairman John Wolfenden, then vice-chancellor of Reading University – began work in August 1954. The task it faced was immense – ultimately the production of what the press immediately dubbed the 'Vice Report' was to take a full three years – and of considerable delicacy. At its first meeting Wolfenden told the committee: 'I have not the faintest idea at this moment what we shall ultimately recommend; but, whatever it turns out to be, my guess is that it will be unwelcome to approximately fifty per cent of Her Majesty's subjects. In short, we can't win.'[1]

It was, though, necessary to fight the battle. Maxwell Fyfe's volte-face and the appointment of the committee had only come about because of another perceptible increase in the public awareness of homosexuality. In 1953 John Gielgud had been convicted for cottaging (he told the court he was 'a clerk' earning just £1,000 a year and might have escaped publicity had he not been recognized by an *Evening Standard* reporter who happened to be in the press box). Memories of the trials of Rupert Croft-Cooke and Lord Montagu were still fresh, not least in the minds of MPs and newspaper editors. Homosexuality had once again become 'an issue' and, in liberal circles at least, this time some form of limited decriminalization even seemed a cause worth fighting for.

A decade before its successful campaign for the withdrawal of the drug thalidomide in the 1960s, the *Sunday Times* had effectively started that particular ball rolling when, in March 1954, it published a leading article anticipating Wolfenden's terms of reference and calling for a complete review of the law as it then stood.[2] It was to prove a rallying call in the fight for what would later be known as 'gay liberation'.

The following week the paper's correspondence column carried a long letter signed merely (but inevitably) 'Yours faithfully, HOMO-SEXUAL' which began by offering its author's 'deeply felt thanks for the ray of hope which your sane approach to the problems of homosexuality offers to the abnormal' and then – in the course of some 2,000 words – tried to identify the most intractable of those 'problems':

As you rightly say, [homosexuality] is a Social Problem; it is also an individual problem, and there is perhaps no such person as 'the typical homosexual'. Newspaper accounts and the proceedings of the criminal courts must together give many ordinary people the idea that all male homosexuals are by definition habitually promiscu-ous, addicted to constant vice and liable to assault any other male, given the slightest opportunity. Yet there must be very many like myself – perhaps even a majority – who, without ever having been approached by another, have known themselves to be irrevocably 'queer' from early adolescence; have for one reason or another – idealism, inhibitions or timidity – denied themselves any physical relationships; and who reach their later twenties or thirties with the energy-consuming stresses, imposed by their unsatisfied emotional needs and the constant mental dilemma of their general situation, heightened every year.[3]

Years later the pseudonymous 'HOMOSEXUAL' identified himself as Antony Grey. At the time of writing he had been a twenty-five-year-old Cambridge graduate and could not have foreseen that publication of his letter would lead to something which (he later wrote) 'was to become my major personal preoccupation, and also my professional occupation, for most of the next two decades'.

~

It is only now, looking back, that we can see why this should have been the case. Grey's letter, couched as it was in a tone of humane *reasonableness*, appeared at a crucial time. For if it had a mollifying effect on those *Sunday Times* readers who had been shocked by the previous week's leader, it also – and rather more importantly – served to make many homosexual men feel better about themselves. However slight, however transient, in itself it offered them another 'ray of hope' in an otherwise particularly benighted decade. Specifically, it came as a welcome corrective to the overwhelmingly negative, homophobically prejudiced or downright ignorant attitudes displayed in much that was being written and said during this latest bout of public concern about homosexuals and homosexuality in general.

Some of it is now barely credible. In Parliament back-bench MPs and back-woods peers regretted having to talk once again about an 'intensely repugnant' subject, something which was 'essentially evil and wicked', but took every opportunity to do so. The press, too, continued to moralize over the further falls of the mighty, most notably after the 'disgrace' of Ian Harvey in the autumn of 1958.

£5 FINE ON IAN HARVEY. HE WILL PAY TO END OF LIFE, ran *The Times*'s headline after the forty-four-year-old MP and Foreign Office minister had been discovered late one evening in St James's Park, 'standing under a tree misbehaving' with a nineteen-year-old Household Cavalry guardsman. The two men were charged with and convicted of only a minor breach of Royal Parks regulations after a gross indecency charge was dropped (the court heard that the guardsman 'was not addicted in this way' and had only gone with Harvey 'out of curiosity'). The nominal fine was, however, only the beginning of what Harvey himself was to call a period of 'Purgatory'. The press eagerly reported how he was forced to resign from his London clubs, relinquish government office (ironically, his ministerial post was filled by John Profumo) and give up his seat in Parliament.

Even ostensibly 'scientific' studies of the subject still described homosexuality as a 'severe mental sickness' and homosexuals themselves as suffering from 'personality deficiency'.[4] 'There are no happy homosexuals; and there would not be, even if the outer world left them in peace,' Edmund Bergler told readers of his unambiguously titled book *The Counterfeit Sex* (1958). 'The reason is an internal one. Unconsciously they want to be disappointed . . .'

'It was not easy for even sensible and socially concerned homosexual people who read [those] words to sustain a high morale,' Antony Grey was later to comment. That, if anything, was a wry understatement. Without the support of a gay community, even while the Wolfenden Committee went about its work, homosexual men very often found themselves in anomic isolation, all too ready to believe everything they read about themselves. (Ironically or not, in his *Sunday Times* letter even Grey described himself as 'queer' and talked about a 'problem' and the 'abnormal'.) Thus in 1958 the luckless Ian Harvey felt compelled to resign his seat in the House of Commons and accept the ostracism of his friends and the irrevocable end of his political career.

His, it might be argued, was a special case, a *cause célèbre*; but such public obloquy as he attracted was only an outward manifestation of the private fear and self-loathing felt by many more ordinary homosexuals at the time. In 1955, for instance, one such man who had also been arrested, brought before the courts on gross indecency charges, conditionally discharged but still sacked from his job, wrote:

If it were not for my mother, I might well take the quickest way out; not that I am ashamed of being what I am, but when one has worked hard from small foundations and built a happy life and environment about one, with various active interests and many hopes, it is so hard to be knocked down again [. . .] I had a friend, but now he is afraid even to write to me, and I am left without any profession, without hope for the future, and without a companion, to lead what seems a pointless life.[5]

'I began to suspect that I was not human. Not inhuman – just not like other human beings,' the poet James Kirkup has written of his period in his life.

> I was beginning to feel that the police must be after me. Was this sheer paranoia, so widespread among gays in the fifties? If so, was it justified paranoia? Was there something wrong with me? Was my behaviour bad, or simply not natural? [. . .] The police *were* after me. I knew that if I stayed any longer in England they would get me. There were bobbies on the beat in Chippenham and Bath, and in Corsham itself there was a plain-clothes officer living in the main street just a few doors away from where my parents and I were staying in Weavers' Cottages, Flemish Buildings. I could not trust some of my colleagues at the Bath Academy of Art . . .[6]

By 1957 everything had got too much for 'Nicholas', the Cambridge undergraduate whom we have already encountered. If he was not unduly frightened of the police, like Kirkup he too felt stifled by the climate of 'Kafkaesque cruelty'. Although he was only in his early twenties, he had had enough: 'I wanted to change I wanted to be "normal". I didn't want to be gay, or "queer", as we called it then – though I hated the term.'

Thus, in his fourth year at Cambridge, beginning work on a PhD, he went to see his doctor – a brave move in itself at the time – and asked for treatment. His and other men's memories of that 'treatment', of aversion therapy which featured the use of the nausea-inducing drug apomorphine and of crude antagonistic counselling, vividly recreate a world in which homosexuality was officially regarded as a mental disorder. (It had been formally classified as such when the World Health Organization was established in 1948, and remained on official British lists of psychiatric disorders until 1993.) 'Nicholas' 's treatment in particular, culminating as it did in a series of interviews with R. D. Laing, the 'media psychiatrist' who would hit the headlines on both sides of the Atlantic during the 1960s, also reveals how little medical, psychological and, more profoundly, social thinking had changed in half a century. Indeed, his account (and the separate experiences of two other men) precisely parallels the treatment undergone by E. M. Forster's Maurice Hall some forty-five years previously:[7]

At the time I thought it was a passing phase. I was beginning to get a bit nervous about it because it was taking such a long time to pass, so I went to see a specialist. He insisted on examining me in the nude, and gave me a full medical examination, running his hand up and down my calves, and so on. Then, when I told him I thought I might be homosexual, he suddenly backed away. He was absolutely horrified!

At last judgement came. [Maurice] could scarcely believe his ears. It was 'Rubbish, rubbish!' He had expected many things, but not this; for if his words were rubbish his life was a dream.

'Dr Barry, I can't have explained –'

'Now listen to me, Maurice, never let that evil hallucination, that temptation from the devil, occur to you again.'

The voice impressed him, and was not Science speaking?

'Who put that lie into your head? You whom I see and know to be a decent fellow! We'll never mention it again. No – I'll not discuss. I'll not discuss. The worst thing I could do for you is to discuss it.'

'I want advice,' said Maurice, struggling against the overwhelming manner. 'It's not rubbish to me, but my life.'

'Rubbish', came the voice authoritatively.[8]

He retreated behind a huge desk and said there was absolutely no one at Cambridge who could 'deal' with this 'condition', but he could send me to the Tavistock Clinic in London where they'd treat me on the National Health. It was an enormous disruption to my work, but I went. [. . .]

I'd also read in one of the Sunday papers about a doctor at the Maudsley Hospital who could cure homosexuality by aversion therapy. So I rang him up and eventually managed to get to see him – this is the extent to which I still wanted to be changed.

I went in not too solemn, trying to be fairly cheerful, even laughing a little bit, but he was grim and treated me like a juvenile delinquent.

I said, 'Well, what'll you do?' and he said, 'I can't really show you naked men, but I'll show you photographs of naked men and then I'll give you an injection or a tablet which will make you feel absolutely nauseated. It's the Pavlovian principle; you'll be so nauseated by the idea of men . . .' So I said, 'I can see how that works, but will the other come? I don't want to end up feeling like vomiting every time I shake hands with a man, and I don't want to be sexually neutral either. I'll do it, but will you be showing me pictures of naked women and giving me wonderful drugs to make me attracted to them?' 'No,' he said, 'it'll just come.' I said, 'But how?' and he could not provide a satisfactory explanation.

I sat in the doctor's room, with an old-fashioned tape recorder. The doctor was asking me questions like Did I realise how offensive it was to be homosexual? Did I realise that anal sex was vile? Did I realise that oral sex was vile? He was trying to make me feel disgusting.

He played the tape back to me and said, Right, this is what we're going to do. And he put me in a room with a male nurse, no windows, a stack of 'dirty books' — as they called them in those days — and pictures of male bodies. They weren't dirty, actually; they weren't particularly disgusting. They were just male bodies. And he said, What do you drink?

In those days I used to drink Guinness, so I had a couple of cases of Guinness stacked up.

So there I am in this bed, listening to a tape which lasts an hour and drinking beer and looking at the books, feeling a bit uneasy, wondering what the hell was going on.

He then gets up and gives me an injection and the injection made me violently ill. I just wanted to throw up. I said, I'm going to be sick, and he said, Go on then. I said, I need a basin. No, just be sick in the bed. I said, You're joking. No, no; just be sick. I was just vomiting everywhere. That lasted an hour. Then they did it another hour and another hour. And every hour they gave me an injection.[9]

'. . . now what do you suppose this picture is of, whom is it of—?'
　'Whom is it of —' [said Maurice.]
　'Edna May.'
　'Mr Edna May.'
　'No, Mr Hall, Miss Edna May.'
　'It's Mr Edna May.'
　'Isn't she beautiful?'

'I want to go home to my mother.' Both laughed at this remark, the doctor leading.

'Miss Edna May is not only beautiful, she is attractive.'

'She doesn't attract me,' said Maurice pettishly.

'Oh, Mr Hall, what an ungallant remark. Look at her lovely hair.'

'I like short hair best.'

'Why?'[10]

He got quite impatient and ratty. He was extremely rude. He really was monstrous. He was the only person I met [while I was getting treatment] who was offensive.

I said I wanted out. If this is supposed to make me better then I don't want to be better. They say, Oh really, but we haven't finished. We want another two days. I went bananas! I've got a temper . . .

They said, But you've got to try the electric treatment. I went, What do you mean – *electrodes*? To me electrodes were Frankenstein! Electrodes were *One Flew Over the Cuckoo's Nest*! Electrodes were the Funny Farm![11]

I had electrodes attached to my arm and my leg and I was shown slides of men and women and asked to say in a scale of perhaps one to ten how sexually exciting I found the slides of the male. Then I was given electric shocks of different velocity [*sic*]. It increased or decreased according to my request, reaction and attraction to the slides.[12]

I told my mother I was having psychiatric treatment and, while I was away, she went to see my doctor and asked his advice. He referred her to someone else, and when I got back I went to see this old chap.

If this new doctor could alter his being, was it not his duty to go, though body and soul would be violated? With the world as it is, one must marry or decay.[13]

It was a most extraordinary experience. There he was in his consulting room. His wife was there, and there seemed to be at least another two or three people around, and he said he wanted a specimen of my semen. So he put me up on to a couch and wanked me off, but I was so embarrassed I couldn't come. Nevertheless he still wrote a report about me: Mr — is young, slim, etc. [. . .]

[After that] I was introduced to several doctors and saw them on a regular basis. Then eventually I was referred on to R. D. Laing. I'd never heard of him; this was several years before he became famous in the Sixties. He had a very bare little office where I saw him twice a week for a year. It was all very formal, as those places were in those days.

That gentleman further relieved him by coming up to his idea of what an advanced scientific man ought to be. Sallow and expressionless, he sat in a large pictureless room before a roll-top desk. 'Mr Hall,' he said, and offered a bloodless hand. His accent was slightly American. 'Well, Mr Hall, and what's the trouble?'[14]

Laing was a very short man, much shorter than me. He used to sit in a chair by his desk puffing very vigorously on a pipe. On my first visit he said, 'You can either lie down on the couch or you can sit.' I sat, I suppose because I thought there was some sort of Freudian cliché that you only lay on the couch if you were ill, *mentally ill.* I knew I wasn't ill, I was just aware that I had 'problems' – and that was the problem, if you see what I mean. But I was too rational for Laing. He wanted me to be a far more deeply disturbed person than I was: I just wasn't mad enough for him, I suppose. [. . .]

He used to say, in that very broad Scots accent he had, 'Mr —, you've never talked about your relationship with *me.* Have you never wanted to marry *me?*' And I'd say, 'No, I haven't; no, I don't want to marry you. You know my position.' 'Mr —, I suggest that you want to have a baby by me. Do you want to humiliate me?' And I said, No, of course I didn't; 'No, I want to look up to you – why should I want to humiliate you? You're going to help me.'

[Maurice] asked 'What's the name of my trouble? Has it one?'
'Congenital homosexuality.'
'Congenital how much? Well, can anything be done?'
'Oh, certainly, if you consent.'
'The fact is I've an old-fashioned prejudice against hypnotism.'
'I'm afraid you may possibly retain that prejudice after trying, Mr Hall. I cannot promise a cure. I spoke to you of my other patients – seventy-five per cent – but in only fifty per cent have I been successful.'[15]

[Laing] was terribly passive, he hardly said anything. He was completely lacking in a sense of humour. Once, I told him my godfather
had given me five pounds and I'd decided I thought it would help
me if I spent it on going to see a prostitute. What did he think
about that? What was his advice? He absolutely refused to commit
himself – why, for God's sake?

I remember [the psychiatrist] once saying to me that she wished
she could say: Go out and do it, have sex with a man! It must have
been terribly frustrating for her.[16]

There were many times when I deluded myself that the treatment
was working. That I wasn't *really* homosexual; that I wasn't *really*
attracted to men, and that I *was* attracted to women. But I was
conning myself. Retrospectively, I can see that so clearly![17]

The next time I saw [Laing] I told him how I'd found a girl
off Park Lane somewhere; how I went back with her to a room
somewhere. It was unbelievably squalid, an unmade bed, ashtrays
everywhere. She was pretty, but a bit skinny. She started to masturbate me, but I couldn't even get an erection. The whole thing was
so sordid! Eventually, I called a halt and said, 'Look, I'm very poor,
I'm only a student. Do I have to pay you the full five pounds?'
'Yes,' she said. So I said, 'Well, can I just kiss you?' 'No, we don't
kiss, dear.' It was a horrible experience. [. . .]
    And he said, 'Mr —, you seem to want my permission for
everything that you do.' I said I wanted his advice. But he wouldn't
say yes and he wouldn't say no. Everything had to be related to
my relationship with him. He never focused on my problems. He
never talked about them: he was totally pre-occupied with my
relationship with *him*.

'You should not resist me,' [said Dr Lasker Jones].
    'Damn it all, I don't.'
    'You are less suggestible than you were.'
    *'I don't know what that may mean, not being an expert in the jargon,
but I swear from the bottom of my heart I want to be healed. I want to be
like other men, not this outcast whom nobody wants —'*[18]

I just wanted to know what was going to happen, and whether he could change me. I'd say to him things like, 'Dr Laing, what's going to be the result of all this? What's going to be the "end product"? I'm doing a PhD thesis; this is all taking up an enormous amount of my time.' And eventually he'd say: 'You're always talking about *the result*. You're too hard on yourself. Go out of here, get married, have a baby.' [. . .]

When eventually I was psychoanalysed I had a dream within about two or three weeks about something which happened when I was three.

'I say, I had a dream when you woke me up [from a hypnotic trance]. I'd better tell it you. I thought I saw a face and heard someone say, "That's your friend." Is that all right? I often feel it − I can't explain − sort of walking towards me through sleep, though it never gets up to me, that dream.'

'Did it get near now?'

'Jolly near. Is that a bad sign?'

'No, oh no − you're open to suggestion, you're open − I made you see a picture on the wall."[19]

He immediately picked up on this and said, 'Something happened when you were three!' A whole year had gone by by then though, and shortly after that I stopped seeing him. It was just getting ridiculous. [. . .]

The last time I saw Laing − just the once − was in 1964. By then he was a distinguished man. He'd published those books.

I said to him that I was still concerned, that I still wanted to be heterosexual. Was there anything else I could do? It was then that he suggested LSD.

I also happened to say to him 'D'you think it's hereditary? I had a great-uncle who was homosexual.' He had a slight outburst: 'Who doesn't have a great-uncle who's homosexual?' he said. 'Why bother to change?' It was the first time he'd ever said anything like that. I'm far too easily influenced by people, and this was the Great Man, as it were − but why couldn't he have said that six years before, when I first went to see him?

❧

The Wolfenden Report, officially the *Report of the Committee on Sexual Offences and Prostitution*, finally appeared on 5 September 1957. (Wolfenden later recorded in his autobiography that 'every sentence in the final document has a history, of discussion, rewording, expansion, deletion, fresh approach, and eventual acceptance').[20] It attracted massive publicity and, as Wolfenden himself had predicted, its authors found themselves in an uncomfortable no-win situation. But that was as nothing compared to the obloquy their report attracted from Parliament and some elements of the Establishment. The cause of all this ire and indignation was, of course, the liberal tone of its proposals ('there must remain a realm of private morality and immorality which is, in brief and crude terms, not the law's business') and specifically its principal recommendation that 'homosexual behaviour between consenting adults in private be no longer a criminal offence'. There were actually another seventeen lesser recommendations directly relating to homosexual offences, but those were all dependent upon acceptance of the first.

Everything came to a head when the report was first formally debated in Parliament, in the House of Lords in December 1957 and in the Commons in November 1958. All the homophobia which had been swirling around for the previous fifteen years finally gushed out – bile mixed with a dash of political 'concern'. 'Incest is a much more natural act than homosexuality,' said one MP. Others chimed in with what might have been intended as 'well-intentioned' remarks – 'I feel sorry for these people. They do not know what they are missing' – but the majority made no bones about their continuing abhorrence of the whole subject: 'I am repelled by the dirtiness of some of those whose conduct is exposed to the public gaze. I want to strip some of this false sentimentality, this false romanticism from homosexuality' ... 'We should keep them out of sight of the general public.'[21]

And that was just the start. The Commons returned to talking about matters homosexual in 1960 – when a motion calling for the implementation of all Wolfenden's recommendations was lost by a majority of more than two to one – and again in 1962. On the strength of the 1960 vote, the government (by then Conservative) stalled, claiming that 'the country' was not ready for the full implementation of the Wolfenden proposals. Nevertheless, the argument or 'process of public consultation' went on and on – by July 1960 one Lady Lloyd had already been moved to write to the *Daily Telegraph* averring that

'All decent people long to see a cessation of [this] discussion. Behind a drawn blind a corpse may be rotting; the blind will not stop the smell, but at least it will hide from the passer-by the horrors of putrefaction.'[22]

Running parallel to all this, the perhaps surprising *Sunday Times* tide of liberalism was getting ever stronger. As early as March 1958 a *galère* of the great and the good, a cross-section of the (predominantly heterosexual) intellectual movers and shakers of the day, had written a letter to *The Times* which began: 'Sir, We, the undersigned, would like to express our general agreement with the recommendation of the Wolfenden Report that homosexual acts committed in private between consenting adults should no longer be a criminal offence.' Bishops and peers of the realm, writers and philosophers (including a not inconsiderable number of women) were among the signatories. It would be invidious now to try to discern private motives for their decision to go public, but the list is worth reprinting if only to show the degree of backstage Establishment support which Wolfenden's proposals enjoyed. Many of the names at the bottom of the letter are still familiar today. In time-honoured *Times* style, in 1958 they were presented in alphabetical order:

> Yours, etc.,
> N. G. ANNAN; ATTLEE; A. J. AYER; ISAIAH BERLIN; †LEONARD
> BIRMINGHAM; ROBERT BOOTHBY; C. M. BOWRA; C. D.
> BROAD; DAVID CECIL; L. JOHN COLLINS; ALEX COMFORT;
> A. E. DYSON; †ROBERT EXON; GEOFFREY FABER; JACQUETTA
> HAWKES; TREVOR HUDDLESTON CR; JULIAN HUXLEY; C. DAY
> LEWIS; W. R. NIBLETT; J. B. PRIESTLEY; RUSSELL; DONALD
> O. SOPER; STEPHEN SPENDER; MARY STOCKS; A. J. P. TAYLOR;
> E. M. W. TILLYARD; ALEC R. VIDLER; KENNETH WALKER;
> LESLIE D. WEATHERHEAD; C. V. WEDGWOOD; ANGUS
> WILSON; JOHN WILSON; BARBARA WOOTON.[23]

The homosexual man was headline news; and while the government dickered over quite how they were going to react to Wolfenden, he – or at least the general idea of 'homosexuality' – looked like remaining so. Predictably, the *Times* letter (actually drafted by the literary critic and academic A. E. Dyson) elicited a response claiming that implementation of Wolfenden's proposals would bring 'a most unsavoury subject into undesirable prominence' and even 'divide the nation'. As Antony

Grey implies, however, in contrast with Dyson's letter, that one was signed by a group of distinctly B-list celebrities. The Bishops of Carlisle and Rochester and Lords Lawson and Winterton hardly had the media clout of the likes of former prime minister Clement Attlee, Julian Huxley, Bertrand Russell, A. J. P. Taylor and Dame Veronica Wedgwood.

Thus, a good case can even be made that, right from the start, there was serious liberal support for what Wolfenden was recommending. In his second book, the less-satisfactory *A Way of Life*, published one year ahead of the report, in 1956, Peter Wildeblood had written:

> The publication of *Against the Law* resulted in a flood of letters, all of which had to be answered. For the first few months an average of one reader in every ten was either writing to me or ringing me up, and I began to wonder whether I should ever have time to write another book The letters were nearly all from 'normal' men and women who did not share, but sympathised with, the problems which I had outlined in the book. There were letters from Judges, magistrates, doctors, barristers and clergymen, housewives and mothers and businessmen . . .[24]

Unfortunately for Lady Lloyd and 'all decent people', the discussion was only just beginning. Indeed, it is still going on.

Amongst homosexual men, reactions to Wolfenden were more complex. For year after year the central problem remained: Wolfenden was just a report; its recommendations were just, well, recommendations. They did not have the force of law. Only Parliament could change that. But there was a ray of hope. Coming as it did in the wake of a clutch of unexpected events which had begun with the defection of Guy Burgess and the bisexual Donald Maclean in May 1951 and included the unusual amount of attention the press gave Peter Wildeblood's account of the Montagu case, *Against the Law*, in 1955, the report could not be ignored for ever. Whatever it was, something would have to be done . . .

Sensing this, almost imperceptibly, the 'gay community' began to emerge in something like its present form. Ur-activists such as Antony Grey seized on Wolfenden and the subsequent debate and used it to bring their plight further into the public consciousness. Indeed, it is possible to trace the origins of the British 'gay liberation' movement from their actions at this time.

We have already seen that the mere appointment of the Wolfenden Committee had changed the course of Grey's life, and given him a 'professional occupation' for the next twenty years. This began modestly enough when he became involved in Britain's first 'gay rights' group, the Homosexual Law Reform Society (HLRS), an ad hoc body which was partly the brain-child of some of the signatories to the *Times* letter – Dyson (eventually its vice-chairman), Stephen Spender, Jacquetta Hawkes and Canon John Collins were among the original members – and partly a mutual support group for openly homosexual men brave enough to make their proclivities known. Chief amongst these were Len Smith and Reiss Howard, at whose home in Liverpool Road, Islington, the HLRS used to meet.

In retrospect, Smith and Howard seem to represent, almost to the level of parody, the 'Julian and Sandy' stereotype of the fifties homosexual couple. Both were pacifists; both, too, had previously been married. Smith was a member of the Independent Labour Party and had been interned as a conscientious objector during the war; Reiss, a Canadian, was an artist. Now, together, they ran an antique shop from the Liverpool Road address. Nevertheless, as Grey points out, their decision to support the HLRS and give it a home and postal address 'was one of signal bravery [because] police surveillance of anyone known or suspected as a practising homosexual was very much a reality in those days, and Len and Reiss knew very well that if they were to be arrested and convicted they would get heavy prison sentences'.[25]

Chief amongst the HLRS's aims and objectives was to change public and political opinion in favour of a reform of the law, broadly along the lines which Wolfenden had recommended. Even that, however, was fraught with difficulties; and the great and the good who had offered their services to the society were not unaware of the irony of their position:

The executive committee for their part were mostly not homosexual themselves; they were very conscious of the delicate, and in some respects potentially dangerous, nature of the task which they had taken on, and they were understandably nervous of being 'railroaded' by a group who, however well-informed and wellintentioned, were all personally vulnerable in the existing state of the law and might do irreparable damage to the Society's cause if they put a foot wrong, individually or collectively.[26]

They need not have worried. Though over the years the HLRS increasingly became a contact point for homosexual men, comparatively few actually joined and fewer still played any active part in its campaigning. In his book Grey singled out A. E. Dyson (later to become famous/notorious as co-editor of the right-wing 'Black Papers' on education policy) and specially praised his work. 'Dyson's brave initiative in launching the HLRS', he wrote, 'should earn him an honourable footnote in the social history of this country.' In the socio-political spirit in which both he and Dyson were working this was undoubtably true. But it was also true that, as early as the late 1950s, the major battles for homosexual law reform were being fought by members of what we would now call the liberal, 'chattering classes'. It had become a Good Cause, an Issue – albeit one which had little or nothing to do with ordinary homosexuals. Indeed, during the 1960 Commons debate Roy (now Lord) Jenkins was to say: 'I am not concerned only with what homosexuals want, or even primarily with what they want. I am concerned with what I think is a reasonable law for a civilised society.'

Thus the whole decriminalization campaign came to be seen by men such as 'Richard' as little more than heterosexual do-gooding – a feeling which intensified when, within days of the foundation of the HLRS, another worthy body came into being. The Albany Trust (which achieved charitable status in 1965) was named after its meetingplace, the set of rooms in Albany, Piccadilly, then occupied by the bluff novelist and wartime *Postscript*-writer J. B. Priestley and his wife Jacquetta Hawkes, both signatories of the original *Times* letter and heavily involved with the HLRS. They and Dyson were among its original trustees.

Things were spiralling away from the man in the street. The Albany Trust actually came close to making a virtue out of the strangely asexual high-mindedness which motivated both it and the HLRS. According to its deeds, its initial objects were 'To promote psychological health in men by collecting data and conducting research: To publish the results thereof by writing, films, lectures and other media: To take suitable steps based thereon for the public benefit to improve the social and general conditions necessary for such healthy psychological development.'

It is easy now to mock these ideas of 'research' and the grandiloquent use of words such as 'thereof' and 'thereon' in this document. But it is notable, too, that nowhere does the word 'homosexual' appear. The HLRS and the Albany Trust lobbyists were doing their best, and from the best of motives; but (as is sometimes the case with Stonewall and Outrage! today) there was increasingly a sense in which the abstract cause threatened to obscure and even overwhelm an essentially human predicament. For men like 'Nicholas', in particular, there was a certain irrelevancy about committee meetings and notions of 'the public benefit'. The pattern of his life, he believed, had been set at an early age. Now, effectively dysfunctional, alone after the failure of the variously well-intentioned medical and psychiatric 'cures' which might just have aided his 'healthy psychological development', he took the only course which seemed open to him. It was yet another ray of hope:

Sophie was the sister of one of my friends. I met her at one of his parties in 1956. She was very young then, about fifteen, but she sat next to me and cuddled me. And then she wrote me a letter saying that she loved me. And she went on writing. Eventually I met her again – this would have been in 1958 – and we started to see each other quite a bit. She'd hold on to me as if she was never going to let go. She'd want a fumble while we were at the theatre; she was very passionate. I'd never come across anything like that, and found it very flattering. So I thought if she feels as strongly about me as this, well, maybe it'll all come right for me. This of course was exactly the advice I'd been getting at that time from the psychiatrists and from the books I'd been reading: you've just got to take the plunge and everything will be all right in the end.

Then I went off to work for an oil company in Pakistan. I tried to 'keep myself' for Sophie, as it were. Then, after about a year, she came out with my mother. She was still only eighteen, but she brought a letter from *her* mother giving her permission to marry me.

I went into it hoping, *hoping* it would work. I told her that I had great problems sexually and I didn't know whether I'd be able to consummate the marriage. I didn't actually say that I had this attraction to my own sex, that effectively I was gay; but I reckoned that what I'd said was enough. I really wanted the marriage to work.

Then, after about four months a very butch, red-haired adventurous sort of boy of about my age came out [to where we were in Pakistan]. I was intensely attracted to him: one evening I was dancing with Sophie and I just wept. I consciously allowed myself to weep. And she said, 'What's happening? Can't you tell me?' And I told her how I was much more attracted to my own sex and how disappointed in myself I was. I didn't or couldn't just come out and tell her 'I'm gay' – for a start I didn't know for sure that I was. I still thought that it would all just blow over; I *hoped* it would. She was in great floods of tears over this, begging me not to send her away. She was very much in love.

So I asked her to marry me. Before we got married I did have sex with her, and I found I could get an erection and penetrate her. It wasn't wildly successful, but I thought it would come. I was still pretty well a virgin, certainly in terms of penetration; I'd just had those fumbling experiences with blokes. But it wasn't disgusting, as I thought it would be. Looking back, though, I suppose a lot of it was me thinking 'Here I am, a young man about to get married', and enjoying the image of a young, handsome masculine body – *my own young, handsome masculine body*[27] – making love. Several gay friends who got married have also mentioned this.

But of course, it wasn't very exciting and I didn't want to do it very much. I did it with her because I wanted to have a child by her. I got married with that hope.

After about a year I got back from a trip one day and found her in quite a state. I don't know what had happened, but she was in tears and eventually she said, 'I want a divorce, I must have sex.' That's the way she put it. I respected that – except that I'd warned her about my problems before we were married. And then she told me that she'd slept with nine men before me. She could remember them all. I'm afraid that did add to the acrimony at the time.

It upset me quite a lot and after she left I started drinking quite heavily. I'd been true to her while we were married, but afterwards

I started to have some sexual experiences. And I began to masturbate for the first time in my life. Odd.[28]

~~~~~

After he saw Lord Brabazon, Antony Grey recalled, he received a note from the peer telling him that he 'will always be welcome here and that I will do all I can to help over this difficult question'. Brabazon was as good as his word. So too were other influential figures after the HLRS and the Albany Trust began a relentless programme of attrition, bombarding Members of Parliament and opinion formers with press releases and digests of the most memorable cases which were still coming before crown, magistrates' and – not infrequently – coroners' courts. The story of the man who killed himself while await- ing trial (January 1959); of the man who told the police that he was being blackmailed, only to find himself arrested; of the soldier who hanged himself rather than face a court martial; of the middle-aged homosexual couple who gassed themselves when the police began investigating what were alleged to be 'unnatural sexual offences' . . .

As a public relations exercise – in an age in which PR had hardly been heard of – it was surprisingly successful. Men like Lord Brabazon of Tara, Roy Jenkins and Kenneth Robinson, MP (who promoted the bill during the 1960 debate), as well as a number of other influential back-benchers, were brought on-side. It is difficult to see how this could have been achieved other than at an 'old boy', 'old school tie' level. In a world in which the majority of Members of Parliament had still been educated in all-male public schools and yet continued to insist that they had never met a homosexual, it was probably the only stratagem which could have worked. The degree of ignorance was staggering, the level of prejudice beyond that which even the cam- paigners had imagined. On a train journey Grey found himself seated with the Conservative MP Godfrey Lagden: 'Lagden [leaned] across to me and said, in a genuinely puzzled voice: "Tell me, is it really true that these homosexuals find the idea of going to bed with a woman distasteful?" Wearily, I replied, "Yes, some of us actually do" . . .'[29]

But even at this stage, tensions were building up among the prosely- tizers, and, in the manner of many ginger-groups before and since, the HLRS and the Albany Trust soon found themselves riven by internal in-fighting. Ironically, the brave homosexual Len Smith was the first casualty. He felt unable to continue and withdrew, leaving its day-to-day running (from new offices in Shaftesbury Avenue) in the hands of the newly appointed secretary of the HLRS, the Revd Andrew Hallidie Smith, his wife and the chairman of both the HLRS and the Albany Trust, the redoubtable *New Statesman* journalist (and one-time police inspector) C. H. Rolph.

This is not the place for a detailed history of gay politics – Antony Grey has, anyway, provided that in *Quest for Justice* – but even the account of this very early skirmish serves to give some indication of what was to come. It has been important, too, in demonstrating just how influential what we must, for want of a better term, call the heterosexual Establishment voice became at a time when the voice from the streets had neither world enough nor time to make itself heard.

For all its influence, however, not even the HLRS could eradicate innate prejudice overnight. As we have seen, the 1960 House of Commons vote after a debate on the Wolfenden Report resulted in an ignominious two-to-one (213–99) defeat – but in the climate of the time it was just possible to claim even that as a moral victory. In an unpublished account of his work at this period Hallidie Smith wrote:

After the debate, the question was no longer *whether* the law would be reformed, but *when*. In three years the word 'homosexuality' had ceased to be a dirty joke and had become a topic for serious discussion. The days when victims of prosecutions were disowned by their parents or friends are almost over, and an increasing number of employers are willing to re-engage convicted homosexuals. In 1895, the name of Oscar Wilde was unmentionable. In 1960, while the law under which he was condemned was being debated in the House of Commons, two of the most popular films in London were sympathetic documentaries of his trials.

9 ⟿

'You'll Pardon the Mess; We Can't Help It, Really; We're Bachelors'

IN RETROSPECT WHAT became known as 'the Vassall affair' was only a small wave in the rising tide of social re-alignment which marked the early 1960s. Public interest began in the autumn of 1962 when an Admiralty civil servant by the name of John Vassall was convicted of spying for the Soviet Union and jailed for eighteen years. There was a sort of weary inevitability in the media coverage, however, even when it became known that Vassall was homosexual, and thus (in the public mind at least) peculiarly vulnerable to blackmail. Unlike the Burgess and Maclean story a decade previously, the 'affair' signally failed to metamorphose into a full-blown scandal. It was alleged that Vassall had been 'too familiar' with the then Admiralty minister, Thomas Galbraith; it was an undeniable fact that Galbraith had resigned (although he was subsequently cleared of any personal or professional impropriety), but the whole case soon dropped from the headlines. Within a matter of weeks it was remembered only in occasional reports of the protracted proceedings of a tribunal set up to look into the 'security implications' of the whole affair. The hapless Vassall himself was equally quickly forgotten.

Another corner had been turned. Although any mention of homosexuality *could* still trigger explosions of indignation and revulsion, in its small way the Vassall affair indirectly played a part in further familiarizing the public with the subject (or, but less often now, the 'problem') of homosexuality. The comparatively cool, matter-of-fact way in which the press and public now dealt with another homosexual scandal seemed to bode well for the future.

In April 1963 the *Sunday Mirror* had still felt it necessary to give its readers a two-page guide on 'How to Spot a Possible Homo' – he'd give them 'shifty glances' and have 'dropped eyes' and 'a fondness for the theatre' – but at around the same time homosexuality had been more reasonably discussed on *Any Questions?* on the BBC Home Service. More and more serious or at least semi-serious books, studies and articles were also being published. The literary and political magazine *Encounter* ran one of the first and most notable of these in November 1962. Sharply contrasting with the *Sunday Mirror*'s shrill alarmism, the tone of Simon Raven's long article 'Boys Will Be Boys – The Male Prostitute in London' was determinedly responsible and measured. Even the guardsman to whom Raven spoke seemed to belong to quite a different generation to the libidinous two-dimensional chancers whom John Lehmann had encountered: ' "Some of us get quite fond of the blokes we see regularly," he said. "You go to their flats and have some drinks and talk a bit – they're nice fellows, some of them, and interesting to listen to. And as for the sex bit, some of the younger ones aren't bad looking, and I've had some real thrills off them in my time." '

What J. R. Ackerley called his 'fairy story for adults', *We Think the World of You*, had appeared in 1960, but even that was whimsical and oblique in comparison with three more new books on explicitly homosexual themes with which it was sharing shelf-space by the end of 1962. There was Rupert Hart-Davis's expurgated but none the less long-awaited edition of Oscar Wilde's *De Profundis*; there was a pseudonymous 'autobiography' – *Another Kind of Loving* by 'Anthony Rowley' – and, perhaps oddest of all, there was a kind of straight man's guide to homosexuality.

In *The Homosexual Society*[1] Richard Hauser claimed, on the basis of no real scientific research, to have identified more than forty different types of homosexual. Many of these will be familiar to anyone who has read this far: there was the Call-Boy, the Sugar-Daddy, the Demoralized Married Man, the Club Type, the Pub Type, the 'Cottage' Type, the Ship's Queer, the War Queer, the Body-Builder, the Religious Homosexual, and so on and so on. Most were no more than broad sketches of the social stereotypes which by then even *The Goon Show* had had in its sights. One of Spike Milligan's scripts, for instance, had parachuted a naive Neddy Seagoon into the arcane world of Grytpype-Thynne and the rough and ever-ready Moriarty:

GRYTPYPE-THYNNE: You'll pardon the mess; we can't help it really; we're bachelors.

NEDDY SEAGOON: Why don't you get married?

GRYTPYPE-THYNNE: *I* would, but Moriarty doesn't love me.

It was hardly more than a pot-boiler, but Hauser's book unwittingly served to mark the confluence of the two streams of homosexuality which we have so far been following. Unlike the *Sunday Mirror* guide, it was fundamentally good-natured. Its patient if hardly original taxonomy reduced the once-shocking 'Sugar-Daddy' (Ned Lathom, say) and 'War Queer' to little more than household familiars. Like Julian and his friend Sandy, the itinerant queens whom Kenneth Williams and Hugh Paddick first began to pay at around this time, they were hardly the type to frighten the horses. Rather, like John Vassall, they seemed to emphasize just how ordinary and ubiquitous the homosexual was. With or without his suede shoes, dropped eyes and shifty glances, he could be a clerk – Vassall had been a clerk – or a member of one of the more effete professions to which Julian and Sandy aspired. Sunday by Sunday on the BBC Light Programme's *Beyond Our Ken* and *Round the Horne* they could be heard as travel or theatrical agents, antique dealers, restaurateurs – 'Could I have a vada at your entrées?' 'Ooooh! 'E's bold, innee?' – or even journalists:

JULIAN: Good morning! I'm Julian, this is my friend Sandy. Hello! Hello! We're from the *Daily Palari*, yes! Can we have five minutes of your time?

KENNETH HORNE: Well, it depends what you want to do with them.

JULIAN: Ooooh! Well, our editor says why don't you troll off to Mr Horne's latty . . .

KENNETH HORNE: That's a flat or house – Translator's note.

JULIAN: . . . and have a palari with him.

SANDY: We like to have something hot and personal . . .

Listeners felt they knew them, or perhaps someone like them. Even the more or less accurate 'palari' in which their sketches were couched seemed to signal how *safe* and almost ordinary Julian, Sandy and their real-life equivalents had become. Indeed, palari itself, by then almost extinct on the gay scene, enjoyed a brief general vogue at this time, leaving men like 'Richard' and 'John', who at least knew the meaning and derivation of the words, looking on in bewilderment. For 'Richard', who began his life in the world of 1930s revue and musical comedy, what he called 'this sudden craze' at least brought back memories:

> We always said 'Girl' at the end of a sentence. It was a sort of full stop. You'd say something like, 'You all right, girl?' or 'Fancy a drink, girl?' But you could get quite technical, too. You could say something like I heard someone say on the radio just the other day: 'Ooooh, will you just vada the bona filiomi ajax!' which meant, 'Oh, just look at the young, slightly effeminate man standing next to you.' It was all camp and rather silly, though; even then. Men talking 'Zhooshing-up'![2]

When Porter and Weeks interviewed 'John', though, he expressed rather more ambivalent sentiments. Another one-time chorus boy, he saw the public appropriation of this jokey private language almost as an invasion of his privacy. It was as if he felt that, as a concomitant to increasing public acceptability, the homosexual was being forced to surrender a bit of his individuality:

> It was originally the language of circus people. There are bits of pig Latin as well. For instance, 'face' is 'ecaf' – well, that's just 'face' backwards. 'Riah' – that's 'hair' backwards. But you have other things; hands are 'lappers', legs are 'lallipegs', breasts are 'jubes', eyes are 'ocals' or 'opals'. It's died out now. I think it was Bruce Forsyth who did a whole song in palari, and then of course Kenneth Williams and Hugh Paddick [used it] in *Beyond Our Ken*. So really it becomes like everything else; everybody does it. So there's no more mystery left.[3]

❦

On Monday 14 January 1963 Kenneth Williams wrote wanly, if rather tetchily, in his diary:

> The papers are full of this Vassall enquiry. The reporters giving evidence all talk about homosexual intrigue & hint at dark secrets in high places. All the muck raking is going on. To no advantage. Homosexuality in itself is no vice, a law which makes it one is evil.

Had the government acted on the findings of the Wolfenden report, this whole nasty episode would never have occurred.[4]

Unfortunately, as we have seen, Harold Macmillan's Conservative government had little intention of acting, least of all while the name Vassall and the red rags of 'blackmail' and 'national security' were still periodically resurfacing in the headlines. And so things dragged on. And on. At the Homosexual Law Reform Society's offices in Shaftesbury Avenue, however (where, following another round of internal disagreements, Antony Grey had taken over as acting secretary), it remained business as usual – and then some. More letters were written, more lectures given, more contacts made, more meetings held, more money raised. But, in the frustrating stand-off – Wolfenden *per se* was not debated at all in the parliamentary sessions of 1963 and 1964 – that was about all. Basically, like the rest of Britain, the society could only sit and wait for the impending General Election.

Looking back, this period of quietude seems extraordinary. It spans the exact period in which England started to 'swing'. 1963 in particular was the year which effectively killed off the old order and gave a five-minute knock on the dressing-room door of the new. It was the year of the Great Train Robbery; the year 70,000 members of the Campaign for Nuclear Disarmament (CND) marched from Britain's Atomic Weapons Research Establishment at Aldermaston in Berkshire to hold their biggest ever rally in London; and the year in which the Beatles first entered the British pop charts ('From Me To You'; 'She Loves You'). Even the poet Philip Larkin found it an 'Annus Mirabilis' – the title of one of his most famous poems:

> Sexual intercourse began
> In Nineteen Sixty-Three
> (which was rather late for me) –
> Between the end of the Chatterley Ban
> And the Beatles' first LP.

If sexual intercourse did not exactly begin for John Profumo, Macmillan's married Secretary of State for War, in 1963, almost alone he was responsible for its recrudescence among the British people. Larkin does not mention it (nor, curiously, in their autobiographies, memoirs, letters or taped recollections do many gay men), but what inevitably became known as 'the Profumo affair' was the *cause célèbre* of the year, what Professor Ben Pimlott has called 'the biggest inquisition into the mores of the governing class since the trial of Oscar Wilde'. It blew apart the notion of Establishment probity, nearly brought down (and certainly fatally weakened) the government, and unwittingly prepared the ground for future revelations directly relevant to this story.

The public first got to hear about things – rumours had been echoing through the corridors of power for weeks, if not months – in March, when Profumo assured the House of Commons that 'There was no impropriety whatsoever in my acquaintanceship with Miss [Christine] Keeler.' That was just the start, however, for it subsequently became known that he was lying – that, at the height of the Cold War, a British war minister *had* been involved with a 'model', whom he had first seen swimming naked in a pool at Cliveden, Lord Astor's country estate. Once it was discovered that Keeler was also involved with Yevgeny Ivanov, the Soviet Military Attaché in London, familiar arguments about the dangers of blackmail were again rehearsed and Profumo was forced to follow the course taken by so many ministers before him. His resignation was accepted on 5 June.

It marked the end of an especially fevered spring:

> In the late spring of 1963 men and women all over Britain were telling, and others were believing, embellishing and repeating, such stories as that nine High Court judges had been engaging in sexual orgies, that a member of the Cabinet had served dinner at a private party while naked except for a mask, a small lace apron and a card round his neck reading 'If my services don't please you, whip me', that another member of the Cabinet had been discovered by police beneath a bush in Richmond Park where he and a prostitute had been engaging in oral-genital activities and that the police had hushed the matter up, that the Prime Minister, Harold Macmillan, had known about some, or all, of these matters but had taken no action, and that a principal member of the royal family had been having sexual relations with one, if not two, prostitutes in circumstances that would have made exposure sooner or later inevitable.[5]

Bernard Levin published those words in 1970 (and it is interesting to note that, although homosexuality did not feature in the Profumo affair, homo-erotic, sado-masochistic elements are prominent in these prototypical urban myths). So extraordinary did the stories seem, even in 1970, however, that Levin felt bound to verify them with a footnote: 'The author heard all of these stories at the time, most of them more than once, and all of them from people who believed, or professed to believe, that they were true.'

In this heated atmosphere Lord Denning, the Master of the Rolls, had quickly begun another government enquiry into the 'security considerations' of the Profumo affair, the usual way of indefinitely kicking a contentious issue firmly into touch. It could not stay there for long, however.

In September people queued all night to buy copies of what was then trendily entitled *Lord Denning's Report* (in sharp contrast, Levin noted, to the general run of government reports which boasted titles such as *Report of the Nyasaland Commission of Inquiry*). It became a runaway best-seller for Her Majesty's Stationery Office. Denning was to blame; he had given a nation then addicted to the world of James Bond – fourteen of Ian Fleming's novels were in print in 1963; the film version of *Dr No* had been released to great success in 1962 – an official report which read like a crime thriller, even if its section headings were more Mickey Spillane than Ian Fleming: 'The Slashing and Shooting', 'Mr Profumo Is Warned', 'The Spaniard's Photography', 'The Man Without a Head'.

Ill and tired, Harold Macmillan was appalled by the whole Profumo débâcle and its seedy aftermath. ('Two, possibly three High Court judges I could believe; but nine, no, no,' he is reported to have said.) At nearly seventy years of age the Old Etonian Great War officer had addressed the House of Commons on 17 June about Profumo's behaviour: 'I find it difficult to tell the House what a blow it has been for me, for it seems to have undermined one of the very foundations upon which political life must be conducted.'

'Wounded', as he put it, he staggered on until, hospitalized by an acute prostate problem, he announced his resignation as Prime Minister on 10 October. Lord Home read the announcement to the annual Conservative Conference, then coincidentally in session. Within hours, the 'customary processes of consultation' having been observed, that same Home – by then plain Sir Alec Douglas-Home – was Prime Minister. After a long convalescence, Macmillan returned to the back benches little knowing that, for him at least, the worst was yet to come. And when it did, it caught him completely unawares.

No one, least of all the former prime minister, was prepared for the bombshell which the *Sunday Mirror* dropped on 12 July 1964. In thick inky black the front page howled: PEER AND A GANGSTER: YARD PROBE.

~

It sounded like another of Levin's *obiter dicta*. Neither the peer nor the gangster was identified by name, but the following article explicitly stated that the police – the 'Yard' – were investigating an alleged 'homosexual relationship between a prominent peer and a leading thug in the London underworld'. There were teasing references to 'Mayfair parties involving clergymen' and 'the private weekend activities of the peer and a number of prominent public men during visits to Brighton'. The dread word 'blackmail' surfaced, too. It did not take long for the identity of the peer, nor even that of the gangster, to leak out. Within a week the *Daily Mirror* announced that it had a 'picture we dare not print' showing 'a well-known member of the House of Lords seated on a sofa with a gangster who leads the biggest protection racket London has ever known'. The German news magazine *Stern* had it too, and gleefully told its readers that the peer was Lord Boothby (the Old Etonian former Conservative MP Robert Boothby, who had been made a Life Peer in 1958) and the gangster Ronnie Kray.

In the light of his comments on Profumo's perfidy in the Commons, it is possible to imagine Harold Macmillan's reactions to this. Boothby was an old friend; but there were deeper issues, too. We now know that for years Macmillan had been aware of, and had accepted with a pained complaisance, the fact that his wife, Lady Dorothy (née Cavendish) had enjoyed a long-term affair with Boothby. Right up until the day of his death Macmillan could never bring himself to talk about any of this.

But if he was a shattered Englishman, the luckless Alec Douglas-Home saw himself as the very likely premier of a shattered nation. Newspaper after newspaper was producing further legally vetted but innuendo-laden stories about Boothby and Kray. Classified government papers released only in January 1995 reveal how worried Downing Street was that the episode could be even more damaging to them than Profumo's had been to Macmillan. Douglas-Home was told that two Tory MPs *knew* that 'Lord Boothby and [Tom] Driberg had been importuning males at a dog track and were involved with gangs of thugs who dispose of their money at the tracks.' His Chief Whip let it be known (confidentially) that 'if a prosecution was impending and was being held up, it should proceed.' In the event, it didn't come to that. The government was let off the hook when Boothby went public in a letter to *The Times* which town-cried rather than merely proclaimed his innocence: 'I am not a homosexual. I have not been to a Mayfair party of any kind for more than twenty years. I have met the man alleged to be the 'King of the Underworld' only three times, on business matters; and then by appointment in my flat at his request, and in the company of other people.'[6]

No one really believed him but, seemingly fearful of even more costly legal action, the *Daily Mirror* caved in, apologized and paid Boothby £40,000 in compensation. To some people the always impecunious peer said he had given this sudden windfall away to charity; to others (Driberg included) he confided that he had used it to buy a country house. As Macmillan had cause to know, Boothby was more than double-faced.

~

Bob Boothby was in his early sixties in 1963; Tom Driberg was fifty-eight. Neither had what was then called 'old money' – both, indeed, fought periodic battles with the Inland Revenue – but they were figures of the Establishment. They had a certain clout, and they undoubtedly used it. Sexual intercourse did not begin for them in 1963, any more than it had for John Profumo; but it was around then that, forever open to blandishment, their elderly lizard eyes began to focus on what was happening in 'swinging London'.

Unfortunately, Driberg's uniquely frank but unfinished autobiography, posthumously published as *Ruling Passions*, does not cover this period of his life. Though otherwise exhaustive, Boothby's autobiographical writings (*I Fight to Live* (1947), and *My Yesterday, Your Tomorrow* (1962)), too, are unrevealing about all that really mattered in his personal life. However, copious secondary descriptions exist of the manner in which middle-aged and even elderly men like Driberg and Boothby battened the remnants of an old-fashioned, patrician homosexuality on to the new youth culture.

They do not tell an especially edifying story. Dignity in particular is signally lacking in the details of the two parliamentarians' involvement with Ronnie Kray. Boothby had apparently first come across him when the gangster called at his flat in connection with an unspecified business deal. As if to demonstrate his own special credentials as a 'swinger' – in October 1959 he had warned the House of Commons that the public regarded MPs as 'practically senile and hopelessly "square" ' – Driberg had met both Ronnie and his twin brother Reggie at an East End nightclub. Fittingly, the introductions on that occasion were made by Joan Littlewood, director of the not inappropriately titled musical *Fings Ain't Wot They Used t'Be* (1959).

Although in early 1963 the Krays – then aged twenty-eight – were not quite the lords of the manor which shotguns, torture and finally murder were to give them, neither encounter was without a certain seediness. Unlike Boothby and Driberg, however, the twins knew what they were doing. Being seen in the company of a Member of Parliament and a Peer of the Realm was not only gratifying in itself; as their confidence in their own invincibility grew, knowledge of the homosexuality of both men – and not least their predilection for rough trade – was an almost bankable asset, a powerful lever which could be pulled if ever the going got tough.

It was another mark of the Krays' self-confidence that Ronnie never felt it necessary to hide his own homosexuality. Their biographer John Pearson has written:

'I'm not a poof, I'm homosexual,' he would say, and [he] was genuinely put out by the antics of effeminate males. 'Pansies', he used to say, with the same Cockney contempt with which he pronounced the word 'women'.

He liked boys, preferably with long lashes and a certain melting look round the eyes. He particularly enjoyed them if they had no experience of men before. He liked teaching them and often gave them a fiver to take their girl-friends out on condition they slept with him the following night. He always asked them which they preferred. He was something of a sadist, but was generous with his lovers [. . .] and, as he proudly insisted, [he] was free from colour prejudice, having tried Scandinavians, Latins, Anglo-Saxons, Arabs, Negroes, Chinese and a Tahitan.[7]

Above all, Ronnie was a snob. He enjoyed kitting out his latest finds at Cecil Gee or any other fashionable tailor before parading them around the West End and plying them with drinks at the Society Club in Jermyn Street. It was fun, too, to entertain new parliamentary, titled and show-business friends at the flat he kept in Cedra Court, Walthamstow. They could play with his collection of north African gewgaws, admire the large painting of a naked boy which dominated one wall, and lounge on their host's elaborate four-poster bed while they popped whatever pills happened to be on offer.

Ronnie's Cedra Court parties even achieved a fame of their own, the suburban bacchanalia at which 'rough but compliant East End lads were served', in Francis Wheen's words, 'like so many canapés', becoming a small but recognized part of London's homosexual scene. At one a television pundit more than made the acquaintance of a famous disc-jockey. At others, as Pearson has described (with a perhaps understandable tact), actors would find themselves rubbing shoulders with 'a world-famous painter, several boxers, the chairman of an engineering firm, an assortment of men from the City, and two young men in dark suits who turned out to be Church of England clergymen'.

This was feasting with panthers on a level which even Oscar Wilde could not have envisaged – but, for the likes of Driberg and Boothby, that was precisely the attraction. It did not matter that Ronnie had got their number and was using them to facilitate entry into what Pearson called 'the useful freemasonry of the similarly inclined'. (Driberg was later to show how useful he could be in that respect by petitioning the Home Secretary on Ronnie's behalf to get a 'friend' transferred to a prison more amenable than Dartmoor.) It didn't even matter that they were risking their careers – as we have seen, even the *Sunday Mirror* could be silenced. The risk was part of the thrill.

Today the involvement of the likes of Boothby and Driberg with such conspicuous members of the *demi-monde* as the Krays seems melodramatic and little short of pathetic, but when seen in context it is illustrative of more than senescent veniality. It is only an extreme manifestation of the way in which homosexuality came to function as one of the levellers of class, age and social boundaries in the new world of the 1960s. Further examples of this process in action are, sadly, not hard to find. We can see it in Brian Epstein's instant infatuation with John Lennon the first time he heard the Beatles play at the Cavern Club in Liverpool. It was at lunchtime on Thursday 9 November 1961 – the very precision of time and date is perhaps indicative of how powerful an epiphany it was. Jewish, fastidious about his appearance, his dark suits and his crisp white shirts, Epstein was then twenty-eight and working in the family department store. Chronically repressed, hitherto his taste for 'rough trade' had led him to adopt a secret nocturnal existence, touring working-class pubs behind the city's Royal Court Theatre in search of compliant dockers or seamen. Now, in one lunchtime, the whole of his life had changed: 'He had fallen in love with John Lennon. He was besotted, not by the pretty-faced Paul [McCartney] or Pete [Best] but by the boy whose façade of crudeness and toughness touched the nerve of his most secret "Rough-Trade" fantasies.'[8]

Lennon was, by all accounts, as adept at avoiding Epstein's advances while still accepting all that he had to offer as Ronnie Kray was with Boothby. Tragically, for Epstein that was all part of his appeal.

Back in London, things were naturally more fluid. A new eclectic aristocracy was evolving, among whom anything – or nearly anything – went. And artfully at the centre of it, literate, LSE-educated, sexually ambivalent and apparently *available*, was Mick Jagger, in so many ways the antithesis of Lennon. Driberg was introduced to the notorious face of the Rolling Stones in 1967, by the gay American Beat poet Allen Ginsberg. He was overwhelmed. After an afternoon in Jagger's company, largely spent staring at his crotch, he announced: 'Oh my, Mick, *what* a big basket you have!' 'I was slightly embarrassed, as Driberg was my guest,' Ginsberg has recalled. 'I was also astounded at his boldness. I had eyes for Jagger myself, but I was very circumspect about Jagger's body. Yet here was Driberg coming on crude. There was a kind of Zen directness about it that was interesting: I suddenly realised that with directness like that you could score many times.'[9]

Or at least you could try. Driberg was far from alone in his pursuit of Jagger. Cecil Beaton, another member of the sixties' charmed circle, took things much further. Then sixty-three years of age, the friend and photographer of royalty first encountered Jagger in March 1967, while he was staying at a hotel in Marrakesh. Suddenly, the Rolling Stones 'together with hangers-on, chauffeurs, and Americans' arrived. There was 'Brian Jones, with his girlfriend, beatnik-dressed Anita Pallenberg – dirty white face, dirty blackened eyes, dirty canary drops of hair, barbaric jewellery'; there was Keith Richard 'and, of course, Mick Jagger'.

In the days that followed Beaton wrote page after page in his diary about the effect Jagger had on him:

> I didn't want to give the impression that I was only interested in Mick, but it happened that we sat next to one another as he drank a Vodka Collins and smoked with pointed finger held high. His skin is chicken-breast white and of a fine quality. He has an inborn elegance. [. . .]
>
> He is very gentle, and with perfect manners. He indicated that I should follow his example and eat the chicken with my fingers. It was tender and good. He has much appreciation, and his small, albino-fringed eyes notice everything. [. . .]
>
> His figure, his hands and arms were incredibly feminine [. . .] I took Mick through the trees to photograph him in the midday sun. I gave his face the shadows it needed. The lips were of a fantastic roundness, the body almost hairless and yet, surprisingly, I made him look like a Tarzan by Piero di Cosimo. He is sexy, yet completely sexless. He could nearly be a eunuch. As a model he is a natural.[10]

In the light of all this, it is not perhaps entirely surprising that many of the homosexual men whom (*pace* Roy Jenkins) the predominantly straight members of the Homosexual Law Reform Society and the Albany Trust were so determined to help rather wished that everyone would just leave them alone. They read about Vassall, Profumo and all the other scandals, and just shrugged; for them the HLRS's Hallidie Smith had been asking the wrong question: for them it was not so much *when* the law would be reformed, but *should it be*?[11]

Ostensibly, this sounds absurd. Right from the start, from its early Liverpool Street days, the HLRS had been something of a lifeline, with its premises acting as an unofficial meeting-place and advice

centre for hundreds of ordinary homosexual men. In subsequent gay
mythology, too, it and the Albany Trust have been portrayed as such
unalloyed Good Things that it is almost heretical to recall the level of
indifference to the work they were doing which existed, even among
those gay men who might have been its casual 'clients'.

Yet there was a feeling that the 'do-gooders' were principally interested in political change, in doing something which would help that
anonymous archetype 'the homosexual' rather than better the lot of
particular individuals. Men like 'Richard' and 'Stephen', for instance,
looked on Wolfenden's recommendations in much the say way as they
did the parallel proposals for a reform of divorce legislation: as something to be welcomed but something which was still not especially
relevant to them. 'Richard' took the imprisonment of Lord Montagu,
Peter Wildeblood and Michael Pitt-Rivers almost as a personal affront
– 'I was shocked at the police action. Persecution, I called it; I still
do. I was appalled' – but he was virtually unmoved by the gay rights
activism of the 1960s: 'I was in favour of decriminalization, of course.
But the Wolfenden debate didn't affect my life very much. I'd been
having rampant sex for years; it didn't exactly make a lot of difference!
In my opinion the most important thing it did was to liberalize the
general atmosphere.'[12]

Moving in completely different social circles, 'Stephen' felt much
the same. Looking back a decade after the majority of the Wolfenden
recommendations had finally passed into law, he was coolly realistic:
'I was, I think, aware of changing opinions – in the wake of the
Kinsey Report, for instance, or the Wolfenden proposals. But, there
again, I wonder if things have changed as much as people make out.
I shouldn't have thought the change in the law affected people's lives
much.'[13]

'Stephen' was, however, something of a special case. A high-ranking
civil servant, he was forty-seven years of age when the Wolfenden
Report was published and in a long-standing 'married' relationship
which had started just after the war. Thus he was, in effect, part of a
continuation of the cosy, pre-war and wartime coterie – the Beatons,
Cowards, Lehmanns, Burgesses and their like – for whom homosexuality had never been a problem. 'The advertisement columns of the
New Statesman were places that one looked at [for] rather carefully
coded advertisements – "Bachelor seeks another to share house", that

sort of thing,' he recalled. In his world one could easily have been forgiven for thinking that the war had never happened:

> There used to be drag parties which were often very grand, because these people usually had enormous flats and lots of money, and it was champagne and that sort of thing. The other thing, of course – a great mecca for the gay world – was Lady Malcolm's servants' ball at the Albert Hall every year. She was some very benevolent lady who believed in doing something for the servants; and so every year, at the Albert Hall, she organised this enormous servants' ball which I suppose several thousand people used to go to, dressed up. And that became a mecca for homosexuals who used to go in all sorts of extraordinary garbs. I went once or twice, I think, and I saw young men dressed in a tiger skin or all sorts.
>
> I was dressed rather respectably, as a matter of fact. I went in an Arab costume which I'd been given during the war, with flowing things and a cord round one's head. Lady Malcolm was horrified by it; and eventually the thing was brought to an end. The other event, of course, was the Chelsea Arts Ball which was a mixed affair, but again sort of largely patronised by the gay fraternity.
>
> Another great meeting place was the gallery at Sadler's Wells. There was the ballet, of course, but one used to go up there and one got in for a shilling and [stood] at the back. That was really quite some pick-up point.[14]

Joe Orton seems to have been equally sanguine, equally at home with the status quo. There is not a single reference to Wolfenden in his published diaries (which cover the period between December 1966 and August 1967). Nor, on the strength of them, did politics or the struggle for homosexual rights overly concern him. Rather, although their centrepiece is a tediously detailed account of the priapic excesses which Orton and his lover Kenneth Halliwell enjoyed during a spring holiday in Morocco, the diaries preserve and highlight images of the quotidian – but hardly mundane – reality of homosexual life as it was developing in the mid-1960s. They give a graphic account of the deterioration of Orton's relationship with Halliwell as well as vivid snapshots of more successful domestic set-ups:

Kenneth Williams said, 'Get Clive and Tom to introduce you to the Holloway set. There's this doctor – queer, but good-natured – and she's bought this house and stocked it with boys. They're all working lads. All from borstal. And she's allotted them their various tasks. One is responsible for the plumbing, another for the electricity. And so it goes on [. . .] There's even a boy responsible for the goldfish,' Kenneth said, more as an afterthought. 'And if any of them neglect their tasks she calls him into her surgery, wags her finger and says, "Now then, Dennis, you've neglected to feed the goldfish. What is your excuse?" And the lad might say, "Well, you see, I had the trade in and I forgot." "Forgot!" this queen will say, "Had the trade in and forgot? You've no right to have the trade until you've fed the fish." '15

Elsewhere, too, far away from the Holloway Road, an inward-looking, domesticated and virtually self-contained world was evolving – a world which seemed to have little need of legislation or would-be legislators. Rather younger than Orton, 'Sam' remembered it only through incidents that are as much a part of a young homosexual's life today as they were in the years immediately before decriminalization:

There was one boy who seemed quite happy to accompany me everywhere I went. I thought perhaps he was interested, and one day I managed to get my hand on his thigh. He knocked it off, but he never said anything.

We went back to the billet and the next thing I knew he and a mate of his came into my room. This boy was a boxer and his mate kept egging him on, and they took me outside.

'I should punch your fucking head in,' this guy says. So I said, 'Well, look; if you want to. You do it if it'll make you feel any better.'

So he hit me, but he must have 'pulled' it, because it didn't hurt me at all. I said, 'Feel better now?' but he couldn't say 'Yes'.

I met one quite nice young boy. I should think he'd [have been] in his early twenties, but he looked about eighteen. We went to bed together; we had sex, and a few days later – cor! It was fortunate for me that I had a friend who worked in the V.D. clinic, so I had quick, easy treatment.16

Eventually a General Election was called, and polling took place on Thursday 16 October 1964. Not entirely unexpectedly – for the last few days of the campaign opinion polls had shown a growing swing in their direction – Labour won. Their overall majority was only five, but they had put an end to 'thirteen years of Tory misrule' largely through the endlessly repeated promise of the new Prime Minister Harold Wilson to forge a new Britain in the white heat of technology.

It is doubtful, however, whether the fundamentally decent but over-ridingly pragmatic Wilson saw the legalization of homosexuality as any more a part of that new Britain than 'Richard', 'Stephen' or Joe Orton. There were far more pressing – and less obviously contentious – issues to be addressed. Without warning, however, there came a new demand for the implementation of the Wolfenden proposals. Up in the House of Lords the eighth Earl of Arran, a hereditary peer who took the Conservative Whip (but was later to cross the floor and join the then Liberal Party), suddenly declared his support for the cause.

'Boofy' Arran was a maverick on the red benches. He kept a pet badger which had the free run of his country house, and he contributed a regular gossip column to the London *Evening News* which, according to Antony Grey, he would compose in longhand, lying full-length on the floor of his office. He was not himself homosexual, he told his noble friends on 12 May 1965, but he had done his homework (under the surprised but delighted tutelage of the HLRS) and now felt 'that, in accepting the law on homosexual practices as it now stands, we are persecuting a minority and we are being unjust. And these things, I think, are unbecoming to our country.'

Startlingly, a number of other lords both temporal and spiritual thought so too, among them the Archbishop of Canterbury (then Michael Ramsey), the Archbishop of York, the Earl of Longford and Baroness Gaitskell, the widow of the former Labour leader. Between them, 'Boofy' and his fellow peers, together with a growing number of members of the House of Commons, worked relentlessly to have Arran's technical 'Moving for Papers' motion transformed into a Bill and then to get that Bill formally tabled.

Circumstances were against them. Not only was there, as we have seen, continuing indifference in large parts of the homosexual com-munity; the overall tone of parliamentary opinion remained stubbornly anti. But slowly a momentum built up. The Arran Bill (the *fons et*

origo, of course, of what was to become the 1967 Sexual Offences Act)
was presented to both houses of Parliament no less than three times.
In 1965 it actually proceeded as far as a vote in the House of Commons
but – 'the Noes have it, the Noes have it!' – was narrowly defeated.
Even the normally buoyant 'Boofy' Arran was beginning to wonder
what he had got himself into. Obscenities had been daubed on the
walls of his London club. 'Frankly,' he told the House of Lords, 'I
admit that many times I would gladly have been shot of the whole
wretched business. There is no fun in it, and sometimes one feels
desperate at some of the letters one receives. Most of my post is
anonymous nowadays, and such letters do not exactly encourage one
to continue.' (One such, opened by his secretary, was no more than
a parcel of human faeces. 'I threw it away, Lord Arran,' she gamely
announced; 'it wouldn't keep.')

There was a certain surrealism about the protracted proceedings as
the arguments dragged on in a world seemingly hermetically sealed
from reality. On the one hand Field Marshal Viscount Montgomery
of Alamein, no less (ironically, a man who was to be posthumously –
and controversially – 'outed'), was fulminating that to vote for the
Bill was to 'condone the Devil and all his works'. It would sap the
moral fibre of the youth of the nation, he said – 'And, Heaven knows!
it wants improving.' On the other there were men like 'Richard', who
had been having rampant sex for years, and Joe Orton. In a radio play
first broadcast as early as 1964, two years before he came to public
notice with his stage play *Loot*, the latter had matter-of-factly incorpor-
ated 'homosexual' rhythms into otherwise heterosexual situations. *The
Ruffian on the Stair* was quintessential 'kitchen-sink' drama, very much
of its time. Set in a London bed-sit, it opens at breakfast-time while
its protagonist, Mike, is shaving and his partner Joyce washing up:

JOYCE: Have you got an appointment today?
MIKE: Yes. I'm to be at King's Cross Station at eleven. I'm meeting
a man in the toilet.
He puts away his shaving materials.
JOYCE: You always go to such interesting places. Are you taking
the van?
MIKE *puts on a made-up bow tie.*
MIKE: No. It's still under repair.

JOYCE *takes the tray to the sink and puts the dishes into a bowl.*
She pours water on them.
JOYCE (*putting on a pair of rubber gloves*): Where did you go
yesterday?
MIKE: I went to Mickey Pierce's. I'd a message to deliver. I had
a chat with a man who travels in electrically operated massage
machines. He bought me a ham roll. It turns out he's on the
run.[17]

WILSON: . . . We were happy, though. [My brother and I] were
young. He was seventeen. I was twenty-three. You can't do
better for yourself than that, can you? (*He shrugs*) We were
bosom friends. I've never told anyone that before. I hope I
haven't shocked you.
MIKE: As close as that?
WILSON: We had separate beds – he was a stickler for convention,
but that's as far as it went. We spent every night in each
other's company. It was the reason we never got any work
done.
MIKE: There's no word in the Irish language for what you were
doing.'[18]

This juxtaposition of the ostensibly bizarre with the prosaic ('Have
you taken up transvestism? I'd no idea our marriage teetered on the
edge of fashion') was to be one of the trademarks of Orton's work –
but it only reflected the reality which, as a young homosexual man, he
saw in the world around him. His diaries are full of strange epiphanies,
although perhaps none is stranger than the long account of an orgy
which he encountered by chance in a north London public lavatory:

. . . A seventh man came in, but by now nobody cared. The number
of people in the place was so large that detection was quite impossible. And anyway, as soon became apparent when the seventh man
stuck his head down on a level with my fly, he wanted a cock in
his mouth too. For some moments nothing happened. Then an
eighth man, bearded and stocky, came in. He pushed the sixth man
roughly away from the fair-haired man and quickly sucked the
fair-haired man off. The man beside me had pulled my jeans down
over my buttocks and was trying to push his prick between my

legs. The fair-haired man, having been sucked off, hastily left the place. The bearded man came over and nudged away the seventh man from me and, opening wide my fly, began sucking me like a maniac. The labourer, getting very excited by my feeling his cock with both hands, suddenly glued his mouth to mine. *The little pissoir under the bridge had become the scene of a frenzied homosexual saturnalia. No more than two feet away the citizens of Holloway moved about their ordinary business.* I came, squirting come into the bearded man's mouth, and quickly pulled up my jeans.[19]

Everything was in a mess, as Grytpype-Thynne might have said. In essence, Orton's diary entry encapsulates the general situation in which homosexuals found themselves as 1966 became 1967 and the 'swinging Sixties' came of age. Just like the citizens of Holloway, the world got on with its own business – protests erupted on both sides of the Atlantic at the increasing level of American military involvement in Vietnam, the Beatles released *Sgt Pepper's Lonely Hearts Club Band*, the government was forced to sanction a devaluation of the pound – largely unaware of the 'frenzied homosexual saturnalia' which was taking place in its midst. Real life was upstaging the legislators. The Wolfenden proposals and successive versions of the Sexual Offences Bill, with their implicitly conservative assumption that decriminalized homosexuality would be predicated on adult, monogamous, hetero-sexual lines, seemed irrelevant at the dawning of the Age of Aquarius. (Thus far and no farther, the ever-circumspect Kenneth Williams seemed to be saying when, in 1977, he told a Campaign for Homo-sexual Equality group: 'The only movement to which I ever attached myself was the Albany Trust, because *its espoused aim was to change the law concerning cohabitation between consenting male adults.*' (my italics))

'Francis' was one of many homosexual men who found themselves caught between two cultures at around this time:

I got arrested in a gay sauna. It was run by some stupid queen who was pissed half the time – a club, you know. And some wretched policeman managed to join and spent a day observing. Then one Friday evening thirty of them came in. This undercover policeman opened the door to them and we were all arrested. I was charged with buggery and arraigned to appear at the Old Bailey, would you believe!

I didn't have any money at the time so I got Legal Aid. Five of us were there for seven days, costing the country hundreds of thousands of pounds, I'd have thought; an enormous sum of money.

After a week one case was dismissed. Another guy was found guilty of indecent behaviour or whatever – he was supposed to have been wanking somebody on the stairs – and the judge gave him a conditional discharge and ordered him to pay seventy-five pounds costs. That's what he thought of it!

Two people were found not guilty, and the jury couldn't agree in my case, even on a majority verdict. So they brought me up again – the sods! The original case had taken eleven months to get there. This time I went along and they asked for an adjournment because one of the witnesses had to go to his grandmother's funeral in Germany. So the judge said that, in view of the trivial nature of the offence and the cost to the Crown and all that, would the prosecution like to . . . So they went off and phoned the D.P.P. [Director of Public Prosecutions] and came back and said they would be offering no further evidence. So the judge said, In that case I shall enter a verdict of not guilty, and I stepped from the court a free man! It wasn't really very traumatic because I didn't feel guilty at all. I think the whole thing was just a nonsense. I was obviously *technically* guilty – but so what?[20]

Despite Lord Arran's forebodings and the implacable corps of opponents both inside and outside Parliament, the champions of law reform remained obdurate in their campaign to get the Sexual Offences Bill on to the statute book, or at least debated on the floor of the House of Commons. But, for session after session, government time was denied them. Any further progress depended on the chance that one of their number would be successful in the periodic ballot of MPs wishing to introduce Private Member's Bills. That chance came on 11 February 1966 when Humphrey Berkeley, a left-wing Conservative MP (who later joined the Labour Party), struck lucky and opted to introduce the Sexual Offences Bill. Supporters from all the major parties rallied round: Liberal leader Jo Grimond; Christopher Chataway and Nicholas Ridley from the Conservatives, Barbara Castle, Shirley Williams and Dick Taverne from the Labour Party. Up in the public gallery representatives of the Homosexual Law Reform Society could only hold their breath as the Commons began what was, unbelievably, their first 'full-dress' debate on the subject of homosexual law reform since 1962.

All the well-worn arguments on both sides were aired, albeit that this time the reformers' were cloaked in the subfusc of social concern. Acceptance of even the bare bones of what Wolfenden had recommended, they pleaded, was a matter of basic human rights. It would obviate the threat of blackmail which hung over every homosexual man and make it easier for him to ask for psychological or social 'treatment', should he so desire it. It would even open the way for measures designed to save small boys from what Leo Abse, MP, a leading advocate of reform, was to call 'the terrible fate of growing up homosexual'.

After five hours during which the authors of this cautious, a priori argument sought to present the utilitarian benefits of reform while down-playing (or consciously ignoring) the more sensational consequences, the House divided on whether to allow Berkeley's Bill to progress to a Second Reading. This time, the Speaker announced, the Ayes had it. One hundred and sixty-four MPs had voted in favour of the motion, 107 (96 of them Conservatives) had opposed it.

Almost unexpectedly – and more than ten years after the appointment of the Wolfenden Committee – the first and most forbidding hurdle on the path to decriminalization had been cleared. No one could quite believe it. 'It certainly surprised me,' Kenneth Williams noted in his diary. 'I would never have dreamed it would get by in a country like this. Certainly it will be enormously encouraging to the people who have worked so hard on the Albany Trust.'[21]

It was. All seemed set fair for campaigners there and in the HLRS. But their celebration were short-lived. Only a matter of days after the vote Downing Street announced that the Queen had approved Prime Minister Harold Wilson's request for a dissolution of Parliament. Westminster emptied as MPs hurried back to their constituencies to prepare for the 'snap' General Election which was to take place on 31 March. Near the bottom of a pile of unfinished business the Sexual Offences Bill languished, now abandoned and forgotten. In parliamentary terms it was 'lost'.

That was 'a blow', Antony Grey commented laconically. Others took the technical knock-out rather harder. It was as if all the effort had been in vain. 'I don't particularly remember the election – Wilson won, so that was good – I just remember the disappointment, the flatness,' one back-stage campaigner recalled. 'It was an unexpected turn of events, but it was still a tragedy. The general feeling was: would we *ever* get it?'

10 ⌒

'Doing Our Bit for the Boys'

LABOUR WON THE GENERAL ELECTION of March 1966 with an overall majority of ninety-seven seats. 'This is make-or-break year,' Harold Wilson had told party colleagues shortly before polling day; and, although the progress of a swiftly resurrected Sexual Offences Bill (now being piloted by Leo Abse) was hardly going to make or break his government, both he and they knew it was hardly going to cover them with glory either. Thus, in an atmosphere of public indifference or worse, they watched rather glumly as, once again, it received a First Reading. In his diary Richard Crossman, the new Leader of the House of Commons, noted:

> Frankly, it's an extremely unpleasant Bill and I myself don't like it. It may well be twenty years ahead of public opinion; certainly working-class people in the north jeer at their Members at the weekend and ask them why they're looking after the buggers at Westminster instead of looking after the unemployed at home. It has gone down very badly that the Labour Party should be associated with such a Bill.[1]

Similarly, in *her* diary Barbara Castle has left a record of how, again and again, the ultimate passage of the Bill was due to old-fashioned Fabian concepts of Duty and Fairness – or, not infrequently, to sheer providence: 'I asked Dick [Crossman] how the Sexual Offences Bill had got through [its First Reading] without a vote. He said that [the Conservative MP, James] Dance, leader of the opposition to it, had been so sozzled he had failed to rise at the right moment!'[2] There was also a certain amount of horse-trading around the Cabinet table – 'I appealed to Roy [Jenkins]: "Back me up." And, purely on *quid pro quo* grounds for my support of the Sexual Offences Bill, he did!'[3] – but there was certainly no general enthusiasm for it:

> At 3pm I said mildly I hoped I shouldn't be prevented from voting at 4pm on the Second Reading of the Sexual Offences Bill. This set George [Brown] off on a remarkable diatribe against homosexuality. As an Anglo-Catholic and Socialist, he thought society ought to have higher standards. As Eric Roll and officials argued with him good-naturedly, he got very passionate: 'This is how Rome came down. And I care deeply about it – in opposition to most of my Church. Don't think teenagers are able to evaluate your liberal ideas. You will have a totally disorganized, indecent and unpleasant society. You must have rules! We've gone too damned far on sex already. I don't regard any sex as pleasant. It's pretty undignified and I've always thought so.'[4]

Even in the face of this, Castle's support stayed commendably solid. In a similar fashion to many of her colleagues, she knew she was Doing the Right Thing, whatever the wider world thought: 'All-night sitting on the Sexual Offences Bill. It was a good job I stayed, tired as I was. At one stage we only carried the closure by three votes. Trailing through the lobby at 4am, I ran into [Labour MP] Lena Jeger who put her arms around me and said in a piercing voice, "Aren't we good, doing our bit for the boys!" '[5]

They were; the Bill was passed at around 5.50 a.m. on the morning of 4 July 1967. It finally received Royal Assent on 27 July 1967. Homosexual acts undertaken in private by two consenting men of twenty-one years of age or over were legalized. Abse, Castle, Jenkins and the other ninety-six Members of Parliament who had voted Aye in the Third Reading division (there were just fourteen votes against), along with such decorous 'activists' as Lord Arran, Antony Grey and Humphrey Berkeley had overturned five centuries or more of legal censure.

That should have been the end of matter. Home Secretary Roy Jenkins certainly thought so. The Bill had been an 'important and civilising measure', he announced. Everything had been neatly tidied up – even if that tidying-up process was in no way, as he put it, 'a vote of confidence or congratulation to homosexuality'.

Once again, though, it had been 'them up there' deciding what was best for 'the buggers at Westminster' and Lena Jeger's 'boys'; even legislation passed and an Act enacted were still nothing more than palliatives. Neither the Wolfenden Report nor the passing into law of the Sexual Offences Act *per se* actually changed anything. Nor, effectively, could they. They certainly didn't change attitudes overnight – society's or even the individual homosexual's. The disc jockey Dave Cash remembers his colleague Kenny Everett at this time: 'He was in a dichotomy first and foremost, because of his sexuality. That was always in evidence; it was always there from Day One. For the first couple of years, when we worked together on the [pirate radio] ships it was being suppressed, and so therefore he lived a dual life until he came out of the closet, which was not until well into the Seventies.' Another friend (actually his bank manager) also remembers this perhaps unexpected side to Everett's character. 'He often used to rant and rave about why God had made him like this. I said to him, Look, Kenny, you can't question what God did or his reasons for doing it. You know that as well as I do. He said, But why did he punish me like this, make me like this? Why can't I be normal?'[6]

We have already seen the extent of this self-loathing in the slightly earlier case of 'Nicholas'. We have seen, too, how there was a palpable if discreet and possibly only retrospectively voiced homosexual antagonism to the campaign for legalization. Now, from 1967 onwards, things began to get even more complicated. In large measure this was due to the fact that, while what was probably a majority of gay men – and the term 'gay' came into general British usage at around this time – were content to remain 'in the closet', a significant minority saw what they had been given as an inch, and began demanding a mile.

Thus in *Quest for Justice*, having minutely chronicled his and other people's fight to get (even a limited degree of) legalization on to the statute book, Antony Grey chose to entitle the chapter which described the immediate aftermath of the passing of the Bill 'Meanwhile, Back at the Ranch . . .'. Lest the implication was lost there, he also prefaced it with a comment from Leo Abse: 'Nothing fails like success.' Similarly, writing fifteen years after the passing of the 1967 Sexual Offences Act, Nigel Warner still found it necessary to highlight how *little* had actually been won:

Two examples of inconsistency in logic stand out particularly: on the male age of consent, having dismissed the 'seduction theory', the [Wolfenden] committee opted for 21 because to fix the lower age would lay young men 'open to attentions and pressures of an undesirable kind'. And yet, four paragraphs earlier, the committee had commented, 'there comes a time when a young man can properly be expected to "stand on his own feet" and we find it hard to believe that he needs to be protected from would-be seducers more carefully than a girl does', clearly implying that 16 was the appropriate age.[7]

'During the 1970s', Warner went on, 'the full implications of the discriminatory philosophy inherent in the 1967 Sexual Offences Act became apparent.' He cited specific instances of this: how the Act set the age of consent for homosexual men at twenty-one, while that for heterosexuals and lesbians was sixteen; how the provisions of the Act did not apply to members of the armed forces, merchant seamen or the residents of the Channel Islands and the Isle of Man; and, more legalistically, how the Act dogmatically stated:

> It is an offence for a man 'persistently to solicit or importune in a public place for an immoral purpose' (s.32 of the 1956 Sexual Offences Act). Homosexual behaviour is deemed an 'immoral purpose' by the law. While in theory s.32 can be applied to both homosexual and heterosexual soliciting, in practice it is applied almost exclusively to the former. It need take the form of no more than smiling at another man a couple of times.[8]

Ironically, 'gay liberation' had its roots in discontent with the very legislation which had tried to bring it about.

～

Or maybe it didn't; maybe it was in the death of Judy Garland in the last week of June 1969. Or, more specifically, her funeral on Friday 26 June. Or, even more specifically, the aftermath of that funeral.

Far more so than she ever was in Britain – at least until she became a staple part of the act of every metropolitan drag-act: quick costume changes for Monroe, Bassey and Garland-*fille* Liza Minnelli in her *Cabaret* schtik – Garland was even then an icon, an image and a role model for the gay scene in metropolitan New York. A weird amalgam of Miss Haversham, Bette Davis, Joan Crawford and Shirley MacLaine (on good nights there were also shades of Jayne Mansfield and Doris Day), even before she died, almost in spite of herself she had been adopted as a sort of materfamilias by New York's burgeoning gay community. Hence the headlines in the long hot summer of 1969:

THOUSANDS LINE UP TO VIEW
JUDY GARLAND'S BODY

Her fans said good-by [*sic*] to Judy Garland yesterday. They arrived before dawn . . .[9]

But that Friday funeral was only the start of a weekend of violence whose repercussions would spread around the world. East Coast newspapers covered it with something approaching bewilderment:

4 POLICEMEN HURT IN VILLAGE RAID
Melee Near Sheridan Square Follows Action at Bar

Hundreds of young gay men went on the rampage in Greenwich Village shortly after 3am yesterday after a force of plain clothes men raided a bar that the police said was well known for its homosexual clientele. Thirteen persons were arrested and four policemen were injured.

. . . Heavy police reinforcements cleared the Sheridan Square area of Greenwich Village again yesterday morning when large crowds of young men, angered by a police raid on an inn frequented by homosexuals, swept through the area.

Their arms linked, a row of helmeted policemen stretching the width of the street made several sweeps up and down Christopher Street between the Avenue of the Americas and Seventh Avenue South. The crowd retreated before them, but many groups fled into the numerous small side streets and reformed behind police lines.

. . . Sheridan Square this weekend looked like something from a William Burroughs novel as the sudden spectre of 'gay power' erected its brazen head and spat out a fairy tale the likes of which the area has never seen.

. . . She sat there with her legs crossed, the lashes of her mascara-coated eyes beating like the wings of a humming bird. She was angry. She was so upset she hadn't bothered to shave. A day old stubble was beginning to push through the pancake make up. *She was a he.*[10]

Rather too hastily, perhaps, later in 1969 the radical New York magazine *Village Voice* tried to sum up what had happened during three nights of near-rioting in the city:

The forces of faggotry, spurred by a Friday night raid on one of the city's largest, most popular and longest-lived gay bars, the Stonewall Inn, rallied Saturday night in an unprecedented protest against the raid and continued Sunday night to assert presence, possibility and pride until the early hours of Monday morning. 'I'm a faggot and proud of it', 'Gay Power!', 'I like boys!' – these and many other slogans were heard all three nights as the show of force by the city's finery met the force of the city's finest. The result was a kind of liberation, as the gay brigade emerged from the bars, back rooms and bedrooms of the Village and became street people.

Nothing quite like this happened in Britain – the Stonewall riots were too intensely *American* an experience, too closely tied to, or modelled on, the civil rights protests which had erupted across the country during the 1960s – but decorous echoes of this latest manifestation of American popular culture soon made themselves felt within Britain's own 'gay brigade'. In November 1970 London homosexuals became 'street people' when what was in all likelihood Britain's first gay rights march took place in the capital. November was hardly the marching season, but 150 men turned up to walk, not through Soho, say, or Westminster, but across Highbury Fields in north London. It was little more than gesture politics – if it was politics at all – and it was certainly not motivated by the pent-up anger which had fuelled the Stonewall riots. Indeed, the event had more effect on the marchers themselves than on the media or the general public. All the same, in retrospect it came to be seen as another defining moment, the time when a fresh infusion of steel entered the soul. 'You got this light going on in people's eyes,' one of the original marchers was to recall. 'It was almost as if you'd started a new religion.'

It was a heady, addictive feeling and soon marching rather than backstage lobbying became the favoured method of gay 'consciousness-raising'. Within two years of that almost-casual amble across Highbury Fields the first 'official' Gay Pride march was announced. Held on 1 July 1972 (the nearest Saturday to the third anniversary of the already fabled Stonewall riots), it attracted 2,000 men, began with a public rally in the West End of London and ended with a big party and picnic in Hyde Park.

This ostensibly unnatural conjunction of agitprop marching and self-satisfied partying set the tone for the next quarter of a century of homosexual lobbying. Banners always went with bands as year by year the numbers of those taking part in the march inexorably rose; to 120,000 in 1993 and to more than 150,000 in 1994. Old scores were forgotten – in 1983 the event was officially renamed 'Lesbian and Gay Pride' – and, as it became more overtly political, even the always vague intentions of the original marchers were subsumed into what by the early nineties had become a general, twenty-four-hour carnival of New Age living, hard-Left politics and 'hi-NRG' music, albeit one at which the authorities tacitly condoned men holding hands and same-sex kissing. Year after year, in the weeks following the event, the correspondence columns of the gay press ran letters praising the drag, disco and Australian soap-opera celebrities who made 'personal appearances' side by side with others deploring the presence on the march of proselytizing members of the Socialist Workers' Party.

In essence, this bifurcation only mirrored what had been going on all the time within the central echelons of the 'gay brigade'. Almost as soon as the 1967 Sexual Offences Bill passed into law a chivvying, impatient, far from complacent clique of guerrillas emerged, whose Marxist-inspired agenda was as confrontationalist as those of the HLRS and the Albany Trust had been 'reasonable' and emollient. The Campaign for Homosexual Equality (CHE, and no reticence about the allusion to the name of the recently executed Che Guevara) was an off-shoot of the less felicitously named North-Western Homosexual Law Reform Committee (NWHLRC) and the first to attract public notice. In Che Guevara's rhetoric, however, it was something of a paper tiger. It was more than a decade ahead of its time when it demanded (rather than requested) that, among other things, major breweries should underwrite its plans for a nationwide network of gay venues to be run by an excruciatingly pi enterprise called Esquire Clubs; it was not until the early 1980s that breweries came to recognize the power of the 'pink pound'.

Back at the Albany Trust, Antony Grey was appalled. The best part of a decade's work was, he thought, being insidiously undermined:

> ... the problems between the Albany Trust and CHE arose out of differences of perception concerning strategy and timing that gradually ballooned into mutual mistrust.
>
> [. . .] my close encounters with the irrational homophobia emanating from the opponents of law reform had convinced me that careful preparation, and not least a possibly protracted period of lobbying for broadly-based religious, political and social work support, was essential before [a viable, realistic social organisation] could be successfully established in this country.[11]

Worms can turn, however; and by the end of 1970 Grey himself had left the Albany Trust and made new friends in the recently founded Gay Liberation Front (GLF). This was far more radical, a direct copy of the post-Stonewall in-your-face gay protest which two left-wing British students had discovered in America. One of them, Aubrey Walter, recalls: 'I got involved in the local politics in New York. And it was there that I met Bob Mellors, another English guy who'd been going along with gay liberation in New York. Bob and I, yakking together, decided that we ought to do something when we got back to England, *try* to do something similar, set something up.'[12]

Their resolution held and, after they got home, the first British meeting of the GLF was convened − fatefully, perhaps, at the then ultra-radical London School of Economics, where Mellors was continuing his studies:

> We both spoke about our activities in the States and what was going on. We did talk about gay pride and the necessity of joining up to fight back [against] our oppression, etcetera. I think we were a little bit dictatorial in the way we spoke to people, like one always is when one's drunk on these things. But [everyone] agreed to go on and have a meeting the following week and the following week, and it all started from there.[13]

The GLF meetings certainly touched a nerve. 'I'd never before seen gatherings of gay people where there was this immense feeling of comradeship and interest and mutual warmth which was not solely, or even primarily, sexual,' Grey later recalled. Nineteen people had turned up for the first meeting, there were around sixty at the third; and right from the start there was a new *charge* in the air, something akin to the 'presence, possibility and pride' which *Village Voice* had discerned on the streets of Greenwich Village a couple of years previously: '[The GLF] created a new language, a new style, a new vocabulary for being gay. *It was about being contemporary, about being incredibly, outrageously, exquisitely radical* and of course – and most important of all – visible; celebrating being gay rather than living an endless existence codified as "something else".'[14] Nobody, least of all Walter and Mellors, knew where this newfound radicalism would lead. Nobody, it seems, actually set out to be revolutionary; but the new mood of exquisite radicalism inevitably took them in the direction of confrontational street politics. Within six months of the group's formation, the GLF's London magazine was reporting:

> Legal reform and education against prejudice, though possible and necessary, cannot be a permanent solution. While existing social structures remain, social prejudice and overt repression can always re-emerge [. . .] We should not confuse legal changes with real structural change. *Legality can always at some point be changed to illegality.*

> We are starting to work alongside women, black people, and now those sections of youth and the working class who see the importance of *our* demands as well as their own, to break the old society which puts us all down and to build a new one on the basis of all our needs.[15]

No gay orgies at the LSE then – no time, no time! Nor in the regional meetings of CHE, which the GLF increasingly and inevitably came to see as 'hilariously over-respectable and prissy':

> . . . someone who was gay came to see me and they said, 'Do you know there's a CHE here?' And I said, No, I didn't. So he said, 'I know the secretary, I'll get in touch with him and tell him to contact you.' He said they met twice a week. I said, 'Well, if you're

going, take me with you, because I don't want to go on my own.'
He said, 'Right, I'll ring the secretary and tell him [and he'll] pick
you up in the car,' and told me what his name was. He took me
into where they had got a room over a pub. We all went in the
bar first, which breaks the ice and the secretary introduces you all
round, to the convenor and everybody and they're all so nice.
When you get in the room they say, 'first of all let us welcome a
new member to the meeting.' From then on it's very nice. Of
course, they all come here to my house. I have an open night once
a month, and they all come here. I've got a bring-and-buy coming
up before I go to Benidorm. Then we have a raffle and, of course,
that's how we get a lot of our money. In the summer we get a
small minibus and go out to places for picnics, to places like Kew
Gardens, Hampton Court. And then we have discos. We hire the
hall and do all our own catering. About a hundred or so come from
all around. We get them from Hastings and Brighton and from the
Medway towns. We get them from as far as Tunbridge Wells.[16]

It was the same old story. While the activists got on with it, the
vast majority of gay men just got on with their lives:

I never got short of sex.
    I don't believe in regretting anything and on the whole I think
I welcomed [the legislation of homosexuality]. I wasn't very sympathetic to the GLF. They were too Left-wing and I'm not. I hate
Socialism. I hate any kind of state control. I'm a libertarian. So
GLF and I didn't see eye-to-eye.
    I did join CHE, but it was just too damned middle-class. You
couldn't get anyone interesting to join the group!
    I was a loner. I had my life to lead. And enjoy: there was no
time for that sort of crap![17]

＊

'Well,' said 'Richard', 'I was only a chorus boy, wasn't I? Pretty much
the oldest in the business by that time, too! *Life* – you know what I
mean – had never been very difficult for us. We'd always known
where to go, and who was who, who offered what; which bars, which
clubs . . .' He had always been, he implied, one of the lucky ones –
and as such well-placed to observe what was happening at around this

time: 'I suppose in the late sixties and early seventies things did get *easier*. Nothing much *changed*, but it was as if all the pressure had been taken off. And then suddenly there were papers and magazines – listings magazines I suppose you'd call them today. It all got easier . . .'[18]

Perhaps it even got too easy. Certainly it was not difficult to find men for whom the mere fact of their own homosexuality had ceased to have any importance at this time, so fully integrated had it already become in their day-to-day lives. 'Sam' was one for whom gayness in others as much as in himself had virtually become the norm: 'I applied for this job, supposedly a sales rep for encyclopaedias. I thought, I'll try that. Well, the young man who was to show me how it was done, *he* turned out to be gay.' It is misleading and too simplistic to say that it was simply 'fashionable' to be gay (or even experiment with gay sex) at around this time, but in London at least it did seem to be a part of the general psychedelia:

> I got friendly with two young lads in the Rainbow Corner Café – Shaftesbury Avenue it was, almost into Piccadilly Circus. It was a Forte place. It's something different now.
>
> I didn't know that these two lads were rent-boys. Then one of them saw someone and said, 'You went with him last night, didn't you? What was he like?' I was talking away to them, but it didn't strike me what they were saying at first.
>
> I said, 'Do you *sell yourselves* then?' 'Course we fucking do! Didn't you know that?' 'Are you gay, then?' 'Oh no! We're not gay.'[19]

> I was involved in all sorts of radical things, like the anti-Vietnam struggle, which was the largest struggle going on at that time – in the Sixties. I was living with my gay lover David for years, never hiding anything, and during that time the 1967 Act didn't even touch me. I wasn't really aware of it. I must have been living in a dream-world, or something.[20]

Fully to re-create the dream-world of the late sixties, early seventies we need to remember a time in which, largely without our knowing it, the old world was giving way to the new; the *Zeitgeist* changing. It was in 1968, for example, that theatre censorship was finally abolished and the Lord Chamberlain was relieved of a right – which had existed since Tudor times – to blue-pencil the script of every new play produced in England. (The 'tribal love rock musical' *Hair* announced the dawning of this new Age of Aquarius with a brief nude scene when it opened in London the day after abolition came into effect.)

And that was just the start. Year after year, the conjunctions become more and more marked. Thus, in the same year (1969) that the BBC dropped its cosy radio soap-opera *The Dales* (it had begun its life, more than twenty years previously, on the Light Programme as *Mrs Dale's Diary*) – a bare fortnight later indeed – Concorde made its first test flight. Propitiously, Thunderclap Newman also had a Number One hit with 'Something in the Air'. Two years later the closure of the decent but desperately old-fashioned *Daily Sketch* seemed to symbolize a final break with the cloth caps, Clement Attlee, Austerity and the anxiety of the fifties. It did: 1971 was also the year in which the self-proclaimed Angry Brigade blew up the home of Robert Carr, then Secretary of State for Employment, and brought terrorism to mainland Britain. It was the year, too, in which Slade, T Rex (formerly Tyrannosaurus Rex), their lead singer Marc Bolan and an epicene, drag-influenced 'glam rock' began to dominate the record charts.

Pace the angry fulminations of the GLF, the demands for MORE! and MORE NOW! (or at least tomorrow), the late 1960s and early 1970s *were* the beginning of homosexuality's brief golden age; the start of a fifteen-year Indian summer which began with legalization in 1967 and ended so abruptly in a welter of lurid antagonistic press reports about the first British AIDS death in the early 1980s. With Marc Bolan or Simon and Garfunkel ('Bridge Over Troubled Water', 1970) playing in the background, for the first time it was possible for men to meet up and talk about 'the gay community', since it really did seem to be developing. Away from the Agitprop hothouses of the London School of Economics and other far-left cells, 'ordinary' gay men were growing in confidence and – quite as importantly and just as the parliamentarians hoped it would – public opinion was also beginning to change, or at least to mellow. One GLF activist from this time has recalled the reactions when the campaign took its increasingly raucous protests on to the streets, only to find themselves preaching to the converted:

The amazing thing was that the public actually responded with humour. That was the crazy thing about it. Occasionally we got attacked – some people got really outraged and hit us with rolled-up newspapers and things like that, but mostly they stopped and stared. And then gradually the smiles came over their faces and they went away laughing to each other and shaking their heads. The whole thing was defused; it was like taking explosives out of a bomb, or something.

Perhaps the most graphic illustration of this new public broad-mindedness was the manner in which West End theatre audiences were prepared to accept the depiction of explicitly homosexual lifestyles (if not of explicitly homosexual acts) on stage. Little has been made of this before, but it is worthy of note that the first major production with an unmistakable gay theme was presented by the Royal Shakespeare Company as early as 1966, i.e. before either the 1967 legislation or the abolition of censorship.[21] (Significantly, too, the script was published as *Penguin Modern Playwrights: Volume One* to coincide with its opening.) Charles Dyer's *Staircase* was described by the author as 'the story of two middle-aged men' and is indeed a two-hander. It takes place in a barber's shop and as the curtain rises Charlie is shaving his partner Harry. Their opening exchange sets the predominantly – and perhaps predictably – bitch, 'queenly' tone:

> CHARLIE: Funny day, Sunday.
> (HARRY *mumbles through the hot towel*)
> Ought to get that gas man in. That gas man. Only asking for trouble.
> (HARRY *mumbles*)
> Oh lovely. Lovely. What! Each time you open the door the flame goes puff.
> HARRY: All nice and homely, dear.
> CHARLIE: Oh witty! Witty. Let's hope you're laughing when they find us stiff and carbonized or whatever happens.
> HARRY: Can you do that blackhead by my jawbone?
> CHARLIE: Oh you are an obscene bag. Where's your culture? Ssssh!
> HARRY: What?
> CHARLIE: There she goes! (*He moves to the staircase*)
> (HARRY *rises and follows. They listen like two little gnomes*)[22]

Three years later, in 1969 (and therefore *after* both legislation and the end of stage censorship), came Mart Crowley's *The Boys in the*

Band. Originally an Off-Broadway show, it is a lacerating real-time account of the tensions which exist in a group of eight young, professional gay New Yorkers who gather together to celebrate the thirty-second birthday of Harold, one of their number. One has brought along Cowboy ('twenty-two, light blond, muscle-bound, too pretty') as a present for Harold:

> EMORY (*indicates* COWBOY *to* HAROLD): *That's* your surprise.
> LARRY: Speaking of beasts.
> EMORY: From me to you, darlin'. How do you like it?
> HAROLD: Oh, I suppose he has an interesting face and body – but it turns me right off because he can't talk intelligently about art.
> EMORY: Yeah, ain't that a shame.
> HAROLD: I could never *love* anyone like that.
> EMORY: Never. *Who could?*
> HAROLD: *I* could and *you* could, that's who could! Oh, Mary, she's *gorgeous!*
> EMORY: She may be dumb, but she's all yours!
> HAROLD: In affairs of the heart, there are no rules! Where'd you ever find him?[23]

Coincidentally, an edition of the script of *The Boys in the Band* too was published while the show was running (Secker & Warburg, 1969). Not quite so coincidentally, Penguin picked it up and produced a paperback edition the following year. Retrospectively, the blurb on the back cover of this explains why – and how, in both commercial and sociological terms, it made perfect sense: 'To say *The Boys in the Band* is a play about homosexuals is wrong. It is a homosexual play, and as such is the first to accept homosexuality as an ordinary fact of life, and then go on to explore the hates, doubts and agonies of love between men.'

Despite this suggestion that the play is no more than a love story, it is difficult today to understand how, with the density of its Americanisms, its references to bath-houses and its she/he ambiguities, *The Boys in the Band* could have been anything other than in advance of conventional West End taste in 1969 – Noël Coward's final play *A Song at Twilight* had, after all, opened only three years previously. But that is to underestimate the extent to which curiosity about homosexuality and a concomitant fascination with 'gender issues' had permeated both the theatre and its audience by that time. They really did believe that, in the words of the urgent, front-line jacket note on a cheap, widely available paperback, homosexuality was 'an ordinary fact of life'. Thus in 1967 – the year which saw the murder of Joe Orton by his lover Kenneth Halliwell – the National Theatre had produced an all-male version of *As You Like It*, which was originally to be directed by John Dexter as a sort of 'magical release from material dominion'. According to one history of the National Theatre company, it was also specifically intended to be 'a production which would reflect the new mood of swinging London. [Dexter] brought in Donovan, the folk-singer, to write some songs. When eventually Clifford Williams took over from Dexter, Ronald Pickup, a Dexter choice for Rosalind, played the part looking surprisingly like Twiggy.'[24]

There were theatrical precedents for such a production, but none for two further incursions at around this time into what might once have been called taste and decency. Continuing its exploration of 'sexual ambiguity', in 1974 the National Theatre gave serious consideration to Dr Jonathan Miller's plan for another all-male production; this time it was to be of Wilde's *The Importance of Being Earnest*. ('I summed up [the meeting] by saying I hoped Jonathan would feel he did not need to do the play with an all-male cast – but that if he decided he must, I and everybody else would back his right to do so,' Peter Hall noted in his diary, bowing to the mood of the times.[25]) In the event, Miller's *Importance* never reached the stage – unlike an equally audacious production at the opposite end of the theatrical spectrum. There, plans for a whole *season* of gay theatre came to fruition in 1975 when the Almost Free Theatre, a fringe venue in the West End, staged the unequivocally titled *Homosexual Acts*. It did not matter that it was all part of 'a crusade' by the newly established Gay Sweatshop theatre company, which had been specifically set up 'to change the world' for gay men. Once again, audiences were undaunted and flocked to the various productions; attendances at the tiny Almost Free Theatre had topped 6,000 by the end of the season.

❦

Everyone seemed intent on doing their bit for 'the boys'. 'Richard' 's comment about there always being plenty of sex for men like him still held true – there was. But there was also more to it than that. Sex wasn't everything. Following legalization many more hitherto frightened gay men (we might think of the luckless 'Nicholas') plucked up the courage to visit pubs long known and even quasi-officially tolerated as the meeting-places of 'the likes of them'. In London there was, most famously, the Salisbury (which had featured in the 1961 film *The Victim*), but there were a dozen or so others too – the Royal Vauxhall Tavern, Bolton's and the Coleherne in Earls Court, the Marquis of Granby in Rathbone Place, the Queen's Head in Chelsea – all offering their own discreet welcomes to men in search of everything from drag/transvestite entertainment to rough trade and the (now fast-disappearing) company of guardsmen. In Manchester there was the Rembrandt, while similar establishments also quietly flourished in towns and cities including Oxford, Norwich, Liverpool, Plymouth and Brighton.

Binding all this together was a sense of communality which had little or nothing to do with the (increasingly political) solidarity of the Gay Liberation Front. Where their fathers (or uncles) had, like 'Nicholas' and E. M. Forster's Maurice Hall, gone through the best years of their lives believing they were unique, freakish beings, a new generation of men were learning within months that they were not alone. Suddenly, in the pages of *Gay News* magazine (found in 1972) they found stories about people like themselves, advertisements for pubs which actually wanted their custom, invitations to meetings and parties being thrown by like-minded souls. They had every reason to be 'Glad to Be Gay'. Although the slogan did not become current for another decade, it well expresses the mood of optimism with which they – and they were predominantly young and well educated – marched off to take up their places as students and undergraduates at Oxford and Cambridge, the red-brick universities and any number of the then proliferating 'glass-and-concrete' polytechnics:

I remember on my first day at — I was looking around at this group of two or three hundred freshers – looking at the men, of course! – and thinking, He's cute! or whatever we said at the time; He's nice!; Mmm! hunky! I wanted to have them all. I knew a lot wouldn't be gay. But I fancied my chances. I reckon I slept with about three or four men, other students, while I was at university.

One fairly regularly for a year or so. A lot of my friends were gay or bi-, but strangely it was only rarely with them. (One, who I kept in contact with, I didn't actually go to bed with until twenty years later, when we were both coming up to forty!)

This was – what? – 1972 until 1975 or 1976. You could get away with it then, before AIDS and everything. We didn't flaunt it though, or force it down people's throats, to coin a phrase; we just felt easy about ourselves, I guess.[26]

⟋

Two quite separate episodes, entirely unconnected in themselves, may serve to sum up the spirit of the 1970s which the last few pages have perforce explored only by snapshots and hasty bulletins from the front. Uniting all the various strands – the homosexual's growing feeling of self-confidence, the growing mood of public acceptance – they give a grassroots account of a society which, if not entirely at ease with itself, both internally and externally was fast coming to terms with one facet of its identity.

Thus, like the former student quoted above, even in Devon in the spring of 1973 undergraduates were feeling easy about themselves. Student Union Gay Societies (GaySocs) were springing up in Exeter every bit as quickly as they were in London, Manchester, Leeds, Brighton or any of the country's other more ostensibly cosmopolitan student nexi. The local newspaper in Exeter was predictably appalled – but only superficially so. It reported this latest manifestation of the spirit of the age with a bizarre mixture of old-fashioned abhorrence and up-to-the-minute broad-mindedness:

We learn that at the University, that seat of learning [. . .] a Gay Society was formed last term. It has, according to its vice-president, a membership of 10 and is still growing.

At St Luke's College, Exeter, another proud institution that has turned out many good teachers in the past, 'there is a movement towards gay rights' and at Exeter College there is 'a fair chance' of a gay society being formed in the future.

What is so nauseating about these disclosures is not that such a situation exists in Exeter [. . .] but that the students are so brazen about it. They want the world to know, apparently, about the activities and proclivities of some of their number [. . .] *We are not moralising here; everyone to his own choice, but . . .*[27]

Even more illustrative of how far things had come since 1967, of how the very homosexual whom the activists had sought to help (remember 'Nicholas') had become no more than the man in the street within a decade, is the story of the Gay Liberation Front and Pride in the 1970s. The ironies are rich, and nowhere richer than in the uncertain fortunes of the Pride march over that period.

The essential facts are clear enough. We have seen that in 1972 the march attracted around 2,000 people; the very next year a mere 300 turned up.

Many reasons can be advanced for this apparent fickleness, not least a failure of the always chaotic planning and administration of the event. But downright complacency probably has as much to do with it, for it was at around this time that a growing number of gay men who had been 'liberated', in many instances *in spite of themselves*, began finding less and less relevance in pressure groups and street politics.

We can picture them, these children of the revolution, almost as the mid-seventies precursors of the straight 'Yuppy' materialists of the eighties. They form a discrete group. Graduates now, and in their mid-twenties – the post-war baby-boomer who turned twenty-one and became a consenting adult the day the Sexual Offences Act came into effect would have been twenty-six in 1972 – their involvement with exquisite radicalism and the gaysocs of their university days is long behind them. For these beneficiaries of nearly two decades of 'action' are now salaried young professionals, affluent, aspirational – and fundamentally conservative. A cynic might say that they have grown up.

They have little in common with, little sympathy for, the GLF street-fighters and their battle against 'social prejudice and overt repression' because they do not themselves feel prejudiced against or unduly repressed. They have their bars – the Salisbury, the Marquis, the Coleherne – the listings in *Gay News* and comparative acceptance in a range of sympathetic professions if they choose to be open or 'out' about their proclivities. A lifestyle predicated not on solidarity with 'women, black people [. . .] youth and the working class' but on advertisements and features in the seductive 'Look!' pages of the *Sunday*

Times and the new colour supplements, on designer clothes and even the Californian 'pool culture' celebrated by David Hockney (the first London retrospective of whose work took place in 1970) was theirs for the asking.

Even before the first words are spoken, an American version of this 'mature' gay lifestyle – the full flowering of the 'dream-world' mentioned previously – is paraded in *The Boys in the Band*. The opening stage directions boil it down to its essentials and in effect present a self-contained cameo:

> *A smartly-appointed duplex apartment in the East Fifties, New York, consisting of a living-room and, on a higher level, a bedroom. Bossa nova music blasts from a phonograph.* MICHAEL, *wearing a robe, enters from the kitchen, carrying some liquor bottles. He crosses to set them on a bar, looks to see if the room is in order, moves towards the stairs to the bedroom level, doing a few improvised dance steps en route. In the bedroom, he crosses before a mirror, studies his hair – sighs. He picks up a comb and a hair-drier, goes to work.*
>
> *The downstairs front-door buzzer sounds. A beat.* MICHAEL *stops, listens, turns off the drier. More buzzing.* MICHAEL *quickly goes to the living-room, turns off the music, opens the door to reveal* DONALD*, dressed in khakis and a Lacoste shirt, carrying an airline zipper bag.*[28]

This is superficial – intentionally so – but indicative of something much deeper, a move towards an atavistic, comfortable monogamy which would not necessarily have offended the parliamentary champions of the 1967 reforms but which Pride and the promiscuous propagandizers of the GLF wholly failed to take into account.

'Does it sound smug if I say that I saw through the seventies and its morality before most people? I can't help that. I tired fairly early of people boasting about their open relationships, and then complaining when that same openness let everything they could have valued trickle away.'[29] So says the narrator of Adam Mars-Jones's later short story 'The Changes of Those Terrible Years'. But what were those things they could have valued? The smartly appointed New York duplex, the phonograph, the liquor bottles, the Lacoste shirt – or at least their British equivalents – and all the other appurtenances of style loomed large among them. As Kenneth Williams (born in 1926 but in gay terms a late-developer) was also discovering in 1972, they represented security, place, identity: 'As all my life is an act and a hollow sham, the concrete things like my belongings & my privacy & my books & things are *necessary* – they're the only reassurance I have.'[30]

With what must have been bewildering rapidity, Williams went through what amounted to the whole growing-up process of his spiritual coevals within the space of just four days while on holiday in Tangier. His diary charts this graphically Pauline conversion:

Thursday, 15 June
We went to the B. Hotel. In the bar we met Norbert (the owner) and three boys. I went off to one of the rooms with Mohammed (Bambi) heartened by Norbert's remark 'All my boys are clean & reliable – you know' and we rolled about amorously & it was all very silly and unfulfilled. The setting was all perfect but I couldn't have an ejaculation or anything [. . .]

Friday, 16 June
Up at about 9 o'c. and of course, found your actual parasite so had to go to the chemist for DDT powder and start *all that*! Then found the skin of the dick was slightly abrased! I thought I felt the teeth last night! Oh! these adventures always leave me disgusted and impaired.

Saturday, 17 June
I think that God did not intend me to have a sexual relationship of any kind, and that is why all these dire consequences occur whenever I defy his ruling.

Tuesday, 20 June
This time, when I get back to London, I really must do something positive about finding a place to live that is *me*. I really must start being selfish for a change and create the kind of surroundings which I really want, instead of living in conditions which give me no peace or aesthetic satisfaction.[31]

In this context it is not surprising that, as the 1970s wore on, the very 'sixties' preoccupations of the Gay Liberation Front seemed increasingly irrelevant. Once people in the street, ordinary passers-by had cheered them on their way (or at worst gone off 'laughing to each other and shaking their heads'). The activists had had reason to believe that a battle had been won, but hardly any time to celebrate. In 1975 no more than 200 people had been on the Pride march. Afterwards, there were suggestions that the whole GLF circus had outlived its usefulness, that it had more than done its bit; even that Pride '75 should be the last. It might have been better if it had been. It wasn't, however, and 1977 brought the final irony. Numbers had picked up – well over 1,000 lesbians and gay men took to the streets that year – but even the gay press noted rather ruefully that 'drinkers outside the world-famous gay pub The Coleherne in London's Earl's Court threw beer cans at [the] demonstrators for flaunting their sexuality'.[32]

11 ～

'I Am Perfectly Normal –
with One Slight Difference'

PROBABLY IRKED BY a television adaptation of Quentin Crisp's *The Naked Civil Servant*, an anonymous gay man was moved to write to the press in January 1976. Crisp's celebration of 'Camp' had 'set the "gay" world back by twenty years', he fumed:

Here we are, all doing our nuts, saying to the hets, 'Let us live our lives as we want to as normal [*sic*] as we can because as far as I am concerned, being 'gay' means that I am perfectly normal – with one slight difference. I prefer to love another man. I am not, and see no point in trying to ape, a female. There are a great deal like me. Our local pub has a good number of 'affairs' and, although in the 'Camp' life it would be boring, our lovers chat about food and clothes [while] the men [talk] about cars, television, etc – just as normal couples do. [This includes] noticing a nice young thing – just as Dad would fancy a young bit of skirt. I put this in to show how normal we really are.[1]

Grammar and punctuation frequently got the better of him, but he did have a point. For the majority of gay men – or at least those who acknowledged their gayness – the mid-seventies were, as we have begun to discover, a period of quietude, consolidation and even domesticity. There is little more than anecdotal evidence to go on (census returns and electoral rolls do not record the nature of the relationship enjoyed by adults sharing the same address), but it is fair to say that something approaching what one might call the Gay Suburban Dream was emerging. Even in 1970 there was an easy, normal mundaneness about many a gay relationship, a cosy domesticity which frequently

241

seemed to mimic a heterosexual marriage's – even if an inherent tension lurked beneath the surface:

> – I was watching you while you were shaving the morning you were going to Leeds. If you'd moved your eyes half an inch you'd have seen me in the mirror. I·was standing behind you studying your neck and my jowls.
> – I saw you.
> – Ah! Well, what did you think of all that, with our Reg, eh?
> – I thought it was creepy.
> – I wonder what your next will be like. Don't be afraid to bring him home, dear, will you? I do worry so.
> – There isn't going to be a next one. At least, not for some time.
> – Ho, reely? I think that's a good plan, h'abstinence makes the 'eart grow fonder.
> – I'm moving in with Reg.
> – I don't think he'll have you, dear, after your indiscretions and sauciness.
> – Yes he will.
> – You'll go running after him, will you? How demeaning!
> – Possibly. But it's better than having him run after me. I've been through that once, I couldn't face it again.
> – You love him then, your butcher's boy?
> – Actually, he's not a butcher's boy, in point of fact. His father teaches maths at the university. His mother's a social worker. They live in an ugly Edwardian house . . .[2]

While newspapers were dominated by accounts of the prosecution of the British publishers of Hubert Selby Jr's *Last Exit to Brooklyn*, an American novel containing several graphic descriptions of homosexual sex, 'serious' novelists were beginning to explore this morally ambiguous Xanadu.[3] Christopher Isherwood, born in 1904 and the archetypal Englishman abroad by this time, had already done it in his present-tense novel *A Single Man* (1964) by placing George, a 'mid-fiftyish' English academic, quite literally at sea in a homo-erotic, Hockneyesque California.

It is a deceptively simple book, the limpidity of its style perversely almost obscuring the profundity of what it is trying to say. A persistent sense of normality runs through it, however, even in its more melodramatic moments. One such: on impulse, after an evening of heavy drinking, George and one of his students, Kenny, strip off their clothes and dive naked into the Pacific for a midnight bathe:

And now Kenny is dragging him out, groggy-legged. Kenny's hands are under George's armpits and he is laughing and saying like a Nanny, 'That's enough for now!' And George, still water-drunk, gasps, 'I'm all right,' and wants to go straight back into the water. But Kenny says, 'Well, *I'm* not – I'm cold,' and Nanny-like he towels George, with his own shirt, not George's, until George stops him because his back is sore. The Nanny-relationship is so convincing, at this moment, that George feels he could curl up and fall immediately asleep right here, shrunk to child-size within the safety of Kenny's bigness. Kenny's body seems to have grown gigantic since they left the water. Everything about him is larger than life; the white teeth of his grin, the wide dripping shoulders, the tall slim torso with its heavy-hung sex, and the long legs, now beginning to shiver.

'Can we go back to your place, Sir?' he asks.

'Sure. Where else?'

'Where else?' Kenny repeats, seeming to find this very amusing. He picks up his clothes and turns, still naked, toward the highway and the lights.

'Are you crazy?' George shouts after him.

'What's the matter?' Kenny looks back, grinning.

'You're going to walk home like that? Are you crazy? They'd call the cops!'

Kenny shrugs his shoulders good-humouredly. 'Nobody would have seen us. We're invisible – didn't you know?'[4]

It is also so simple, so automatic, so matter-of-fact, so *mundane*. So, too, is the life of Dick Thompson, the writer-hero of Francis King's laceratingly candid novel *A Domestic Animal* (1970). Again, the book is 'middle-class' – this time an exploration of the destructive power of the (unrequited) love which Thompson feels for the straight, young Italian philosopher he takes in as a lodger. Again, too, its power comes from the sheer amount of 'corroborative detail'. Thompson's infatuation – and his homosexuality – is just another aspect of a messy life dominated by the imperatives of taking the dog for a walk, getting the builders out, and knocking up a quick spaghetti bolognese when neighbours arrive unexpectedly for supper:

> Until the night of my house-warming party, several days later, 'love' was never a word either of us used to describe my devotion to him. 'You care too much for me,' he would say; or 'you should not feel this way about me'; or 'I cannot return the kind of friendship you have for me.' In turn I would use similar euphemisms – 'the affection I have for you', 'I've never felt like this for any man before', 'this absurd attachment'. I think that both of us sensed subconsciously that if that monosyllable 'love' passed between us then this curious relationship, still fluid between us because it was never defined, would come to a crisis; and that crisis, oddly, was what he as much as I wished to avoid.[5]

～

By 1970, too, real people were living similarly 'ordinary' lives – just as they always had, only more so:

> At school I was very friendly with a chap called —— ——. He wasn't particularly attractive, but we were very close and once, during the holidays, I was staying with him and he said, Have you ever masturbated? And I said, Well, no, not really. What do you mean? I was suddenly interested and wanted him to pursue this subject further! He described everything in detail and I said, Well, show me! He said he wasn't going to show me 'out front', but underneath his duvet he started fondling himself and described what he was doing. In the end we were doing it together next to each other under the duvet, although we didn't show each other what we were doing.
>
> And then later we used to have competitions – we used to support our towels on our cocks when they were rigid, and the person who could keep it up the longest would win. We actually got quite good at this, but he always seemed to win; he had a slightly bigger cock than me and awesome staying-power.
>
> And then I invented forfeits. Some of them were completely unsexual, but many of them involved having to snog each other. If I lost I'd have to snog him. I used to pretend to protest at this – but then went ahead and did it! He'd say, Well, you don't have

to, you know. And I'd insist and say, Fair's fair, I have lost; we agreed. And we'd have long snogs.[6]

For the teenager coming on 'the scene' at any time from the beginning of the 1970s until the mid-eighties life presented a seemingly endless range of opportunities. The living was easy. Gay businesses were opening up – gay travel agents, gay plumbers and gay builders were among the first. There were gay lawyers, gay doctors, gay accountants and gay dentists. There were gay films if one knew where to find them (*Nighthawks*, the story of a gay secondary school teacher, *Pink Narcissus*, David Hockney's *A Bigger Splash*, Derek Jarman's *Sebastiane*), and pulp gay novels by David Rees (*The Milkman's on His Way*) and other writers, together with *Gay News* and a top-shelf range of mostly American magazines in 'specialist bookshops'. Most obviously, there was an ever-growing number of gay pubs, clubs and sauna-bars, where anything could happen:

Wednesday, 1st September 1982
Frustrated and depressed. Went into town on the last of my money, recklessly aware I wouldn't have enough to get home.

What a marvellous evening it turned out to be!

After chatting to several people I knew to try and cheer up – including one of the [pub] staff who bought me a drink – I spoke to Ashley to see if he could help. After an unsuccessful attempt to fix me up with a 19-year-old, he finally introduced me to 20-year-old Robert.

He was quite beautiful, with short, wiry black hair and blue eyes. He listened to my problems and cheered me up. I had no money, but without too much trouble succeeded in getting an invitation to stay the night with him.[7]

I was at a party in a nightclub one night and this man I slightly knew came up to me and said, Are you rich? I said, No; and he said, If I was to pay you five hundred pounds would you masturbate me? I said I'd probably do it for free![8]

In the years before AIDS was heard of there was a certain innocence abroad. Everything seemed possible. 'Time and the younger generation are on our side,' Ian Harvey averred in *Gay News* in 1976. Even if the forces of law and order did occasionally intervene – in 1977 *Gay*

News and its editor Denis Lemon were found guilty of blasphemous libel for publishing a poem by James Kirkup describing the homosexual fantasies of a centurion guarding the crucified body of Jesus Christ – nothing seemed capable of stopping the revolution, of halting a 'subversive gay potential'.

In the mid- and late seventies there was a lot of this sort of rhetoric around, not least in the columns of *Gay News*. Its protestations that to be gay was *ipso facto* to be political, its exhortations to gay men to 'empower' themselves and seize the moment were very much of their day. Even now they have a period charm, and are vividly redolent of a time when Britain was convulsed by sometimes violent change – the years when the surprise resignation of Harold Wilson (and the inevitable departure of Liberal leader Jeremy Thorpe after allegations that he had conspired to murder a former male model), the Sex Pistols' takeover of an early evening television programme and the Anti-Nazi League's sometimes violent clashes with National Front supporters were played out to a soundtrack of punk rock:

. . . My sexuality is socially important. It takes no account of gender roles. It is not justified because of its reproductive possibilities. It can give a powerful support to the women's movement. It can show the way to newer and more joyful sexual behaviour for all human beings.[9]

. . . Gay pornography [. . .] is by and large a positive fulfilment that counteracts the nightmarish fears of our adolescent years and, as such, is politically progressive.[10]

. . . freed from the confines of a barbaric law, man would turn irrevocably from woman to the superior attraction of homosexuality with the whole country brought to its birthless end as an orgy of gay sex.[11]

. . . Live your life openly as being gay. Let other people see you are an ordinary guy and that you and your boyfriend can be and are as happy with one another as your straight friends and colleagues are with their husbands or wives.[12]

. . . I keep my treasure in my arse, but then my arse is open to everyone.[13]

. . . gay people don't need any improvement; they're so complete, so intact, so well-developed.[14]

These were, of course, minority views; even at the height of the publicity generated by the blasphemy trial *Gay News* never sold more than about 22,000 copies and, as we have already seen, the final years of the 1970s marked the low point in popular support for Pride. In the sheer earthiness of their imagery, however, the fragments quoted above (and chosen almost at random) convey something of the frantic venery and erotic *potential* implicit even in the humdrum minutiae of the relationships we have thus far examined. 'I was watching you while you were shaving' . . . 'and, Nanny-like, he towels George, with his own shirt, not George's' . . . even the fastidious Dick Thompson is reduced to snuffling in the wardrobe of his unreciprocating lodger in a desperate attempt to *have* and hold the un-havable.

Significantly, however, the reminiscences and diaries of those directly involved with 'the scene' at this time – with what we would now call the 'sex industry' – reflect little of this gleeful urgency. Rather, the overall tone is matter-of-fact, necessarily 'liberated' but hardly nostalgic for a golden era of arse and orgy:

I tried various jobs, but couldn't stand any of them. I couldn't find anything I could bear to do. Then [in the mid-seventies] I went along to see some lad – I expect he was a whore – a masseur, who advertised in *Gay News*. He didn't turn me on in the least; but he gave me a wank and he told me he'd taken this massage course which enabled him to advertise his services. So I thought that would be interesting because I live mainly in my head, and it might add something to the physical side of my life, which was then a bit deficient.

So I went along and took the course: six lessons for thirty quid. I had to do my final examination on a woman! She was wearing a bra and, never having unhooked one in my life, I hadn't the faintest idea what to do.

I soon found out that massage meant you were really supplying sex – a quarter of an hour on the front, a quarter of an hour on the back. In those days I seriously enjoyed doing the massage. The physical touch was good for me. But with half the clients – or more – you'd get away with five minutes of massage and then they'd start touching your cock or something, making it quite plain that the massage was just the excuse as far as they were concerned.

It was no problem – basically, I'd have sex with anyone who asked me. I could never see the point in saying no. It was 'massage and relief' in those days. So English! Not pleasure, *relief*!

I found I was really a social worker. Men would tell me things they would never tell anyone else – perhaps they had no one else to tell. Quite a lot of them were married, of course – I was a shoulder. In well over fifty per cent of the men who came to see me, the sex was the excuse and not the reason. They were seeking gay company, perhaps a gay touch, but sex . . .

Very few were 'out'; there were so few out gay men in those days. They were nearly all 'closet-jobs'. The youngest I saw was seventeen, which got me a bit paranoid. I think I charged him a quid or something. The commonest were men in their fifties. I didn't make a fortune, but I made a living. I got so bored, though! It got so tedious!^[15]

[1983]
Having eventually arrived after a long train ride – made lighter by the commentary of the Indian driver who crowned his act, to the uproar of the passengers, with 'This is London, and the weather outside is very, very nice' – went for coffee, then on to the basic and somewhat untidy office [. . .] at the top of a very *unsuspicious* building. Then we got started.

—, a middle-aged, slender man with thinning hair but a humorous, kind disposition (chicken-chaser?) proceeded to take snaps of me getting undressed. I then had to lie on a most uncomfortable wooden bench and hold rather uncomfortable positions as I thrust my buttocks towards his lens and tried desperately to put some life into my penis, which seemed to take umbrage at being ordered to 'get really stiff!' — tried 'fluffing' me, to little avail. Things only got better when he left the room for something. While he was gone the old willy – to use his affectionate reference to my unco-operative appendage – began to take interest. Three rolls of film later – time passed very quickly between three and five – we emerged from the studio, a back room full of an enormous piece of orange paper (the background) and lights hanging from the ceiling, and did the

necessary deeds regarding my fee of £50. We were looked upon
with blatant disinterest, and I left feeling just a little bit like used
toilet paper; very useful at the time but, once used, flushed away
as quickly as possible.[16]

'To me, of course my gayness is very important, twenty-four hours
a day, seven days a week,' Jeffrey Weeks had told *Gay News* in 1976.
And of course it was; but it seems fair to conclude that he was speaking
of a homosexual *sensibility* rather than the sort of priapic absorption
with which his fellow-contributors were concerned. 'Richard' the
masseur notes how few gay men were 'out' at this period (and indeed
how many of his clients were married). Then, as now, what he calls
the 'closet-job' was far from being an isolated – or necessarily pitiable
– individual. Isherwood's George was one; Francis King's Dick
Thompson another. Close friends would have known about them and
their 'little secret', but no one else. They were not overtly camp,
would never have been seen on a Pride march, and to anyone other
than intimate friends seemed perfectly 'normal' – as of course they
were: 'Michael Hart had never married; certainly he had never slept
with a woman and possibly he had never slept with a man. I had
always thought of him as a homosexual eunuch; but the homosexuality,
like the death he knew to be imminent, he always kept from a friend
as old, as intimate and as understanding as myself.'[17]

The generality of the gay experience lay somewhere between the
two extremes, between the endless 'orgy of gay sex' and the stubborn
outward denial of the 'homosexual eunuch'. There was a midpoint
between the primal desire for arse and the no-less-visceral fear of the
legal consequences of going too far, at which, more or less happily,
it was possible to exist twenty-four hours a day, seven days a week as
a sentient homosexual. Rather in advance of the times in this, as in
everything else, Joe Orton had arrived at this stasis a full decade earlier.
As early as 1967, moping around the north London flat he shared with
his lover Kenneth Halliwell (who was to batter him to death in a
frenzy of sexual and professional jealousy less than three weeks later),
he described in his diary a day on which his gayness was just another
element in his (literally) global consciousness:

Tuesday, 25 July
Grey day. Nothing much happened. Detroit is torn by rape and

rapine. There is an empty church around the corner from Noel
Road which was burned to the ground last night. Loot and the sack
of empires is in the air. DETROIT BURNING! was one headline.
Science fictionville. [Television producer Peter] Willes rang to say
that the ITA would allow [his play *Entertaining Mr] Sloane* to be
performed on telly. 'I feel it's dated!' Willes said. I rang Clive at
five o'clock. Talked for a bit. He's the young man I was introduced
to by K[enneth] Williams. Spoke about Morocco. He was off-
putting about having dinner. Came to the real point of the telephone
call: 'How about me coming up to your place about five tomorrow
for a cup of tea?' He went strange. 'I've got to go to the doctor's
tomorrow. It's awkward, see.' 'I'll ring you sometime then,' I said,
putting the phone down. 'Another one crossed off the list,' I said
to Kenneth H. Kenneth shrugged. 'I don't know why you bothered
ringing.' 'Well,' I said, 'I wouldn't've minded fucking him. He had
a nice body. But if sex is out, he can get stuffed. I'm not interested
in him for any other reason'.[18]

~

Throughout an extraordinary military and diplomatic career, 'Neil'
elegantly personified the homosexual's compromise between private
life and public self, between the rampant Freudian Id and what was
in his case a necessarily and particularly censorious Ego/Superego.

Obviously, there was no way any of us could be openly gay in the
forces, [he says] it would have been a total disaster. Homophobia,
jokes about 'nancy-boys' and aggression were part of the atmosphere. You had to be so bloody careful! It was a bit like being a
member of the Resistance in occupied France – you were leading
a secret, hidden life; you were engaged in activities which could
bring about your downfall. You were living in continuous danger;
your alarm system was continually primed.

Despite – or maybe precisely because of – being forced to lead this
double life, 'Neil' was able to achieve high security clearance. One
confidential reference written by a very senior military officer stressed
that his work 'was of great importance in an allied command in
Europe'. Another called him 'a loyal, extremely capable and intelligent
individual who could put his hand successfully to a wide variety of

tasks'.[19] Although quietly subversive – 'In the military, every gay orgasm was a salvo fired for freedom' – he was posted to a sensitive NATO capital at the height of the Cold War, where he was able to integrate his private and public personae to a degree unmatched at the time even by many civilians:

The British ambassador in —, no less, asked the Air Ministry to appoint me to his staff as Assistant Air Attaché with full diplomatic status, and this was done.

Among the diplomats and military officers from various countries who were serving in —, there were some gays. I formed friendships which led to sex with some of them. But I ceased to do this when I met an American called Martin, a lieutenant commander in the US navy.

In those days accommodation in — was extremely expensive, so it was quite usual for officers to share a house to save money. But what made our relationship unique was that Martin was American and I was English. We shared a house for getting on for three years, I suppose. It was absolutely ideal; we fucked each other from the start, we had the same sense of humour and the same outlook on life. Martin had even lived in London and knew all kinds of stage and screen stars. (On one occasion when I was in London on leave, he arranged for me to meet Hermione Gingold for lunch. I'd never had a meal with a star before, so I was rather intimidated. I met her at an expensive restaurant, where she made a sensational entrance – furs, jewels, a hat and God knows what! Everybody was looking, I stood up and she swept towards me and said, 'You must be Martin's boyfriend!' There were lots of glances cast in my direction, but I realized that they were of envy and not of anything else at all.)

It was a thorough-going love affair, Martin's and mine; the biggest love affair of my life, really, and the happiest period of my life too.

Martin and I were recognized as a pair. We were invited out to parties several times a week – *as a pair*. Martin loved giving parties, so we did quite a lot of entertaining too. One of our parties was a big costume 'do' at which all the guests – ministers, attachés, *everyone!* – had to come dressed as a Great Sinner of history or fiction. I was Satan, stripped to the waist, with diabolical make-up and a cloven hoof; Martin was Mr Hyde, with intermittent moments of Dr Jekyll.

I really don't know how many people guessed that Martin and I were gay. Obviously the other gays in the diplomatic community did, because we knew about them – we had separate, purely gay, parties too. Among the rest, I think some people may have been suspicious, but I don't know. Certainly, some people never suspected a thing.

There was one party we gave at which both the British and American ambassadors were present. The British ambassador made a short speech saying how pleased he and the American ambassador were – in view of the 'special relationship' between Britain and the United States – to see a British and an American officer living together. All the people who were in the know cast their eyes down, rather furtively; Martin and I kept straight faces. Nobody – thank God! – cheered or applauded. But it was clear that he just didn't know what he'd said.[20]

～

To the public at large 'Thatcherism' did not so much evolve as spring fully formed upon Britain after the Conservatives won the General Election of 1979. In fact it had been conceived several years earlier and undergone a prolonged gestation in a behind-the-scenes huddle of 'think-tanks' and policy studies institutes. Moreover, it was only the purest irony which led to its apparently immaculate parturition exactly coinciding with the glorious efflorescence of what we now look back on (through the *trompe l'oeil* perspective of less than two decades) as the Golden Age of the British homosexual.

It was, however, a conclusion devoutly to be wished for, even – irony or ironies – a marriage made in heaven. Never really more than a pale derivative of its West Coast American archetype (the pattern-books of which, Armistead Maupin's *Tales of the City* and *More Tales of the City*, were respectively published in Britain in 1978 and 1980), the gay scene by the end of the 1970s was, as we have seen, essentially commercial in nature. Despite polemical calls to arms in *Gay News* and other organs of the radical Left, the era was not characterized by San Francisco-style 'street culture'; back-rooms and, still less, bath-houses were never really significant elements. Rather, the British 'Golden Age' was one of ostentatious consumerism. If they were in work (and living in or within reach of a major town or city), in 1980 and 1981 and 1982 single gay men and an increasing number of long-term gay couples prospered as much as their Yuppy or Dinky ('double income, no kids yet') straight equivalents in their very own Thatcherite version of the world of *The Boys in the Band*. This was the era of boom and buoyant property prices − of well-paid 'service industry' jobs in estate agency, retailing, the music business; of holidays in Sitges or Playa del Inglés arranged by the gay tour company Uranian Travel; of 'tasteful' flats furnished from Peter Jones and the Habitat catalogue. Style was all; details were important. In *Coming Clean*, an award-winning play first produced in 1982, the gay central character condemns another gay man purely by reference to his living room:

> . . . More money than sense. His flat's horrendous. An emetic com-
> bination of Salvador Dali and the Ideal Home Exhibition. Gallons
> of dark-blue paint everywhere, with hundreds of mirrors, and glass-
> topped tables, and concealed lighting. He was so proud of his
> dimmer-switch. Kept re-adjusting it to get the mood just right. I
> nearly said, the only thing that'd improve this room'd be a power
> cut.[21]

Above all, this was the era when burgeoning self-confidence ineradicably replaced the simpering Julian-and-Sandy stereotype of the gay man with the tougher, more masculine figure of 'the clone'. Owing something to the Action Man dolls of his childhood, but rather more to America and the blue-eyed Marlboro Man masculinity of Steve McQueen and the Paul Newman of *The Hustler* and *Cool Hand Luke*, the clone arrived in Britain at around the same time as Margaret Thatcher arrived in Downing Street − when an American group called the Village People appeared on *Top of the Pops* singing their song 'YMCA'. 'There's a cowboy who wears chaps and smiles a lot; a construction worker in hardhat and mirrored sunglasses; a black motorcycle cop; a black G.I., who looks like a Vietnam Vet − kind of hard-bitten − in fatigues; and a biker in black leather with the peaked cap, the chains and the eagle badges . . .'[22]

Described by the poet Adam Johnson as a 'stylish thug', the clone marked out the territory, soon claiming bars, clubs and the very pavements of Earl's Court in London and the developing 'Village' in

Manchester as his own. For him the whole of Thatcher's Britain became a giant YMCA: 'It's fun to stay at the YMCA,' sang the Village People, 'They have everything there for young men to enjoy . . .' Throughout the early eighties his was the kingdom, the power and the glory. 'His rise was irresistible,' Freddie Mercury and Tim Rice were to write in their song 'The Golden Boy'; and they could well have had the early eighties clone in mind:

His road in life was clearly drawn, he didn't hesitate
He played, they saw, he conquered as the master of his fate.

There was an overt sexuality about the clone which was at once uniform – the tight T-shirt or vest; the button-fly Levi 501 jeans; the cropped hair and clipped moustache – and individual. His Clone Zone shops (a chain established in 1981) stocked all the costumes as well as a range of props – variously coloured handkerchiefs, fetish gear, American magazines, specialist reading matter, bottles of 'poppers' (Amyl and Butyl Nitrate stimulants), a connoisseur range of condoms – which, for those in the know, differentiated and deliciously delineated the pleasures in store.

For 'Georgie' and his friends in Eire, Thatcher's lean, macho Britain and the clone's lean, macho torso were almost too good to be true. 'If it isn't hurting, it isn't working'; 'Bop 'til you drop!' – the message was just the same:

I went to London to check it out, couldn't believe how good it felt, a real sense of freedom. I quit my job and room and headed for the smoke.

What can I say? I arrived in London and here it all was. The Scene [. . .]

All our lives seemed to start over. We made a stack of friends, good friends. It was a wonderful thing, the scene at that time. You felt free and understood, and very strong. I really got on good terms with myself. Sex was part of that; it gave me confidence. Everybody I knew, gay and straight alike, seemed to be well into sex. If you got caught out, got a dose or some 'visitors', a trip to the clinic or chemist was sufficient remedy, and the severest consequence was a week or two off the booze.

Really, that party kept running – '78, '79, '80, '81, '82, '83.[23]

1983 looked set to be the apogee, the golden year. Margaret Thatcher and the Conservatives won a second term in office that year with promises of more, and more of the same. The party just kept running. The American writer Edmund White published *A Boy's Own Story*, a sensitive (if rather sentimental) novel which the gay community immediately took up as a sort of contemporary *Catcher in the Rye*. The Village People were long forgotten (although 'YMCA' was still on the play-list in every decent disco-bar), but by then the equally egregious Boy George was riding high in the charts with his song 'Karma Chameleon' . . .

Within less than half a decade 1983 had acquired mythic status – but only because – as Alan Hollinghurst recognized when he chose to set his 1988 novel *The Swimming Pool Library* in that *annus mirabilis* – parties, by their very nature, cannot run for ever. Had they but eyes to see, all the revellers should have noticed, like Hollinghurst's hero William Beckwith, that midnight was fast approaching: 'My life was in a strange way that summer, the last summer of its kind there was ever to be. I was riding high on sex and self-esteem – it was my time, my *belle époque* – but all the while with a faint flicker of calamity, like flames around a photograph, something seen out of the corner of the eye.'[24]

At first the portents of doom were scarcely noticeable, hardly more than flickers indeed. 'Brad' – who, ten years on, freely admits that the continuing threat of AIDS has not prevented him from leading 'an active sex-life in London, Los Angeles, Sydney, Paris and Amsterdam' – was at boarding-school at this time:

> As far as I was concerned, it was just another news story then. We'd have all the newspapers in the Day Room and they'd be filled with accounts of how 'queers' – that's how we referred to them – were dying because they'd been having sex with monkeys or something; monkeys or South African airline pilots, I seem to remember. Ironically, at the time I found it all quite funny.[25]

'Then in '84 I started noticing articles in the press about this new disease hitting gay men in America,' 'Georgie' remembers. Although it was banned from the BBC's play-list because of its homosexual overtones, Frankie Goes to Hollywood had a Number One hit with their notorious single 'Relax' in 1984, but it was becoming increasingly difficult to do so. Paul Cons has recalled a new climate which was overtaking the club scene, in Manchester as everywhere else: 'In the late eighties there [was] a major depression on the gay scene through AIDS and through what had happened to the sort of people who were partying in the early eighties; the decimation that had occurred. That put a major downer on the whole gay clubbing experience for a number of years.'[26] The flames were beginning to take hold. Fewer and fewer men were singing along with Tom Robinson that they were glad to be gay. In 1984 it was established that the HIV virus (then still known as HTLV–III) *did* cause AIDS; by then thirty cases had already been diagnosed . . . 'If I sneezed or coughed I'd often make a quip about AIDS and laugh it off. I never thought about it in any detail and none of my friends talked about it with me until I became ill. That was in '85.'[27]

'Georgie' 's experience echoed in miniature those of the wider gay community. They looked on helplessly as AIDS increasingly became a fact of life and, significantly, the new Thatcher government appeared to be doing little or nothing to support them. Instinctively prudish in matters sexual (in 1989 she was personally to veto the idea of a national survey of sexual behaviour), Thatcher herself 'could only watch with pursed lips what was going on, and disapprove', one-time health minister Edwina Currie observed. (Nor, later, did she so much as mention AIDS – 'potentially the greatest health risk of modern times', according to her own government – in her memoirs, *The Downing Street Years*.) Currie's predecessors at the Department of Health, too, 'were not only not interested, but actively hostile'.

Against this background, large numbers of homosexuals – in common with many youth, ethnic and minority groups – lost faith in Thatcherism (Edmund White's 1988 follow-up to *A Boy's Own Story* was to be entitled *The Beautiful Room Is Empty*). Thenceforth, the tone within the gay community, so recently one of blithe complacency, became one of increasing hostility. Where only two or three years previously Thatcherism had seemed to offer a comfortable oyster-bed, now it was transformed into the irritant grit. Its *laissez-faire* non-interventionism came to be seen as little more than callous complacency, and almost overnight a reaction against its own incipient conservatism erupted among large sections of the gay community. Signalling this new impatience, Pride '85 (attendance 10,000) had as its centrepiece a water carnival on the Thames with the statuesque drag-artiste Divine symbolically shouting defiance from a launch moored only a few hundred yards from the Palace of Westminster.

AIDS rapidly and inevitably became the issue uppermost in the mind of this new generation of agitators and, selfishly, as some saw it, they began trying to keep it for themselves, even positively embracing once-gibed-at references to a 'gay disease'. Gay men were, after all, inescapably the 'victims' of a brutal blend of prejudice and medical over-reaction:

> The doctor said he'd give me an 'Aids test', took my blood, and said the results would take eight or nine days. Would I wait in the hospital? Two days later, there's me in my pyjamas in the corridor on the telephone and these two zombies walk up with their space suits on, the whole bit, top to bottom. I was near the operating room and thought, 'God! I wonder what they've been doing in there.' [But] they came and took the phone out of my hand, picked me up, carried me to my room, and locked the door. I thought, 'Ah, I wonder if I can guess the results of the test.'
>
> Five hours later the door opened. It was my doctor, who looked as if he had seen a ghost. He'd developed a stutter and he fiddled with a pencil. He said he had some bad news. 'You have Aids.'
>
> 'I've got Aids.' And I didn't think anything else. I didn't know what it meant. I just numbed out.
>
> I stayed in that room for nearly a month and was barrier nursed. The doctor came in capped and gowned and masked, with plastic bags on his feet, and nobody was allowed in without doing the same. Food was left outside the door. Paper bags of shit built up because nobody came to take them away, and there were no extractor fans in the room, just this huge window to open. I froze.
>
> All they told me was that I had 'Aids', and that everything that went out of the room had to be burnt. Nothing else.[28]

Actual cases were rare. In 1983 there had been between thirty and forty confirmed diagnoses of AIDS (a total which included a number of intravenous drug-users and haemophiliacs infected by 'contaminated blood products'). By the beginning of 1986 the cumulative total was 670; by the year's end it had risen to a little over 2,000, but even that was well below official predictions. Despite the publicity, AIDS was still a distant, albeit terrifying, prospect for the majority of British homosexuals; something to watch with appalled fascination in a series of American feature films which effectively began with *Longtime Companion* (1990) but only achieved international box-office success with *Philadelphia*, and read about in novels such as Oscar Moore's *A Matter of Life and Sex* (1991). Insidiously, however, AIDS was having a direct effect on a far greater number of otherwise healthy men as life began to imitate art and those men were forced to share the experiences of less fortunate friends:

—'s been moved into a private room. The only sound emanates from a rotating fan and a discreet machine which seems to inflate and deflate his mattress. A bag of dextrose and saline solution and something more sinister drip down lines into his left arm. That in itself is so thin the shadow of the needle, fine as it is, stands out like a weal on his wrist. A catheter drains bile-orange urine into a bag half-hidden beneath the bed. Impossible to imagine he has just turned twenty-eight.

15 May
Stayed all night at the hospital. — now completely unconscious, a little pump administering shots of diamorphine every minute or so through a line which disappears into the wall of his stomach. Oxygen mask over his face.

His mother and I take turns – roughly two-hourly – to sit with him, holding his hand and occasionally stroking his hair. He is hot, with tiny beads of perspiration on his face, neck and chest. Very pale.

For long periods the only sign of life is the heaving of his chest as he struggles to breathe. Then suddenly he grips my hand, holding it surprisingly strongly for a few seconds. This happens roughly every fifteen minutes. Once, just once, he half-opens his eyes, again only for a few seconds.

Dawn breaks without anyone noticing it.

At around 7.30 I make coffee and toast – from which his mother and I snack around —'s bed.

Shortly afterwards two nurses arrive to turn him. We may stay in the room, they say. It would have been kinder if they'd asked us to leave. Although they do what they can to preserve his modesty, it is impossible to miss his naked thighs, shrunken now to about the size of my upper arms but hairier, furrier, than I remember them – than my own, indeed.

I *know* then that he cannot recover. Even to turn this shadow the nurses have to give him an intravenous shot of Diazepam. This quickly relaxes him.

Decide about 8.30 that it is time to go. Take —'s hand, kiss him on the forehead and whisper Goodbye. Leave pretty certain that I will never see him alive again. Cry a bit, and sleep off and on for most of the next twenty-four hours.[29]

In the face of this and a perceived government indifference – it was not until 1989 that Whitehall and the Health Education Authority (HEA) sanctioned and grudgingly began to fund AIDS-awareness campaigns explicitly targeted at gay men – any atavistic selfishness quickly became enlightened self-help. Battling, as it saw it, for its very survival, the gay community quickly established a range of bodies offering practical help and advice to those directly and indirectly affected by the condition. In London alone, the Terrence Higgins Trust, Body Positive and the London Lighthouse AIDS hospice (1988) were only the headline-making organizations among a plethora of smaller regional and locally funded groups which were to unite under the generic title Gay Men Fighting Aids (GMFA) in 1991.

Their aim was nothing less than the complete re-education of the entire homosexual community. The Terrence Higgins Trust pioneered a programme of frank 'practical support, help, counselling and advice for anyone living with or concerned about Aids and HIV infection'. Leaflets, posters, advertisements in the gay press and a best-selling videotape stressed the importance of condom use and gave explicit advice on what constituted 'safe' (later prudently amended to 'safe*r*') sex in the demotic language of which the government and the HEA had always fought shy. 'Safer sex is great sex,' it insisted, making no apology for unlocking the bedroom door on a whole Kama Sutra of contemporary homosexual practice:

> You could suck, kiss, lick, touch, fondle, bite, nibble and squeeze all over his body – his nipples, arse, calves, toes, neck, ears, thighs, nose, crotch, balls, armpits, fingers . . .
>
> You could give him a soft sensual massage or get tougher with wrestling, rough-and-tumble or spanking . . .

You could wank each other off – dry or using lots of lube [lubricant] – or press, rub and slap your dick against his dick, buns, face, chest, thighs . . .[30]

It was (and continues to be) an effective programme. In 1995 a seventeen-year-old gay Londoner told a newspaper: 'I haven't been any more promiscuous than any [straight] teenager my age, but I think I know a lot more about safe sex.' Rather older, other gay men were also heeding the message, modifying praxis and developing expedients of their own:

Men did start using condoms – 'johnnies' – round about then [1985–6] – or didn't, if you see what I mean.

You'd go to the pub – *I'd* go to the pub – and you'd meet this bloke. There were two I saw pretty regularly around this time. There was one I called the Beckenham Hunk, because he was a hunk and he came from Beckenham. I only ever met him in the gents in this pub, but it was two or three times a week. None of my friends there knew about him – he wouldn't have been 'their sort of person' – but at the end of the evening I'd find some excuse and slope off to see him. We didn't do much; just grab each other's cock and have a quick wank and hope no one came in while we were at it. I don't think we said more than about six words to each other in all the time I knew him; but we were close, in a sort of way.

I guess that was a sort of conscious nod towards safe sex – on my part at any rate. Before, *yes*; I think I would have taken him home, and let him roger me rotten if we're going to be honest!

Another chap I met at the same pub was a nurse: blond, hairy chest, *definitely bed-able*! But it was the same with him. He lived somewhere near me, but never invited me back, like I didn't invite him back. We'd just walk home together after closing time. Sometimes he'd put his hand down inside the back of my trousers, which was fun and exciting because it was illegal, out there on the 'public highway'. There was a dark alley off the road – it's all been pulled down now – and we'd automatically stop off there. It was probably safer than the cottage at the pub! We'd masturbate each other, kiss and have a bit of a cuddle and sometimes suck each other off. Sad, really; safe, though.[31]

I used to go to gay clubs occasionally. I'd have snogs and that sort
of thing, but never anything more than that. There were a few
occasions in some alley-way or some bloke's place. We'd be really
drunk and get off with each other . . . but somehow this sixth sense
told us when to stop. Nothing serious happened for a number of
years: I didn't have any *sex* or intercourse or anything. It was
just fondling, groping, kissing, stroking. With a number of chaps,
though.[32]

People said that the gay community was 'showing the way'; that it
had 'come of age', or at least 'grown up'. Certainly its general readiness
to accept the social implications of HIV and its realistic – if not always
enthusiastic – adoption of 'safer sex' practices were well in advance
of those of the general public. But, although the government's alarmist
health education programmes featuring images of tombstones and ice-
bergs had gone out of their way to be even-handed – 'There is now
a deadly disease. *It is a danger to us all*,' the commentary to a television
advertisement had begun – the very fact that gay men had publicly
recognized that they were at particular risk counted against them. In
the public minds 'AIDS' and 'gays' continued to have more than an
assonant at connection, and a sizeable, vocal and sometimes influential
homophobic constituency was quick to seize on the so-called 'world-
wide AIDS pandemic' to reinforce it.

At a time when, despite the government's health education programmes, polls suggested that around 14 per cent of the population
still believed AIDS could be 'caught' from sharing towels or using
cups and plates which had previously been used by an infected person,
Sir Alfred Sherman, a Downing Street adviser during Margaret
Thatcher's premiership, fulminated that it was 'mainly sodomites' who
were spreading it. 'Perverts to blame for gay plague', the *Sun* told its
readers in 1986.

From there it was only a short step to attacking homosexuals merely
for being homosexual – for 'putting [their] penis into another man's
arsehole', as the Conservative MP Sir Nicholas Fairbairn was to tell
the House of Commons they did. A former chief constable of Great
Manchester, James Anderton, claimed to be speaking for God when
he described homosexuals as 'swirling around in a cesspool of their

own making'. They were a 'menace to society', said the *Sun*, again; while another Conservative MP, Geoffrey Dickens, called publicly for anal sex and all other homosexual acts to be re-criminalized . . .

On the streets, too, the term 'queer' (and less frequently the American 'faggot') began to be used derogatively once more, and a journalist was quick to report how fear of AIDS was directly rekindling anti-gay feeling: 'After one of my son's teachers died of Aids, I told a school governor how grieved I was. "But he was a homosexual," she replied tartly, as though this made his death all right.'[33] In the aftermath of Margaret Thatcher's call for a return to 'Victorian values' there was even a pursed-lipped recourse to the Victorian notion of the Love That Dare Not Speak Its Name: '. . . the Blitz spirit flared briefly when Kensington residents were faced with the prospect of a memorial to the late gay icon (and local householder) Freddie Mercury on public land [. . .] "Mr Mercury may have lived in the Borough," sniffed a near neighbour of the deceased, "but one could hardly call him a Kensington person." '[34]

It was the biggest setback to gay toleration which activists could remember in Britain since the days of the Wilde trial. Gay characters, most notably Colin – the graphic designer played by Michael Cashman – in the BBC's *EastEnders*, disappeared from popular television drama. A *Daily Mail* opinion poll discovered that 55 per cent of people agreed with James Anderton's views, and for the first time in a generation gay men – and particularly young gay men – found themselves deprived of any meaningful role models. 'Tim', a sixteen-year-old then living in Manchester, experienced the full force of this reversionary prejudice at first hand as his parents blindly tried to come to terms with his gayness:

My mum and dad didn't help me; they treated me like dirt. They didn't know what it was like. Nobody did.

[. . .] I told my mum about all my problems – e.g., being gay, not talking to anyone and being a loner, etc. She said, 'I love you whatever you may be.' 'Yes,' said dad.

Then one day I found the telephone number of the Gay Centre. I phoned up and they gave me directions to get there. I started going to the youth group and made a few friends. I enjoyed myself so much and found it was a great opportunity to meet other young

gay people. But all the time I was going to the Centre I was telling
my parents I was going to friends'.

When they found out they said they didn't mind, and accepted
it. Then, after a few months I walked in and was five minutes late.
My dad got up and started saying things like, 'That place is taking
over your life; don't you give a shit what the neighbours say? [. . .]
When you're seventeen you can piss off and do anything with those
other poofters!' He said much more, then slapped me round the
face. It wasn't the slaps that hurt and made me cry, it was the hatred
in his eyes and what had come out of his mouth. [. . .]

One day when I got home my mum said, 'Why do you do it?
We are going to take you to a head-shrinker. You're not gay,
you're a transvestite!' I couldn't explain [to my parents] because
they would probably hit me. Then my dad said, 'There is no such
thing as gay. It's *queer*, as far as I am concerned. Don't go to that
Centre again. If you do, I'll paste you and burn it down. It's them
queers that have made you turn this way. We know you've been
going there all the time. You've been with dirty old men. Anyway,
we're going to get your brain sorted out.[35]

More crucially, many gay men – and an increasingly vocal body of
lesbian women – came to believe that they and their lifestyles were
under concerted and even centralized attack. The press was seen to
be obsessed by the profligate funding which supposedly subversive
gay and (especially) lesbian groups were receiving from 'Loony Left'
councils. Baleful motives were detected behind its reports that primary
school libraries were stocking *Jenny Lives with Eric and Martin*, a Scandi-
navian picture-story book about a young girl being brought up by her
gay father and his male lover; and that a London headteacher had
vetoed a school trip to a performance of Prokofiev's *Romeo and Juliet*
because the ballet was 'totally heterosexual'. Even routine court proceedings were seen as part of a grand and sinister plan, with judges
and magistrates 'cracking down' and handing out dire warnings – or
worse:

> . . . two men who were kissing in a King's Cross street [. . .] had
> been arrested by a police officer who 'realised how offensive this
> can be to ordinary members of the public'. The men were bound
> over for £100 each after charges of 'gross indecency' against them

were dropped. The judge, Thomas Pigott QC, told them they were lucky to escape a prison sentence: 'This kind of thing is intolerable,' he said, 'and you had better tell your friends that they risk a prison sentence if they do it.'[36]

Seemingly substantiating this notion of establishment control was the discovery that, through an obscure section in a local government Bill bought before Parliament in 1987 (the notorious 'Clause 28'), the government was specifically seeking to outlaw 'the promotion of homosexuality [. . .] and the promotion of the teaching of the acceptability of homosexuality as a pretended family relationship' by schools and local authorities.

None of this *was* primarily motivated by anti-gay spleen or AIDS-inspired homophobic atavism. Rather, it was all part of a continuing government battle to 'trim the wings' of 'spendthrift' – and predominantly Labour-controlled – local authorities. Nevertheless, in an increasingly acrimonious climate, Clause 28 in particular was seen as a draconian and uniquely vindictive measure; and that was enough. Ironically blind to what a later commentator has called the 'danger of over-representing the power that it had',[37] activist groups responded by invoking civil liberties arguments and a radical rhetoric which had not been heard since the 1960s: 'Society marks homosexuals out as separate people deserving of different, discriminatory treatment. We have to respond to that by defending our right to be gay and to be treated with dignity – we have to defend homosexuality in order, ultimately, to abolish it.'[38] There were rallies and (not infrequently) bad-tempered demonstrations in every part of the country (in London, an angry Pride '88 attracted an attendance of 36,000) but ultimately, of course, it was all in vain. Inexorably, Clause 28 passed into law as Section 28 of the 1988 Local Government Act.

A battle had been lost – but the war, a war, *any* war went on. Indeed, as the 1980s became the 1990s, as Margaret Thatcher quit the scene and, for a new generation of young people, AIDS became just another fact of life, the most notable legacy of the Clause 28 campaign was the pettish, dyspeptic qui vive attitude it engendered. Newly established, post-'28' bodies such as the AIDS Coalition to Unleash Power (Act-Up), the short-lived Organization for Lesbian and Gay Action (OLGA), Stonewall and OutRage! reared up against any perceived denial or infringement of homosexual rights. Campaigns which began on the streets but more and more frequently ended in the House of Lords or on the long road to the European Court of Justice and the European Court of Human Rights sought to highlight and bring an end to – among other injustices – the continuing existence of the 1967 Act's 'discriminatory' age of consent for homosexual men; the Church of England's 'hypocritical homophobia'; police 'harassment'; anti-gay prejudice in the media and the workplace; the ban on lesbians and gay men serving in the armed forces; local authorities' refusal to extend fostering, adoption and parenting rights to lesbians and gay men; and the illegality of homosexuality in the Isle of Man, the Channel Islands, Gibraltar and the merchant navy.

No issue was too large or too small; but, almost unnoticed in all the sound and fury, the underlying emphasis had shifted. OutRage!'s early 1990s' programme of 'outing' allegedly gay churchmen, judges and politicians whose support for 'anti-gay' policies they deemed harmful to other gay people, may have grabbed the morning headlines and made the television news bulletins, but for all its stridency it had little or nothing to do with gay activists' demands for 'fuck and arse' and that unending 'orgy of gay sex' of little more than a decade previously. Rather, OutRage! and the more conservative, media-friendly lobbying which Stonewall had been undertaking since 1988 were variations of that same desire to 'abolish' homosexuality – at least in a discriminatory, legal sense.

Stonewall's description of itself as a 'national lobbying & campaigning organisation working for legal equality and social justice for lesbians & gay men' perfectly chimed with the less confrontational mood of the times. All the sound and fury only masked the ultimate aims of OutRage! too. 'We don't claim to speak on behalf of every member of the lesbian and gay community,' explained one of its activists, which was true; but it was Peter Tatchell, its most high-profile member, who put things into context when he revealed to a journalist in 1994 that his 'one dream' had always been 'to have a house with a garden in a quiet street in a safe neighbourhood'.[39]

More pressing than anything else in the battle for equality and invisibility before the law was the issue of the homosexual age of consent. Some rationalization of a situation which allowed girls to engage in sexual activity from the age of sixteen while denying the right to young gay men until they reached the age of twenty-one had been proposed by a government advisory committee as early as 1979. It was not until 1994, however, that anything reached the House of Commons order paper. Even then it had taken months of careful planning. Stonewall in particular had mounted a lobbying campaign as meticulous as anything undertaken by the Homosexual Law Reform Society in 1967. Nothing had been left to chance. All-party support for 'sixteen' had been secured. The media had even been given their 'Bosie' for the night, in the person of a petulant but personable teenager called Hugo. The cameras were all in place. Crowds had gathered in Parliament Square, sure that history was about to be made, certain that 'sixteen' it would be.

'Everyone felt jubilant,' recalls the writer Edmund Hall, who was there.[40] 'It was a phenomenal atmosphere. When I arrived, I guess there were two thousand people there with banners – OutRage! banners, Stonewall banners, it didn't matter. All the [gay activist] groups had come together for the night. It was pretty well unique. We were going to win!'

So sure of that were they, in fact, so noisily, jubilantly sure, that few in the crowd heard Will Parry, Hugo's partner, when he emerged into Parliament Square. It wasn't sixteen, he said. They'd lost. It was eighteen. Someone pressed a microphone into his hand: 'It's eighteen!' he said again, quietly. 'We've lost. It's eighteen. The bastards!' Somehow the microphone caught his words, and then Hugo's – clear amidst the prematurely triumphalist din: 'The *bastards*! The BASTARDS!'

I was in the Central Lobby at this point [Hall goes on], and suddenly you could hear this banging on the door, this incredible rhythmic banging. This door was being forced against the bolts. It looked like it was going to come in.

Outside there was such a sense of anger and shouting. There were a couple of hundred extremely angry men and women screaming, still trying to reason with anyone inside. It looked as though the people were two or three high, which they can't have been, but there was this *slope* of people with banners and lights and torches and candles and fog-horns – lots of fog-horns! – trying to beat down the doors of the Palace of Westminster. There was a group trying to climb over the gate, and another group lying down across the road, so all the traffic was shut off in Parliament Square. It was a riot!

❧

It might have been a riot; it might have been rout. Whichever, in retrospect, as the crowds picked their way through what Edmund Hall describes as 'the detritus of the event, the bits of banners, the used-up flares, the posters trodden underfoot, the old sparklers', the fudged compromise on a homosexual age of consent of eighteen seemed to sum up the dilemma facing a gay man in a liberal but heterosexual democracy.

Ironically the debate itself had been held 100 years – almost to the week – after the Marquess of Queensberry's first attack on Oscar Wilde (although, typically, no one seemed to remember the fact). Socially and politically, a great deal had happened since 1895; homosexuals had become more visible than ever before, but at the same time they had signally failed to 'abolish' the negative connotations of homosexuality.

E. M. Forster's 'Happier Year', in which 'two men [could] fall in love and remain in it for the ever and ever that fiction allows', was still fully to dawn. Real equality, too, seemed as far away as ever.

Public-sector and a growing number of private-sector jobs *were* being offered to candidates irrespective of their sexual orientation. The image of a latter-day Ben Butley watching his partner shaving *had* become an unremarkable media norm. For a decade or so, finance companies had been offering joint mortgages to gay men. Newspapers, too, occasionally featured gay couples celebrating twenty-five years together as well-respected pillars of the community – but public opinion surveys rather more often revealed that around 40 per cent of the adult population still found the sight of two men kissing in the street 'offensive' and continued to believe that same-sex intercourse was 'distasteful or morally wrong'.[41]

Despite this, there were significant signs that young gay men at least had come to regard themselves as 'perfectly normal – with one slight difference' – albeit in a different way to the one envisaged by that contributor to *Gay News* twenty years previously. Section 28 still lay ominous (but unused) on the statute book, around 13,000 cases of AIDS had been recorded in the UK, of which less than 200 had been due to heterosexual sex; but in Manchester's rather self-conscious canal-side 'gay village' Paul Cons was watching the arrival of 'a new generation of young lesbians and gay people who had taken on board the lessons of AIDS and were ready to have a good time'.

A potent sign of this was the fact that, month after month there and in and around Old Compton Street in London, more and more new gay clubs and pavement cafés were springing up. Others, significantly catering for a so-called 'mixed clientele' of gay and straight young people, were beginning to flourish in smaller metropolitan centres as what was perceived as 'gay style', and an overtly 'gay sensibility' came to dominate the fashion and music industries, inspire the typographical anarchy of 'lifestyle' magazines and, through series such as *Out This Week* and *Gaytime TV*, make themselves felt on BBC radio and television.

Pride, too, was enjoying a new lease of life. In the mid-1990s attendances at what had become Europe's largest annual gay and lesbian festival regularly topped 40,000 – but only, cynics equally regularly pointed out, because the march had been stripped of any political significance and served merely as the prelude to a free festival where straight bands played, straight 'gate-crashers' made it impossible to move in the disco-tents and banners bearing the logos of mainstream sponsors fluttered alongside the rainbow flags of Pride.

One hundred years after Oscar Wilde was humiliated by being publicly named as a sodomite, a new generation of gay men, for the most part born after homosexual acts had been decriminalized, had taken to wearing T-shirts bearing the legends 'QUEER AS FUCK' and 'I CAN'T EVEN THINK STRAIGHT' – as fashion statements. And ironically, if anything it was 'the scene', the Moloch which continued to demand they be seen to belong and yet to be seen to be different, which was to come closest to bringing about the very abolition of the homosexual sensibility as it had traditionally existed.

The never-quite-coherent theories of Edward Carpenter, the ideals of the 'special friend' and 'lad-love' and the notion 'manliness' seemed absurdly pompous and earnest in an age in which 'gayness' had become a bolt-on fashion accessory. It was noticeable that, eight years after Colin first kissed Guido, when *EastEnders* revisited homosexuality it was not through the experience of Mark, its – straight – HIV-positive character, but via a storyline in which another young man's admission of his gayness (again signalled by no more than a male–male kiss) was seemingly precipitated by a previous immersion in the club and drug scene.

In 1889 W. S. Gilbert had pointed out that 'When everyone is somebodee,/Then no one's anybody'. In 1996 it seemed that being gay meant no more than living for the moment, being one of the 'boyz', being at the cutting edge of fashion. By then Neil Tennant of the Pet Shop Boys was telling a national newspaper: 'We've invented this thing called homosexuality and now everybody is either gay or straight. I mean fifty years ago I'd have been married with three children and having affairs with men on the side and frankly, I'd probably be happier.'[42]

It was a sign of the times. There had been more than enough self-delusion in the come-on-in propagandizing of the Golden Age activists. (It serves no purpose now to remember that back in 1977, in *The Naked Civil Servant*, Quentin Crisp had made the omniscient pronouncement: 'There is no great dark man'.) Without precognition, oblivious of the events which would later hobble their progress, they could reasonably have looked forward to a *future* – or at the very least a 1995 in which the 100th anniversary of Oscar Wilde's conviction and imprisonment would be marked as a milestone in an onward march, a development, an evolution.

But too many now were dead; their mantle had been assumed by a shrill, tiny army for whom AIDS and Ecstasy had telescoped history and foreshortened any future. Beating time on the dance-floor, they were self-appointed Edgars, intent on hammering full-blown tragedy out of private tantrums:

> The weight of this sad time we must obey,
> Speak what we feel, not what we ought to say.
> The oldest hath borne most; we that are young
> Shall never see so much, nor live so long.

Thus, in his 1991 novel *A Matter of Life and Sex*, while awaiting the results of an HIV test, Oscar Moore's all-too-autobiographical hero Hugo Harvey contemplated life from a post-modernist position way beyond the traditional space-time continuum. Like most of his friends, he perceived himself doing little more than 'looking forward to the days when you will look back fondly on the days you spent looking forwards'.[43] Wasted in other ways, the central characters in the 1992 film *The Living End*, saw things more simply: 'We're victims of the sexual revolution. The generation before us had all the fun. We get to pick up the fucking tab.'

It wasn't quite as bad as that, neither as solipsistic nor as melodramatically self-indulgent. Things had moved on, all manner of panics and prejudices had been overcome; querulous and, too often, still pipingly adolescent, the love that dared not speak its name had nevertheless found a voice. When Oscar Moore died in the summer of 1996 the *Guardian*, for which he had been writing a graphic diary of his fight against AIDS-related illness, was surprised by the level of heterosexual appreciation he attracted. Quietly, memorials to Wilde and A. E. Housman had been unveiled in Westminster Abbey. And, although research conducted for the Broadcasting Standards Council in 1994 had discovered that 50 per cent of adults sampled still disliked watching 'gay scenes' on television – and 22 per cent felt that gay characters should not be seen at all – the *Pink Paper* took not a little pride in quoting a BBC spokesman as saying that 'The Programmes Complaints Unit didn't get a single complaint after *EastEnders* gay kiss'.

It was Oscar Fingal O'Flahertie Wills Wilde who once wrote that 'there is only one thing in the world worse than being talked about, and that is not being talked about.' In the present context it is doubtful if even the egregious Oscar would have minded being proved wrong. Just for once.

Notes and Sources

Publishing details for books quoted frequently in these Notes are to be found in the Bibliography.

INTRODUCTION

1. Letter published in *The Pink Paper*, 11 October 1996.

ONE: 'FOR THE PUBLIC BENEFIT'

1. André Gide, *Oscar Wilde*, p. 14; p. 29.
2. See Richard Ellmann, *Oscar Wilde*, p. 412 and footnote.
3. H. Montgomery Hyde, *The Trials of Oscar Wilde*, pp. 344–5 (my italics).
4. Ibid., pp. 142–3.
5. Ibid., p. 175.
6. Cf. the street-cries of 'Quentin!' which followed the transmission of the television adaptation of Quentin Crisp's *The Naked Civil Servant* in 1975.
7. Wilde's enduring legacy as a homosexual icon is traced in Alan Sinfield, *The Wilde Century: Effeminacy, Oscar Wilde and the Queer Movement*.
8. Peter Wildeblood, *Against the Law*, p. 105.
9. Oscar Wilde, *The Importance of Being Earnest*, Act I.
10. Gide, op. cit., pp. 31–3 (my translation).
11. H. Montgomery Hyde, *The Cleveland Street Scandal*, p. 87 (my italics).
12. *Le Temps*, 7 April 1895; quoted in Ellmann, op. cit., p. 428.
13. Quoted in Ellmann, op. cit., p. 425.
14. Montgomery Hyde, *The Cleveland Street Scandal*, p. 49.
15. John Betjeman, 'The Arrest of Oscar Wilde at the Cadogan Hotel'.
16. Martin Fido, *Oscar Wilde*, pp. 111–12.
17. Ellmann, op. cit., p. 427.
18. For a more detailed account of the origins and aims of Aestheticism, see

Holbrook Jackson, *The 1890s* (1913), Cresset Library, 1988, and my own book, *The Fitzrovians*, pp. 6–17.

19. *Punch*, 14 February 1880.
20. *Patience*, Act I, lines 415–20.
21. Ibid., Act I, lines 206–9.
22. *Punch*, 12 February 1881.
23. Quoted in Montgomery Hyde, *Cases That Changed the Law*, pp. 150–51.
24. Quoted in Montgomery Hyde, *The Trials of Oscar Wilde*, p. 68.
25. Quoted in ibid., p. 69 footnote.
26. Montgomery Hyde, *The Cleveland Street Scandal*, p. 26.
27. Ibid., p. 22.
28. Ibid., p. 96.
29. Ibid., p. 39.
30. *Pall Mall Gazette*, 12 September 1889; quoted in ibid., pp. 45–6.
31. Criminal Law Amendment Act, 1885 (48 & 49 Vict. c. 69), sec. 11.
32. Montgomery Hyde, *The Trials of Oscar Wilde*, pp. 179–87.
33. Ibid., p. 275 (my italics).
34. Ibid., pp. 192–3.
35. Ibid., p. 276.
36. Ibid., pp. 199–200.
37. Ibid., p. 281.
38. Ibid., p. 315.
39. Ibid., p. 316.
40. Ibid., p. 318.
41. Ibid., p. 339.
42. Alan Sinfield, op. cit., pp. 3–4.
43. Montgomery Hyde, *The Trials of Oscar Wilde*, pp. 281–2.
44. Ibid., p. 335.
45. Henry Harland to Edmund Gosse, 5 May 1895; quoted in Ellmann, op. cit., p. 430.
46. Ellmann, op. cit., p. 430.

TWO: 'YOU AND I ARE OUTLAWS'

1. *Imperialist*, 26 January 1918; quoted in H. Montgomery Hyde, *Cases That Changed the Law*, pp. 177–8.
2. Quoted in *Cases That Changed the Law*, p. 177.
3. See Victoria Glendinning, *Vita: The Life of V. Sackville-West*, Weidenfeld & Nicolson, 1983, and Nigel Nicolson, *Portrait of a Marriage*, Weidenfeld

& Nicolson, 1973. Harold Nicolson's letter, written on 15 September 1919, is reproduced in Nigel Nicolson (ed.), *Vita and Harold: The Letters of Vita Sackville-West and Harold Nicolson*, Weidenfeld & Nicolson, 1992, p. 98.

4. See Bryan Connon, *Beverley Nichols: A Life*, p. 40. Frustratingly, Connon has 'deliberately avoided footnotes or an appendix of sources' in this full and otherwise exemplary biography.

5. John Betjeman, 'Narcissus', 1966.

6. Quoted in Bevis Hillier, *Young Betjeman*, pp. 116–17.

7. Michael Davidson, *The World, the Flesh and Myself*, p. 71 (my italics; the incident at the Southampton swimming pool need not concern us).

8. A. E. Housman, *A Shropshire Lad*, LI.

9. Ibid., LVIII.

10. A. E. Housman, *Last Poems*, XII.

11. E. M. Forster, *Maurice*, p. 236.

12. Ibid., p. 16.

13. Ibid., pp. 42–3.

14. Ibid., p. 37.

15. Ibid., p. 117.

16. Ibid., pp. 92–3.

17. Ibid., p. 236.

18. Ibid., p. 125.

19. Davidson, op. cit., p. 31.

20. Forster, op. cit., p. 134.

21. Ibid., pp. 136–7.

22. Ibid., p. 138.

23. Quoted in Michael De-la-Noy, *Denton Welch: The Making of a Writer*, Viking, 1984, p. 91.

24. Quoted in ibid., p. 93.

25. Forster, op. cit., p. 93.

26. Ibid., p. 223.

27. D. H. Lawrence, *Women in Love*, Penguin, 1960, p. 232; p. 310.

28. Forster, op. cit., p. 235.

29. Havelock Ellis, *Studies in the Psychology of Sex*, I, Case VII; quoted in Paul Delany, *The Neo-Pagans*, p. 10.

30. Forster, op. cit., p. 235.

31. Quoted in Kevin Porter and Jeffrey Weeks (eds), *Between the Acts: Lives of Homosexual Men, 1895–1967*, p. 24.

32. Ibid., pp. 24–5 (my italics).

33. Forster, op. cit., p. 70.

34. Ibid., p. 8.
35. Ibid., p. 53 (my italics).
36. Ibid., p. 15 (my italics).
37. Ibid., p. 73.

THREE: 'I'M AWFULLY PROUD TO THINK HE'S MY FRIEND'

1. W. H. Auden, 'Doggerel by a Senior Citizen'.
2. E. M. Forster, op. cit., p. 73.
3. There is, for instance, no mention of homosexual activity in Lyn Mac-donald's on-going social histories of the Great War (*Somme, They Called It Passchendaele, 1914*, etc.). Nor, apparently, was there any officially voiced concern akin to that of the army high command who, during the last year of the Second World War, felt compelled to move against what they called 'Lack of Moral Fibre'. (See my book *Heroes, Mavericks and Bounders*, Michael Joseph, 1991, pp. 168–71.)
4. Stephen Spender, 'Ultima Ratio Regum', *Collected Poems, 1928–1985*, Faber, 1985, p. 69.
5. R. C. Sherriff, *Journey's End*, Act I.
6. Shoeing Smith C. H. Williams, quoted in Lyn Macdonald, *1914–1918: Voices and Images of the Great War*, Michael Joseph, 1988, p. 188.
7. R. C. Sherriff, op. cit., Act I.
8. Ibid.
9. Quoted in Harold Owen and John Bell (eds), *Wilfred Owen: Collected Letters*, Oxford University Press, 1967, p. 441.
10. Michael Davidson, *The World, the Flesh and Myself*, pp. 77–8, pp. 81–2 *passim*. As a corollary addendum to this and the previous extract, it is perhaps worth including here a passage from the robustly heterosexual Robert Graves's *But It Still Goes On* (1931): 'Do you know how a platoon of men will absolutely worship a good-looking gallant young officer? If he's a bit shy of them, and decent to them, they get a crush on him. He's a being apart: an officer's uniform is most attractive compared with the rough shapeless private's uniform. He becomes a sort of military queen bee.' Maybe we should note, too that it was Graves who published an early (and now thankfully forgotten) collection of war poems entitled *Fairies and Fusilliers* in 1917.
11. *Between the Acts*, p. 16; pp. 17–18.
12. Ibid., p. 25.
13. Ibid., pp. 5–7 *passim*.
14. Ibid., p. 16.
15. Davidson, op. cit., pp. 77–8; pp. 81–2 *passim*.

16. *Between the Acts*, p. 6.
17. Davidson, op. cit., p. 134.
18. H. Montgomery Hyde, *The Other Love*; quoted in James Gardiner, *A Class Apart: The Private Pictures of Montague Glover*, p. 52.
19. Anonymous, quoted in Macdonald, op. cit., p. 262.
20. Quoted in ibid., p. 263.
21. *Between the Acts*, pp. 74–5.
22. Davidson, op. cit., p. 86.
23. Ibid., p. 92 (my italics). In Bryan Connon's biography of Beverley Nichols there is an account of a similar episode. Nichols is at formal, regimental gathering: 'At dinner, a captain said, apropos of nothing, "Talking of buggery."
    'The major opposite grinned. "What about it?"
    ' "I never understood why, if a chap wants to go in for buggery, he doesn't bugger a woman?"
    'Much laughter greeted this, but Beverley kept quite and got on with his meal' (Connon, op. cit., p. 57).
24. Davidson, op. cit., pp. 121–2.
25. Ibid., p. 93.
26. Quoted in Connon, op. cit., p. 61.
27. A. E. Housman, *Last Poems*, XXXV. I have omitted the final stanza.
28. Davidson, op. cit., p. 47.
29. Housman, *Last Poems*, XXIII.
30. *Between the Acts*, p. 7.
31. Ibid., pp. 7–8 *passim*.

FOUR: 'SUIVEZ-MOI, JEUNE HOMME'

1. Several of these phrases have dropped out of common currency. 'Nonce', for instance, seems now only to be used within prisons as a cant term for child sex offenders. Pejorative terms remain, however, especially in the police and armed forces. As late as 1992 Surgeon Commander Richard Jolly, OBE, principal medical officer at Britannia Royal Naval College, listed a few which he regarded as still 'common' in the navy: 'Brownhatter; Shirtlifter; Porthole-gazer; Uphill gardener; Beef bosun; Boweltroweller; Botty-bandit; Arse grabber; Raving nosh; Turd burglar' (quoted in Edmund Hall, *We Can't Even March Straight: Homosexuality in the British Armed Forces*, p. 73).
2. In common parlance in Britain, the use of the word 'gay', both adjectivally and as a noun ('a gay'; 'gays') as a euphemistic – and later, politically correct – synonym for 'homosexual' seemingly began in the early 1970s.

The present author can certainly recall having heard it employed at around that time.

It was an American import, although the word has always had a certain redolence and was very probably part of a private homosexual argot ('palari') long before the 1970s. Eric Partridge noted that, since at least the early nineteenth century, 'gay' had connotations of both (female) prostitution and intoxication ('gay and frisky' was rhyming slang for 'whisky'). Published in 1961, the last edition of his *Dictionary of Slang and Unconventional English* includes no reference to its homosexual usage, however – although a gloss that in nineteenth-century slang the term 'the gaying instrument' referred to what he called the 'male member' reinforces the idea that for a long time the word has enjoyed a double – or even a triple – life.

3. Godfrey Winn, *The Infirm Glory*, pp. 262–3.

4. Richard Buckle (ed.), *Self-Portrait with Friends: The Selected Diaries of Cecil Beaton*, p. 30.

5. Quoted in Hugo Vickers, *Cecil Beaton*, p. 107.

6. They are quoted in Ellmann's *Oscar Wilde* (p. 38) and are thus assured of immortality.

7. Ifan Kyrle Fletcher, *Ronald Firbank: A Memoir* (1930); reprinted in Mervyn Horder (ed.), *Ronald Firbank: Memoirs and Critiques*, Duckworth, 1977. pp. 134.

8. See Humphrey Carpenter, *The Brideshead Generation: Evelyn Waugh & His Friends.*

9. Carpenter notes (pp. 112–13) that Waugh inserted this description of Howard into the novel (originally published in 1945) only when he came to revise it in 1960, two years after Howard had killed himself.

10. Harold Acton, *Memoirs of an Aesthete*, pp. 119–20.

11. Provenance unknown; quoted in Bryan Connon, *Beverley Nichols*, p. 76. Connon's biography is the only serious study of Nichols's life and work which has so far appeared. My information about Nichols's circumstances at this time is largely drawn from chapters four to ten of the book. His own six volumes of autobiography are notoriously unreliable and at times demonstrably misleading.

12. Quoted in Cole Lesley, *The Life of Noël Coward*, p. 80; p. 82.

13. Quoted in Connon, op. cit., p. 144.

14. Ibid., pp. 122–3.

15. Quoted in ibid., pp. 179–81 *passim*.

16. Quoted in Charles Castle, *Noël*, pp. 61–2.

17. Quoted in ibid., p. 64.

18. John Gielgud, *An Actor and His Time*, Sidgwick and Jackson, 1979, p. 46.

19. John Lahr (ed.), *The Orton Diaries*, p. 251 (23 July 1967). Williams's own account of the incident is recorded in Russell Davies (ed.), *The Kenneth Williams Diaries*, p. 307 (14 July 1967).
20. William Gerhardie, *God's Fifth Column*, Hodder and Stoughton, 1981, p. 307.
21. Simon Blow, *Broken Blood: The Rise and Fall of the Tennant Family*, p. 177.
22. *Self-Portrait with Friends*, p. 392.
23. Ibid., p. 25.
24. Cole Lesley, op. cit., p. 218.
25. Quoted in *Between the Acts*, p. 98.
26. Ibid., pp. 121–2.

FIVE: 'THE HOMINTERN'

1. Cyril Connolly, *Harper's Magazine*, June 1973.
2. Anthony Powell, *To Keep the Ball Rolling*, Penguin, 1983, p. 98.
3. Rather pathetically, as it seems today, in his autobiography *Memoirs of an Aesthete* (1948) Harold Acton devotes almost nine pages to descriptions of the fashionable luncheon, dining and literary clubs and societies to which he belonged: '. . . at first I was drawn to them like a moth. I fluttered my wings at the Italian Circle, the Spanish Society, the Ordinary . . .' (p. 120).
4. The radicalization of otherwise Establishment public schoolboys at this period is a theme which has been explored in various works of fiction over the past thirty years. Lindsay Anderson addressed it in his film *If. . .* (1968). More subtly, it underlies Julian Mitchell's play *Another Country* (1981), a thinly disguised account of Guy Burgess's last terms at Eton.
5. W. H. Auden, *Forewords and Afterwords*, Faber, 1973, p. 514.
6. See Ben Pimlott, *Harold Wilson*, HarperCollins, 1992, pp. 42–5 *passim*.
7. W. H. Auden, 'Consider this and in our time', *Selected Poems*, Faber, 1979, p. 15.
8. Tom Driberg, *Ruling Passions*, p. 71.
9. Ibid., p. 50.
10. Ibid., p. 56.
11. Recollection by A. J. P. Taylor, quoted in Francis Wheen, *Tom Driberg: His Life and Indiscretions*, p. 41.
12. Driberg, op. cit., pp. 75–7 *passim*.
13. These were, as he must have known, unrealistic expectations. At least three posthumous biographies have appeared in Britain or America. Few, if any, of his correspondents burnt his papers, and substantial archives of his letters and manuscripts are anyway held by the Berg Collection at

the New York Public Library and the universities of Oxford and Texas (the Humanities Research Center).

14. Stephen Spender, *World Within World*, p. 53.
15. Humphrey Carpenter, *W. H. Auden*, George Allen & Unwin, 1981, pp. 47–9 *passim*.
16. Spender, op. cit., p. 53.
17. Christopher Isherwood, *Lions and Shadows* (1938), New English Library, 1968, p. 112; p. 121.
18. Stephen Spender, *The Temple*, p. 7.
19. See poems such as 'The Truly Great' and 'Trigorin'; *Collected Poems*, pp. 30 and 22 respectively.
20. Ibid: 'Us', p. 32; 'What I Expected', p. 24.
21. The referencing of Auden's work has always been difficult. In the first editions of his early work the poet presented his poems untitled. In subsequent editions, titles were inserted. Thus, in his *Collected Shorter Poems* (Faber, 1966) this couplet comes from a poem entitled '1929'. Mendelson's definitive editions revert to Auden's original form, remove such titles and index these poems by their first lines. I follow his practice.

    See, therefore, 'It was Easter as I walked in the public gardens', W. H. Auden, *Selected Poems*, Faber, 1979, p. 7.
22. W. H. Auden, 'Watch any day his nonchalant pauses, see' (tellingly, but only latterly entitled 'A Free One'), ibid., p. 4. Mendelson dates this poem to March 1929.
23. Cecil Beaton's diary, 9 October 1923; quoted in Hugo Vickers, *Cecil Beaton*, p. 40.
24. Quoted in Barrie Penrose and Simon Freeman, *Conspiracy of Silence: The Secret Life of Anthony Blunt*, p. 48.
25. Quoted in Vickers, op. cit., pp. 27–8.
26. Quoted in *Conspiracy of Silence*, p. 145.
27. Ibid., p. 47.
28. Jack Hewit, quoted in ibid., p. 51.
29. Cyril Connolly, *The Missing Diplomats*, p. 18.
30. Quoted in Andrew Boyle, *The Climate of Treason*, p. 72.
31. The climax of Julian Mitchell's play *Another Country* (1981, and later filmed) descants on this theme. A homosexual public schoolboy, Guy Bennett (an obvious fictionalization of Burgess), has been turned down as a prefect. He rails at his left-wing friend Judd:

    JUDD: There's no reason you have to be any kind of prefect at all.
    BENNETT: Yes, there is. If I'm spending the rest of my life hiding my true nature from the rest of the world, I'm taking every comfort that's going while it *is* going.

JUDD: Oh, well, if that's your attitude –

BENNETT: Besides, being absolutely *objective*, it would dish me once and for all, wouldn't it?

JUDD: You can't have things both ways, Guy.

BENNETT: What do you want me to do – march about the streets shouting slogans with you? I wouldn't get past the first pub. [*He picks up 'Das Kapital'*] As for this – [*He drops it*] Too heavy.

JUDD: Either you accept the system, or you try to change it. There's no alternative.

BENNETT: [*Suddenly gay*] Why not? Why not both? Pretend to do one, while you really do the other? Fool the swine? Play along with them! Let them think what they like – let them despise you! But all the time –

(Act Two, Scene Six)

32. Goronwy Rees, *A Chapter of Accidents*, Chatto and Windus, 1972; quoted in *Conspiracy of Silence*, pp. 86–7.

33. See Driberg, *Guy Burgess: A Portrait with Background*, p. 18.

34. Ibid., pp. 17–18.

35. Jack Hewit, *Sunday Times* magazine, 7 April 1991.

36. Stephen Spender, *World Without World*, p. 255.

37. W. H. Auden, unpublished poem; quoted in *Sunday Times* magazine, 7 April 1991.

38. W. H. Auden, 'September 1, 1939', op. cit., p. 86. With particular reference to the last line quoted in the text, in the 1960s Auden disowned much of his early work, calling it 'trash which he is ashamed to have written'.

39. John Lehmann, *In the Purely Pagan Sense*, p. 35; Goronwy Rees, op. cit., p. 188.

40. Quoted in *Conspiracy of Silence*, p. 219.

SIX: 'I HAD THE TIME OF MY LIFE'

1. Patrick Hamilton, *Twenty Thousand Streets Under the Sky*, Constable and Co., 1935, pp. 16–17.

2. Michael Davidson, op. cit., pp. 134–5.

3. Jack Hewit, *Sunday Times* magazine, 7 April 1991.

4. See A. H. Halsey (ed.), *Trends in British Society Since 1900*, Macmillan, 1972, p. 533.

5. Quentin Crisp, *The Naked Civil Servant*, p. 83.

6. Ibid., p. 24.

7. Virginia Woolf, letter to Jacques Raverat, 24 January 1925.

8. Terence Greenidge, *Degenerate Oxford?*, Chapman and Hall, 1930.

9. Virginia Woolf, diary entry, 31 August 1928; quoted in Quentin Bell, *Virginia Woolf*, Vol. 2, Hogarth Press, 1972, p. 138.

10. Quoted in Nigel Nicolson (ed.), *The Sickle Side of the Moon: The Letters of Virginia Woolf, Volume V – 1932–5*, Hogarth Press, 1979, p. 273.

11. Quoted in Martin Gilbert, *Second World War*, revised edition, Fontana, 1990, pp. 256–7.

12. Quoted in Detlev J. K. Peukert (trans. Richard Deveson), *Inside Nazi Germany: Conformity, Opposition and Racism in Everyday Life*, Batsford, 1987, pp. 166–7.

13. Christopher Isherwood, *Christopher and His Kind*, p. 10.

14. John Lehmann, *In the Purely Pagan Sense*, p. 45.

15. Quoted in Anne Olivier Bell (ed.), *The Diary of Virginia Woolf, Volume IV – 1931–35*, Hogarth Press, 1982, p. 129.

16. Letter to Quentin Bell, 21 December 1933; quoted in Nicolson (ed.), op. cit., pp. 261–2.

17. Quoted in *Between the Acts*, pp. 137–8.

18. See Lee Bartlett (ed.), *Letters to Christopher: Stephen Spender's Letters to Christopher Isherwood, 1929–1939*, Black Sparrow Press, Santa Barbara, USA, 1980, p. 57.

19. The term 'steamer' seems to have been a short-lived part of the homosexual *patois*. Although in his *Dictionary of the Underworld* (1950) Eric Partridge defines the verb 'to steam' as meaning 'to prepare a "mug" for a fleecing' and notes a first printed usage in 1936, it meant nothing to any of the homosexual men I interviewed in the course of my research for this book.

20. Stephen Spender, *World Within World*, p. 175.

21. 'John', quoted in *Between the Acts*, p. 139.

22. Spender, op. cit., pp. 176–7.

23. Crisp, op. cit., pp. 25–6.

24. Ibid., pp. 27–8.

25. 'John', quoted in *Between the Acts*, p. 138.

26. Crisp, op. cit., p. 28.

27. Ibid., p. 29.

28. 'Trevor', quoted in *Between the Acts*, pp. 61–2.

29. 'John', quoted in ibid., p. 139.

30. Lehmann, op. cit., pp. 35–6.

31. Quoted in *Between the Acts*, p. 64.

32. Spender, op. cit., p. 266.

33. Crisp, op. cit., pp. 117–18 *passim*.

34. 'Neil', interview with the author, 10 October 1994.
35. Spender, op. cit., p. 270.
36. Tony Whitehead, letter to the *Guardian* 'Weekend', 23 March 1996; W. P. Coughlin, letter to the *Independent on Sunday*, 28 May 1995.
37. Anonymous speaker, BBC Radio 5, 31 December 1995.
38. Dudley Cave, *Life* magazine, 7 May 1995.
39. 'John', quoted in *Between the Acts*, p. 142.
40. Dudley Cave, interview with the author, October 1995.
41. 'David', quoted in *Between the Acts*, p. 45.
42. 'Neil', interview with the author, 10 October 1995.
43. 'Cecil', quoted in *Between the Acts*, p. 87 (my italics).
44. Lehmann, op. cit., p. 130.
45. 'Tony', quoted in *Between the Acts*, p. 149.
46. Nichols, op. cit., p. 200.
47. Angus Calder, *The People's War: Britain 1939–1945*, Jonathan Cape, 1969, p. 63.
48. Crisp, op. cit., pp. 157–8.
49. Lehmann, op. cit., p. 53.
50. Ibid., pp. 49–51 *passim*.
51. 'David', quoted in *Between the Acts*, p. 45.
52. 'Roy', quoted in ibid., p. 78.

SEVEN: 'THE HORRORS OF PEACE WERE MANY'

1. George Beardmore, *Civilians at War: Journals 1938–1946*, John Murray, 1984, pp. 194–5.
2. Naomi Mitchison, (ed. Dorothy Sheridan), *Among You Taking Notes*, Victor Gollancz, 1985, p. 321.
3. *Observer*, 13 May 1945, *passim*.
4. Crisp, op. cit., pp. 176–7.
5. Crisp, quoted in the *Independent on Sunday*, 7 May 1995.
6. Crisp, op. cit., p. 179.
7. Ibid., pp. 171–3 *passim*.
8. David Hughes, 'The Spivs', in Michael Sissons and Philip French (eds.), *Age of Austerity*, Hodder and Stoughton, 1963; Oxford University Press, 1986, p. 77. Writing less than a generation after the time he was describing, Hughes possibly pushes the idea of the spivs as post-war inheritors of the mantle of the pre-war 'beautiful people' too far. Nevertheless, his comparison – and vocabulary – is illuminating:

The spivs descended on the wreckage of central London during 1946, as if by magic, to fill the gap left by the exodus of the toffs. The West End has never been abandoned for long without an élite, a carefree cynosural focus for the tired eyes of sightseers, a brand image for the idea of a great, gay capital. Before the war, the upper crust, still residential, attended functions in full drag; now, patriotic to the last clothing-coupon, they dressed dowdily and the spivs had assumed their plumage as well as their habitat [. . .]

However, the barrow-boys – as flashy as neon, as exaggerated as the cut of their suits – were only the façade that stuck out with such vitality against the scarred hungry background of a city down on its uppers. They over-compensated for the drabness, becoming almost feminine in the process, tricked out in the patterns and shades of cheap bulls-eyes, all their tough swagger just a device to conceal a soggy cowardice beneath. For such pansy braggadocio surely meant that these characters only flirted with crime, never embraced it; and this was largely true [pp. 77–8].

It is interesting too that in Angus Wilson's early novel *Hemlock and After* (1952) the homosexual Terence Lambert, a middle-aged stage designer, disparages younger, better-looking men as, among other things, 'golden spivs' and 'butterfly spivs' (Penguin, 1992, pp. 93–100 *passim*.).

9. Earl Jowitt, quoted in *Hansard*, 19 May 1954.
10. Bishop of Southwark, ibid.
11. Sir Dirk Bogarde, interview, BBC Television, June 1995.
12. The phrase may not be precisely *echt*. It occurs in Frederick Raphael's loosely autobiographical novel *The Glittering Prizes* (Penguin, 1976) which opens in the Cambridge of the early 1950s, but it meant nothing to any of the men I interviewed for this book. That notwithstanding, it is vividly illustrative of the fear which the police inspired in many homosexuals of the period:

'You don't happen to have the cheque stubs with you, Denis, I suppose? Because –'
'Oh I wouldn't carry anything like that in the *street*,' Denis said.
'You never know when Mavis will stop you and search you, do you?'
'*Mavis?*' Cadman said. 'Who's Mavis?'
'Mavis. The *Polizei*, dear. Mavis *Polizei*. The girls in blue. Oh never mind' [p. 89].

13. Angus Wilson, op. cit., p. 108.

14. Colin Spencer, interview, Channel Four Television, 22 August 1995.

15. James Kirkup, *A Poet Could Not But Be Gay*, p. 19.

16. Peter Wildeblood, op. cit., p. 32.

17. Ibid., pp. 34–5.

18. 'Richard', interview with the author, 19 October 1994.

19. 'He remarked on your absence from the gay scene. I didn't, of course, know you were so often there' (Wilson, op. cit., p. 56). This is the earliest general British usage of the phrase in its now-familiar sense which the present author has come across.

20. Ibid., p. 89.

21. Wildeblood, op. cit., p. 36.

22. Letter to Annette Kerr, 13 April 1955, quoted in Russell Davies (ed.), *The Kenneth Williams Letters*, p. 46. Williams's comments were provoked by a performance of Julian Green's play *South*.

23. Wilson, op. cit., p. 108.

24. 'Nicholas', interview with the author, 21 September 1994 (my italics).

25. Ibid.

26. Quoted in John Lahr, *Prick Up Your Ears*, Allen Lane, 1978, pp. 90–92 *passim*.

27. 'Trevor', quoted in *Between the Acts*, pp. 65–6.

28. Anonymous; material supplied to the author.

29. Simon Raven, interview with Peter Parker, 2 July 1987; quoted in Parker, *Ackerley*, p. 337.

30. Quoted in Parker, op. cit., p. 338.

31. *Sydney Morning Telegraph*, 25 October 1953.

32. 'Nicholas', interview with the author, 25 October 1994.

33. 'Tony', quoted in *Between the Acts*, pp. 147–9 *passim*.

34. Michael Davidson, op. cit., pp. 298–9.

35. Wildeblood, op. cit., p. 40.

36. Ibid., p. 52.

37. Ibid., p. 55.

38. Ibid., p. 26.

39. Ibid., p. 24. Wildeblood gives no source for the survey, and I have been unable to trace it; but its findings accord with other literature of the period.

40. Ibid., p. 60.

41. Ibid., p. 92.

42. Ibid., pp. 92–3.

43. Ibid., p. 84.

44. Ibid., p. 65.

45. Ibid., pp. 94–5.

46. Undated letter, quoted in Nigel Jones, *Through a Glass Darkly: The Life of Patrick Hamilton*, Scribners, 1991, pp. 328–9.

EIGHT: 'THE RAY OF HOPE'

1. John Wolfenden, *Turning Points*, The Bodley Head, 1976, pp. 134–5.
2. *Sunday Times*, 26 March 1954.
3. *Sunday Times*, 2 April 1954. The complete letter is reprinted as an appendix to Antony Grey's book *Quest for Justice: Towards Homosexual Emancipation*, p. 279ff.
4. See, inter alia, D. J. West, *Homosexuality*, Duckworth, (first edition) 1955, and Tudor Rees and Harvey V. Usill (eds), *They Stand Apart: A Critical Survey of the Problem of Homosexuality*, Heinemann, 1955.
5. Anonymous letter, quoted in Peter Wildeblood, *A Way of Life*, pp. 20–21.
6. James Kirkup, op. cit., pp. 13–15 *passim*.
7. To illustrate this, in what follows I have interpolated 'Nicholas' 's story, and the specific experiences of two other men, with quotations from *Maurice*. Although slightly re-ordered, Nicholas's words remain as the almost-verbatim transcript of an interview he gave me on 21 September 1994. Neither Forster nor *Maurice* was mentioned on this occasion. The editorial juxtapositions are entirely mine.
8. E. M. Forster, op. cit., pp. 145–6.
9. Anonymous man, *Dark Secret*, BBC Television, 8 August 1996.
10. Forster, op. cit., p. 169.
11. Anonymous man, *Dark Secret*, BBC Television, 8 August 1996.
12. Ibid.
13. Forster, op. cit., p. 156.
14. Ibid., pp. 166–7.
15. Ibid., p. 167.
16. Anonymous man, *Dark Secret*, BBC Television, 8 August 1996.
17. Ibid.
18. Forster, op. cit., p. 195.
19. Ibid., p. 169.
20. Wolfenden, op. cit., p. 138.
21. The quotations are taken, respectively, from speeches given by William Shepherd, MP; Dr A. D. D. Broughton; MP, F. J. Bellenger, MP; and Dr Broughton again, during a House of Commons debate held on 26 November 1958.
22. *Daily Telegraph*, 5 July 1960.
23. *The Times*, 7 March 1958.

24. Wildeblood, *A Way of Life*, p. 20.
25. Grey, op. cit., p. 28.
26. Ibid, p. 29.
27. Elsewhere in his interview with the author, 'Nicholas' remembered a conversation with his father. In the light of the stress he put on this phrase, it might be seen to have some psychological bearing:

> When I was about thirteen or fourteen my father said to me, '[Nicholas], you must be careful when you go to the lavatory in a railway station or somewhere like that, that some man doesn't come along and have a look at your tiddly-om-pom.' I was appalled! I couldn't believe anyone would want to do something as awful as that. So he said there were these people known as homosexuals, and he explained what they did and said that it was against the law. 'Why was that?' I asked. 'Because if it wasn't, everybody would be doing it,' he said, 'and the human race would disappear. Having sex with a man is more attractive than having sex with a woman, because a man's body is firmer and more muscular.' I often thought I must have dreamt that, but then fifteen or twenty years later my mother said, 'Oh, Daddy always used to say . . .', and she repeated the same conversation.

28. 'Nicholas', interview with the author, 19 October 1994.
29. Grey, op. cit., p. 45.

NINE: 'YOU'LL PARDON THE MESS . . .'

1. Richard Hauser, *The Homosexual Society*, The Bodley Head, 1962.
2. 'Richard', interview with the author, May 1995.
3. 'John', quoted in *Between the Acts*, p. 138.
4. *The Kenneth Williams Diaries*, p. 206.
5. Bernard Levin, *The Pendulum Years: Britain and the Sixties*, p. 49.
6. *The Times*, 2 August 1964.
7. John Pearson, *The Profession of Violence: The Rise and Fall of the Kray Twins*, pp. 140–41.
8. Philip Norman, *Shout!: The True Story of the Beatles*, Hamish Hamilton, 1981, p. 157.
9. Quoted in Francis Wheen, op. cit., p. 356.
10. *Self-Portrait with Friends*, pp. 381–3 *passim*.
11. The present author can recall having heard similar sentiments expressed by a few gay men when AIDS was first making headlines in the early 1980s. Then the argument ran that, if homosexuality were *re-*

criminalized, to all intents and purposes it would effectively disappear from the public gaze, and things could go back to 'normal'.

12. 'Richard', interview with the author, 19 October 1994.
13. 'Stephen', quoted in *Between the Acts*, p. 115. The Kinsey Report, *Sexual Behaviour in the Human Male*, which was first published in America in 1948, claimed that the incidence of male homosexuality in the general population was much higher (approximately 10 per cent) than had previously been thought.
14. Ibid., pp. 113–14.
15. *The Orton Diaries*, p. 147 (30 April 1967).
16. 'Sam', interview with the author, 20 October 1994.
17. Joe Orton, *The Complete Plays*, Methuen, 1976, p. 31. This and the following extract come from the only published text, which is that of the first *stage* version of *The Ruffian on the Stair* (Royal Court Theatre, June 1967).
18. Ibid., pp. 49–50.
19. *The Orton Diaries*, p. 106 (entry for 4 March 1967; my italics).
20. 'Francis', interview with the author, October 1994.
21. *The Kenneth Williams Diaries*, p. 273 (entry for 11 February 1966).

TEN: 'DOING OUR BIT FOR THE BOYS!'

1. Richard Crossman, *The Diaries of a Cabinet Minister*, Hamish Hamilton and Jonathan Cape, Vol. 2, p. 407 (entry for 3 July 1967).
2. Barbara Castle, *The Castle Diaries 1964–1976*, Macmillan Papermac, 1990, p. 100 (entry for 20 December 1966).
3. Ibid., p. 139 (entry for 13 July 1967).
4. Ibid., p. 54 (entry for 11 February 1966).
5. Barbara Castle, *The Castle Diaries*, Weidenfeld and Nicolson, 1984, p. 273 (entry for 3 July 1967).
6. Both quotations from a BBC radio interview, 1995.
7. Nigel Warner, 'Parliament and the Law', in Bruce Galloway (ed.), *Prejudice and Pride: Discrimination Against Gay People in Modern Britain*, p. 84.
8. Ibid., p. 98.
9. *New York Times*, 27 June 1969.
10. Newspaper reports taken from the *New York Times*, *Village Voice* and the New York *Daily News* respectively, 28 June 1969 *et seq.* (my italics).
11. Antony Grey, *Quest for Justice*, p. 154.
12. Aubrey Walter; material supplied to the author, September 1995.
13. Bob Mellors; material supplied to the author, September 1995.
14. Anonymous, BBC interview, 1995.

15. *Come Together*, London GLF newspaper, No. 2, December 1970 (my italics); No. 5, March 1971.

16. 'Sam', quoted in *Between the Acts*, op. cit., pp. 107–8.

17. 'Stephen', interview with the author, 1994.

18. 'Richard', interview with the author, 1995.

19. 'Sam', interview with the author, 20 October 1994.

20. Anonymous contributor, *Out This Week*, BBC Radio 5, 17 September 1995.

21. It should be remembered, too, that John Osborne's *A Patriot for Me*, with its notorious drag-ball scene, had been given a private performance (i.e. one not subject to the censorship of the Lord Chamberlain) by the English Stage Company at the Royal Court Theatre a full year previously, in the summer of 1965.

22. Charles Dyer, *Staircase*, Penguin, 1966, pp. 9–10.

23. Mart Crowley, *The Boys in the Band*, Penguin, 1970, p. 47.

24. John Elsom and Nicholas Tomalin, *The History of the National Theatre*, Jonathan Cape, 1978, p. 196.

25. John Goodwin (ed.), *Peter Hall's Diaries*, Hamish Hamilton, 1983, p. 81 (entry for 7 February).

26. Anonymous; material supplied to the author, 1994.

27. *Exeter Express and Echo*, May 1973 (my italics).

28. Crowley, op. cit., p. 9.

29. Adam Mars-Jones, 'The Changes of Those Terrible Years', reprinted in *The Faber Book of Gay Short Fiction*, Faber, 1991, p. 392.

30. *The Kenneth Williams Diaries*, p. 432 (entry for 22 September 1972).

31. Ibid., pp. 427–8.

32. *Pink Paper*, 17 June 1994.

ELEVEN: 'I AM PERFECTLY NORMAL'

1. Purely for the sake of clarity, I have extensively repunctuated this passage which, either by editorial choice or failure of sub-editorial function, originally appeared as a sort of stream-of-consciousness rant. My interpolations (here as elsewhere in the text) are contained within square brackets. (Slightly abbreviated, the original text is reproduced in Patrick Higgins (ed.), *A Queer Reader*, p. 208).

2. Simon Gray, *Butley*, in *The Definitive Simon Gray*, I, Faber, 1992, pp. 62–3. *Butley* was first performed in July 1971 at the Criterion Theatre, London. I have intentionally removed character names and stage directions from this extract.

3. Mary Renault, of course, had written *The Charioteer* as long ago as 1953.

4. Christopher Isherwood, *A Single Man*, Methuen, 1964; Eyre Methuen, 1980, pp. 138–9.

5. Francis King, *A Domestic Animal*, p. 127.

6. 'Edward', a public school pupil in the early 1980s, interview with the author, 8 October 1995.

7. Diary made available to the author.

8. 'Edward', as above.

9. *Gay News*, February 1976.

10. Michael Denneny, 1979; quoted in *A Queer Reader*, p. 212.

11. Nicholas de Jongh, *Gay News*, January 1976.

12. Jeffrey Weeks, *Gay News*, January 1976.

13. Mario Mieli, *Homosexuality and Liberation*, 1980; quoted in *A Queer Reader*, p. 213.

14. David Starkey, *Gay News*, January 1977.

15. 'Richard', interview with the author, 19 October 1994.

16. Diary made available to the author.

17. Francis King, op. cit., p. 51.

18. *The Orton Diaries*, p. 253.

19. Both these confidential Ministry of Defence letters have been seen by the author.

20. 'Neil', interview with the author, 10 October 1994. This was the only conversation undertaken as part of my research for this book which was not conducted on a private, one-to-one basis. This interview was conducted jointly by Edmund Hall and myself at 'Neil' 's home in southern England. As with other direct quotations from interviews in this book, his words are here transcribed from a tape recording. Further information about 'Neil' 's military career is contained in Hall's *We Can't Even March Straight*, p. 129ff.

21. Kevin Elyot, *Coming Clean*, Faber, 1984, p. 12. The play, which won the 1982 Samuel Beckett Award, was first produced at the Bush Theatre, London, in November 1982.

22. Peter York, 'Machomania', *Harpers and Queen*, February 1979. The article is reprinted in York's book *Style Wars*, Sidgwick & Jackson, 1980, p. 153ff.

23. 'Georgie', quoted in *Bodies of Evidence: Stories about Living with HIV*, Camerawork/The Photo Co-Op, 1989, unpaginated.

24. Alan Hollinghurst, *The Swimming-Pool Library*, p. 3.

25. 'Brad', interview with the author, 30 June 1995.

26. Paul Cons, interview with Granada Television, 1995.

27. 'Georgie', quoted in *Bodies of Evidence*.

28. Anonymous, quoted in *Bodies of Evidence*.

29. Entries from the diary of the author, May 1993.

30. *Safer Sex for Gay Men*, leaflet produced by the Terrence Higgins Trust, 1991.
31. Forty-year-old man, interviewed by the author, 23 May 1994.
32. 'Edward', as Note 6.
33. Clare Tomalin, *Independent on Sunday*, 1 April 1990.
34. *Independent* magazine, 25 November 1995.
35. 'Tim', interview with the Albert Kennedy Trust, 1991.
36. *Gay Times*, June 1989.
37. Sue Sanders, quoted in the *Pink Paper*, 24 May 1996.
38. Peter Tatchell, quoted in the *Independent on Sunday*, 11 December 1994.
39. Ibid.
40. Edmund Hall, interview with the author, 8 October 1995. Additional information provided to the author by Will Parry.
41. *Independent on Sunday*, 21 January 1996.
42. Ibid., 21 April 1996.
43. Oscar Moore, *A Matter of Life and Sex*, p. 310.

Bibliography

This is no more than a check-list of those books to which I have had most frequent recourse, and to which reference is made in the Notes.

The publication details are, in general, first editions. Where these are now difficult to obtain and more recent and/or revised editions generally available, the latter, too, have been listed.

Except where otherwise stated, place of publication is London.

Acton, Harold: *Memoirs of an Aesthete*, Methuen, 1948; Hamish Hamilton, 1984

Blow, Simon: *Broken Blood: The Rise and Fall of the Tennant Family*, Faber and Faber, 1987

Boyle, Andrew: *The Climate of Treason*, revised edition, Coronet, 1980

Buckle, Richard (ed.): *Self-Portrait with Friends: The Selected Diaries of Cecil Beaton*, Weidenfeld & Nicolson, 1979

Carpenter, Humphrey: *The Brideshead Generation: Evelyn Waugh & His Friends*, Weidenfeld & Nicolson, 1985

Castle, Charles: *Noël*, W. H. Allen, 1971

Connolly, Cyril: *The Missing Diplomats*, Queen Anne Press, 1952

Connon, Bryan: *Beverley Nichols: A Life*, Constable, 1991

Crisp, Quentin: *The Naked Civil Servant*, Fontana, 1977

Danziger, James: *Beaton*, Secker & Warburg, 1980

Davenport-Hines, Richard: *Sex, Death and Punishment*, Collins, 1990

David, Hugh: *The Fitzrovians*, Michael Joseph, 1988

Davidson, Michael: *The World, the Flesh and Myself*, Arthur Barker, 1962, GMP Publishers, 1985

Davies, Russell (ed.):*The Kenneth Williams Diaries*, HarperCollins, 1993
– *The Kenneth Williams Letters*, HarperCollins, 1994

Delany, Paul: *The Neo-Pagans*, Macmillan, 1987

Driberg, Tom: *Guy Burgess: A Portrait with Background*, Weidenfeld and Nicolson, 1956

– *Ruling Passions*, Jonathan Cape, 1977

Ellmann, Richard: *Oscar Wilde*, Hamish Hamilton, 1987

Fido, Martin: *Oscar Wilde*, Hamlyn, 1973

Forster, E. M.: *Maurice*, Edward Arnold, 1971

Galloway, Bruce (ed.): *Prejudice and Pride: Discrimination Against Gay People in Modern Britain*, Routledge & Kegan Paul, 1983

Garfield, Simon: *The End of Innocence: Britain in the Time of Aids*, Faber and Faber, 1994

Gardiner, James: *A Class Apart: The Private Pictures of Montague Glover*, Serpent's Tail, 1992

Gide André: *Oscar Wilde*, Mercure de France, Paris, 1925

Grey, Antony: *Quest for Justice: Towards Homosexual Emancipation*, Sinclair-Stevenson, 1992

Hall, Edmund: *We Can't Even March Straight: Homosexuality in the British Armed Forces*, Vintage, 1995

Hillier, Bevis: *Young Betjeman*, John Murray, 1988

Higgins, Patrick (ed.): *A Queer Reader*, Fourth Estate, 1993

Hoare, Philip: *Noël Coward: A Biography*, Sinclair-Stevenson, 1995

Hollinghurst, Alan: *The Swimming-Pool Library*, Chatto & Windus, 1988

Hyde, H. Montgomery: *Cases That Changed the Law*, Heinemann, 1951

– *The Cleveland Street Scandal*, W. H. Allen, 1976

– *The Trials of Oscar Wilde*, Hodge, 1948

Isherwood, Christopher: *Christopher and His Kind*, Eyre Methuen, 1977

Johnson, Adam: *The Playground Bell*, Carcanet Press, Manchester, 1994

King, Francis: *A Domestic Animal*, Longman, 1970

Kirkup, James: *A Poet Could Not But Be Gay*, Peter Owen, 1991

Lahr, John (ed.): *The Orton Diaries*, Methuen, 1986

Lehmann, John: *In the Purely Pagan Sense*, Blond & Briggs, 1976; GMP Publishers, 1985

Leavitt, David: *The Lost Language of Cranes*, Alfred A. Knopf, Inc., New York; Viking, 1987

Lesley, Cole: *The Life of Noël Coward*, Jonathan Cape, 1976

Levin, Bernard: *The Pendulum Years: Britain and the Sixties*, Jonathan Cape, 1970

Moore, Oscar: *A Matter of Life and Sex*, Penguin, 1992

Parker, Peter: *Ackerley: A Life of J. R. Ackerley*, Constable, 1989

Pearson, John: *The Profession of Violence: The Rise and Fall of the Kray Twins*, second edition, Granada, 1972

Penrose, Barrie, and Freeman, Simon: *Conspiracy of Silence: The Secret Life of Anthony Blunt*, Grafton, 1986; revised edition, 1987

Pickles: *Queens*, Quartet, 1984; Penguin, 1995

Porter, Kevin, and Weeks, Jeffrey (eds.): *Between the Acts: Lives of Homosexual Men, 1885–1967*, Routledge, 1991

Sinfield, Alan: *The Wilde Century: Effeminacy, Oscar Wilde and the Queer Movement*, Cassell, 1994

Spencer, Colin: *Homosexuality*, Fourth Estate, 1995

Spender, Stephen: *The Temple*, Faber, 1988

– *World Within World*, Faber, 1951; 1977

Tatchell, Peter: *We Don't Want to March Straight: Masculinity, Queers and the Military*, Cassell, 1995

Vickers, Hugo: *Cecil Beaton*, Weidenfeld & Nicolson, 1985

Wheen, Francis: *Tom Driberg: His Life and Indiscretions*, Chatto & Windus, 1990

Wildeblood, Peter: *Against the Law*, Weidenfeld & Nicolson, 1955

– *A Way of Life*, Weidenfeld & Nicolson, 1956

Winn, Godfrey: *The Infirm Glory*, Michael Joseph, 1967

Index

DJ

Lc   28·8·97